The Sufi Answers
to the 'Salafi' Calumnies

The *Sufi* *Answers* to the *'Salafi'* *Calumnies*

'False hadiths'
'Grave-worship'
'Miracles of the Awliya'
'Knowledge of the unseen'
and more

Gibril Fouad Haddad

Foreword by
Sayyid Yusuf Hashim al-Rifai

INSTITUTE FOR SPIRITUAL & CULTURAL ADVANCEMENT

Adapted and expanded from the author's book in Arabic entitled *Tuḥfat al-labīb bi-nuṣrat al-Ḥabīb ʿAlī al-Jafrī fī dhikri baʿḍi adillat al-tawassul wal-tabarruk wa-ghayrihimā min al-masāʾil al-ṣūfiyya* (Damascus: Dār Ṭaybat al-Gharrāʾ, 1428/2007).

First published in the US by
Institute for Spiritual & Cultural Advancement
17195 Silver Parkway #401, Fenton, MI 48430, USA
Tel: (888) 278-6624
Fax: (810) 815-0518

Email: info@sufilive.com
Web: http://www.sufilive.com
Purchase online at: http://www.isn1.net

Cover picture: Mawlana Shaykh Muhammad Hisham b. Muhammad Salim Kabbani (1945-2024) visiting the honored grave of Mawlana Shaykh Muhammad Nazim al-Haqqani (1922-2014) in Lefke, Cyprus.

Cover design by author. The author wishes to thank Camille Mallat, MA for proofreading part of the typescript.

ISBN: 978-1-938058-86-8

Cataloging-in-Publication Data

Haddad, Gibril Fouad, 1960- ; Yusuf Hashim al-Rifai, 1932-2018

The Sufi answers to the 'Salafi' calumnies: 'false hadiths,' 'grave-worship,' 'miracles of the Awliya,' 'knowledge of the unseen' and more. Foreword by Sayyid Yusuf Sayyid Hashim al-Rifai.

190 p. 23 cm.

1. Damascus (Syria) -- Sufism. 2. Islam -- Intercession. 3. Islam -- Graves. 4. Islam -- Saints. 5. Islam -- Hadith. 6. Sufism -- Principles. 7. Wahhabism -- Polemics. I. Author. II. Title. III. Title: *Tuḥfat al-labīb bi-nuṣrat al-Ḥabīb ʿAlī al-Jafrī fī dhikri baʿḍi adillat al-tawassul wal-tabarruk wa-ghayrihimā min al-masāʾil al-ṣūfiyya.*

بسم الله الرحمن الرحيم

Dedicated to the pious memory and pure soul of my teacher Sultan al-Awliya Mawlana al-Shaykh Hisham Kabbani

روى الحافظ أبو محمد عبد الله بن محمد بن جعفر بن حَيّان الأنصاري المعروف بأبي الشَّيخ الأصبهاني في (طبقات المحدِّثين بأصبهان والواردين عليها)،
وروى الحافظ أبو القاسم عبد الرحمن بن محمد ابن مَنْدَهْ العَبْدي الأصبهاني في (الأحوال والإيمان بالسؤال)،
وروى الحافظ أبو القاسم إسماعيل بن محمد بن الفضل القرشي الطَّلْحِي التَّيمي الأصبهاني الملقب بِقِوَام السنّة في (سِيَر السَّلَف ومناقبُهم من الصحابة والتابعين ومَن بَعدهم من الصالحين)، جميعهم بسندهم:

عن سَلَمَةَ بْنِ شَبِيبٍ، قال: سمعتُ أبا حمّادٍ الحفّارَ، وكان ثِقَةً وَرِعاً، قال:

دَخَلْتُ مَقْبَرَةً بِمَكَّةَ بِالْهَاجِرَةِ - نسخة: دَخَلْتُ يَوْمَ الْجُمُعَةِ الْمَقْبَرَةَ نَصِفَ النَّهَارِ - فَمَا مَرَرْتُ بِقَبْرٍ إِلا وَسَمِعْتُ مِنْهُ قِرَاءَةَ الْقُرْآنِ.

Salama b. Shabīb said, "I heard Abū Ḥammād al-Ḥaffār say—and he was trustworthy, scrupulous—'I entered a cemetery in Mecca at noontime [one version has, I went into the graveyard on a day of Jumu'a at midday], and I did not pass by a single grave but I heard coming from it the recitation of the Qur'ān.'"

Narrated by Abū al-Shaykh, *Ṭabaqāt al-muḥaddithīn bi-Aṣbahān*; Ibn Mandah, *al-Aḥwāl wal-īmān bil-su'āl*; Qiwām al-Sunna, *Siyar al-Salaf.*

Contents

Dedication and Epigraph 7
Foreword and Commendation by Sayyid Yūsuf al-Rifāʿī 11
Preamble 13

Part One
Sunni principles of Hadith validation

I The claim that Sufis misquote Prophetic Hadiths 21
II The claim that Sufis authenticate inauthentic hadiths 27
III Sufis follow Consensus in accepting weak hadiths 31
IV Even a very weak hadith may convey a sound meaning 37
V Do not call a lie a hadith—and do not call a hadith a lie! 41

Part Two
Love of the Prophet's Family and denunciation of their enemies

VI The Messenger of Allah, the Companions and the Successors all warned about the Umayyads 45
VII Sufism and Sunnism are both defined by the inseparable love and respect of *Ahl al-Bayt* and the Companions 51

Part Three
Grave structures and visitation to the people of *barzakh*

VIII The *Salaf* built structures over graves and visited them 63
IX Grave structures for ulema, Awliya and *Ahl al-Bayt* 65
X Travel to visit graves for *duʿā*, *tabarruk*, *tawassul* is a Sunna 67
XI Visit of the Prophet's Grave is piety unrelated to the report "One does not travel other than to the three Mosques" 71
XII The hadiths "Do not make my grave a *ʿīd*" and "Whoever visits my grave, my intercession must take place for him" 79

XIII The hadith "They took the graves of their Prophets as places of prostration" has a mainstream sense and a misleading one 81
XIV Touching and kissing the grave out of love and for blessing is desirable according to Imam Aḥmad b. Ḥanbal 87
XV The life of Prophets in their graves and the Prophet's awareness of his Umma are categorical knowledge in Islam 93
XVI Belief in the life of Prophets in *Barzakh* explained from the book *Methodology of the Salaf in understanding texts* 99
XVII The sound hadith "Your works are shown to me" and the Prophet's witnessing of the Umma from *Barzakh* 105
XVIII Visiting the Messenger of Allah–upon him the blessings and peace of Allah–and his grave for the fulfillment of needs 111
XIX The *Salaf* and *Khalaf* visited Awliyas' graves to fulfill needs, especially the Ḥanbalīs with Imam Aḥmad's grave 127
XX Advice when visiting the graves of Prophets and Awliya 135

Part Four
The miracles and divinely-gifted knowledge of the Awliya

XXI Miracles of Awliya are truth and part of the Sunni creed 137
XXII Awliya conversing with Allah and even seeing Him 141
XXIII Awliya do not legislate but they infer sound rulings 145
XXIV Prophets and their inheritors do receive God-given knowledge of the unseen; meaning of *Nabī* and *Nubuwwa* 149
XXV Affirmation of the Awliya's knowledge of the unseen by the putative founders of "Salafism" 155
XXVI Affirmation that 'Alī b. Abī Ṭālib had *ladunnī* knowledge 159
XXVII 'Alawī b. 'Abbās al-Mālikī's fatwa on *kashf* (unveiling) 163
XXVIII The human being is the vicegerent of Allah on earth 167
XXIX Epilogue and Supplications 175

Bibliography 179
Index of Hadiths 185

Foreword and Commendation by
Sayyid Yūsuf b. Sayyid Hāshim al-Rifāʿī
for the author's original Arabic version
published in Damascus in 2007

بسم الله الرحمن الرحيم

In the Name of Allah All-Beneficent, Most Merciful.
We praise Allah Most High and invoke blessings and peace on His noble Messenger and his Family.

To proceed: I have looked at the blessed epistle entitled *Tuḥfat al-labīb bi-minaḥ al-Ḥabīb* (The gift to the insightful of the Beloved's bestowals) by Shaykh Gibril b. Fouad Haddad al-Naqshbandi al-Haqqani. I was gladdened by what I read in it and I found it to reflect the genuine credal doctrines of the *Ahl al-Sunna wal-Jamāʿa* who are the vast majority of the mercied Muhammadan Umma. I found it to be supported and reinforced by the noble Prophetic reports that are documented with their trusted sources in the books of Hadith. I therefore thank the author for his excellent effort in composing it and I ask Allah Most High to reward him and recompense him for that in the best way. May Allah Most High bless and greet our liege lord Muhammad and his Family!

Written with his mortal hand by
al-Sayyid Yūsuf al-Sayyid Hāshim al-Rifāʿī al-Ḥusaynī
–may Allah Most High forgive him.

Damascus, 2 Rajab 1425 / 17 August 2004

In the Name of the One God, the All-Beneficent, the Most Merciful

Preamble

Praise belongs to the One God, the nurturing Lord of the worlds! May blessings and greetings of peace be upon our liege lord Muhammad, the truthful and trustworthy one who was sent as a mercy to the worlds, and upon his family and all his Companions.

To proceed: Allah Most High said in the revelation He sent down,

﴿ فَاتَّقُوا اللَّهَ وَأَصْلِحُوا ذَاتَ بَيْنِكُمْ وَأَطِيعُوا اللَّهَ وَرَسُولَهُ إِن كُنتُم مُّؤْمِنِينَ ﴾ من سورة الأنفال الآية ١

so beware the One God, and mend unity among yourselves, and obey the One God and His Messenger if you are believers (Anfāl 8:1), and it is related from ʿIyāḍ b. ʿAmr al-Ashʿarī that when the following verse was revealed, *then the One God shall bring forth a people whom He loves and who love Him, humble towards the believers, hard against the unbelievers, striving with jihad in the way of Allah, and fearing not any blame from any blamer. That is the bounty of the One God which He gives whomever He pleases; and the One God is All-Embracing, All-Knowing* (Mā'ida 5:54), the Messenger of Allah–upon him blessings and peace of Allah–said, "They are your people, O Abū Mūsā!" and he signaled with his hand to Abū Mūsā al-Ashʿarī. Ibn Saʿd, Ibn Abī Shayba and al-Ṭabarānī narrated it—al-Haythamī said its narrators are all the narrators of the *Ṣaḥīḥ*—as well as al-Ḥākim in the wording below, and he said it was sound by Muslim's criterion.

عن عِيَاضِ بْنِ عَمْرٍو الأَشْعَرِيِّ لَمَّا نَزَلَتْ ﴿فَسَوْفَ يَأْتِي ٱللَّهُ بِقَوْمٍ يُحِبُّهُمْ وَيُحِبُّونَهُۥٓ أَذِلَّةٍ عَلَى ٱلْمُؤْمِنِينَ أَعِزَّةٍ عَلَى ٱلْكَٰفِرِينَ يُجَٰهِدُونَ فِى سَبِيلِ ٱللَّهِ وَلَا يَخَافُونَ لَوْمَةَ لَآئِمٍ ۚ ذَٰلِكَ فَضْلُ ٱللَّهِ يُؤْتِيهِ مَن يَشَآءُ ۚ وَٱللَّهُ وَٰسِعٌ عَلِيمٌ﴾ من سورة المائدة الآية ٥٤. قَالَ رَسولُ الله ﷺ: **هُمْ قَوْمُكَ يَا أَبَا مُوسَى!** وَأَوْمَئَ ﷺ بِيَدِهِ إِلَى أَبِي مُوسَى الأَشْعَرِيِّ. رواه ابن سعد وابن أبي شيبة والطبراني وقال الهيثمي: رجاله رجال الصحيح. والحاكم بهذا اللفظ وقال: صحيح على شرط مسلم.

It was also related in the sound hadith from Anas that the Prophet–upon him the blessings and peace of Allah–looked towards Iraq, Syro-Palestine and Yemen then said, "O Allah! Bring over their hearts to obedience of You and back them up with Your mercy." Ṭabarānī narrated it—through the narrators of the *Ṣaḥīḥ* per Haythamī except 'Alī b. Baḥr and he is trustworthy—as did Ibn al-Muqri' in his *Mu'jam*, al-Ḍiyā' al-Maqdisī in *al-Mukhtāra* and al-Sam'ānī in *al-Taḥbīr* and *Faḍā'il al-Shām*.

عَنْ أَنَسٍ أَنَّ النَّبِيَّ ﷺ نَظَرَ قِبَلَ العِرَاقِ وَالشَّامِ وَالْيَمَنِ فَقَالَ: **اللَّهُمَّ أَقْبِلْ بِقُلُوبِهِمْ عَلَى طَاعَتِكَ وَحُطَّ مِنْ وَرَاءِهِمْ بِرَحْمَتِكَ.** رواه الطبراني في معاجمه الثلاثة ومسند الشاميين وابن المقرئ في معجمه وقال الهيثمي رجال الطبراني رجال الصحيح غير علي بن بحر وهو ثقة وأورده الحافظان الضياء المقدسي في الأحاديث المختارة والسمعاني في التحبير وفضائل الشام.

He also said, "The best of men are the men of the people of Yemen, and belief is Yemeni, and I am Yemeni." Aḥmad narrated it in his *Musnad* from 'Amr b. 'Abasa.

وقال ﷺ: خَيْرُ الرِّجَالِ رِجَالُ أَهْلِ الْيَمَنِ، وَالإِيمَانُ يَمَانٍ، وَأَنَا يَمَانٍ.

رواه الإمام أحمد في مسنده عن عمرو بن عَبَسَة

It is also related from Anas b. Mālik that the Messenger of Allah–upon him blessings and peace of Allah–said, "Tomorrow there shall come over to you companies of people who truly have softer hearts for Islam than you do." He said, "Then the Ash'arīs came, among them Abū Mūsā al-Ash'arī. When they drew near to Medina they started reciting this *rajaz* poetry:

tomorrow we meet the beloved,
Muhammad and his company!

"Then, when they arrived, they started exchanging handshakes. So they were the very first who innovated the mutual handshake." Aḥmad narrated it.

عَنْ أَنَسِ بْنِ مَالِكٍ قَالَ: قَالَ رَسُولُ الله ﷺ يَقْدَمُ عَلَيْكُمْ غَدًا أَقْوَامٌ هُمْ أَرَقُّ قُلُوبًا لِلإِسْلَامِ مِنْكُمْ. قَالَ: فَقَدِمَ الأَشْعَرِيُّونَ، فِيهِمْ أَبُو مُوسَى الأَشْعَرِيُّ. فَلَمَّا دَنَوْا مِنَ الْمَدِينَةِ جَعَلُوا يَرْتَجِزُونَ يَقُولُونَ:

غَداً نَلْقَى الأَحِبَّهْ مُحَمَّداً وَحِزْبَهْ

فَلَمَّا أَنْ قَدِمُوا تَصَافَحُوا فَكَانُوا هُمْ أَوَّلَ مَنْ أَحْدَثَ الْمُصَافَحَةَ رواه أحمد.

It is also narrated in the two *Ṣaḥīḥ*s of Bukhārī and Muslim from Abū Mūsā that the Prophet–upon him the blessings and peace of Allah–said of the people of Yemen, "They are part of me and I am part of them."

وعن أبي موسى قال النبي ﷺ في أهل اليمن:

هُمْ مِنِّي وَأَنَا مِنْهُمْ. في الصحيحين

Damascus the well-guarded was gifted of **the rescuing wind of the All-Beneficent** that the Messenger of Allah–upon him blessings and peace–described as **hailing from Yemen** [Abū Hurayra and Salama ibn Nufayl al-Sakūnī in Aḥmad, Ṭabarānī and others], with the visit of the caller to Allah, al-Ḥabīb ʿAlī Zayn al-ʿĀbidīn b. ʿAbd al-Raḥmān al-Jafrī–Allah preserve him– –in the month of Rabīʿ al-Awwal 1425 from May to August 2004. He received in it a splendid welcome on the part of its people— the general public and the ulema—all concurring on love for him and the acknowledgment of his special spiritual status. There is no doubt the cause for such acceptance on earth was the occurrence of acceptance for him in the heavens first, whereby the *Shaykh al-qurrāʾ* (head authority in the teaching of the Qurʾān) of Damascus, Shaykh Kurayyim Rājiḥ, complimented him by praising Habib ʿAlī al-Jafrī's eloquence to the skies and said, "Each of us speaks from the earth to the sky except Habib Jafrī, for verily he speaks from the sky to the earth, and he is an inspired servant." He echoed the way Imam Ibn ʿAbd al-Salam had described Ibn ʿAṭāʾ Allāh al-Sakandarī's speech by saying, "It is verily a discourse fresh from its nurturing Lord." That is, he compared it to divine inspiration due to its purity. And it was truly a wonderful and true compliment in light of the statement of the Messenger–upon him the blessings and peace of Allah– "Belief is Yemeni and wisdom is Yemeni," narrated from Abū Hurayra and Anas by Aḥmad and it is also in the two *Ṣaḥīḥs*.

الإِيمَانُ يَمَانٍ وَالْحِكْمَةُ يَمَانِيَةٌ متفق عليه عن أبي هريرة وأنس

Despite this vibrant welcome some spurious objections soon emerged against Shaykh ʿAlī al-Jafrī from certain quarters. We were shocked to hear it was the very same praiser cited above who was voicing them. We do no know how he allowed himself to give voice to them without verification or ascertainment of the truth beyond giving credence to one of his Wahhabi students sowing strife and accusations of corruption and misguidance. Allah knows the contents of hearts, but the results of such actions showed malice. Allah Most High has said,

﴿ يَٰٓأَيُّهَا ٱلَّذِينَ ءَامَنُوٓاْ إِن جَآءَكُمۡ فَاسِقُۢ بِنَبَإٖ فَتَبَيَّنُوٓاْ أَن تُصِيبُواْ قَوۡمَۢا
بِجَهَٰلَةٖ فَتُصۡبِحُواْ عَلَىٰ مَا فَعَلۡتُمۡ نَٰدِمِينَ ٦ ﴾ الحجرات

O you who believe! If some depraved person has come to you with a piece of news then investigate, lest you should assail a group of people in ignorance then later find yourselves regretting what you have done (Ḥujurāt 49:6). Allah Most High also said of the propagators of falsehood that spread lies so as to reject the knowledge that they do not possess because of their ignorance,

﴿ بَلۡ كَذَّبُواْ بِمَا لَمۡ يُحِيطُواْ بِعِلۡمِهِۦ وَلَمَّا يَأۡتِهِمۡ تَأۡوِيلُهُۥۚ ﴾ يونس ٣٩

Rather they belied that whose knowledge they did not encompass when its upshot had still not come to them (Yūnus 10:39). And the poet said, as related by al-Bahā' Ṭāhir b. Aḥmad al-Qazwīnī, known as al-Najjār (d. 580/1184) in *Sirāj al-'uqūl fī minhāj al-uṣūl*—a book on Ash'arī credal doctrine:

أَتَـانَـا أَنَّ سَهْلاً ذَمَّ جَهْلاً عُلُوماً لَيْسَ يَدْرِيهِنَّ سَهْـلُ
عُلُوماً لَوْ دَرَاهَا مَا قَلاَهَا وَلَكِنِ الرِّضَىٰ بِالْجَهْلِ سَهْلُ

we heard Sahl had blamed—in ignorance—
types of knowledge Sahl had no inkling of,
which, if he grasped them, he would not hate;
but settling on ignorance is an easy thing.

The role gossipmongers play in disputing the merits of people is notorious and denounced by all. The secret behind their temporary success is "the spread of the most vicious illness devastating the well-being of this Umma" in the words of the shahid Muhammad Sa'īd al-Būṭī–Allah have mercy on him–"namely that which Ibn 'Aṭā' Allāh has mentioned in one of his wise aphorisms when he said, *the taking hold of whim in the heart is the most lethal and terminal disease.*" Būṭī explained it thus in his published 1990s classes on the *Ḥikam Ibn 'Aṭā' Allāh*: "It is the disease of fanaticism for a school and for oneself that leads the diseased one to ride on the *dīn* for the sole purpose of promoting himself and, to that end, belittle and despise the immense goodness that pleases Allah—by which He benefits the Umma and for which He employs whomever He wishes of His servants—and blow out of proportion petty matters and ijtihad-related foibles that might befall anyone that is below the rank of Messengers and Prophets."

It would have been more appropriate for the objector to address the leaders of false campaigns carrying misleading slogans that have disgraced the pulpits of Damascus in recent times in the name of what they called "renewal," "liberation," "unity of faith-communities," "contemporary readings of the Qur'ān" and "justice and monotheism."[1] Instead, the objector turned to target someone whose discourse benefits the spiritual life of all and strengthens the light of belief! How truly does the truthful and trustworthy one speak–upon him blessings and peace–saying, **"There will be towards the end of time anti-Christ arch-liars who shall bring you sayings neither you nor your forefathers ever heard before. Beware of them and keep away from them! Never let them lead you astray or seduce you!"** (Abū Hurayra by Aḥmad and Muslim), **"those that call others at the gates of Hellfire, whoever answers them they cast into it, people with our complexion saying the same exhortations as we do and speaking our languages"** (Ḥudhayfa in the two *Ṣaḥīḥs*).

يَكُونُ فِي آخِرِ الزَّمَانِ دَجَّالُونَ كَذَّابُونَ يَأْتُونَكُمْ مِنْ الْأَحَادِيثِ بِمَا لَمْ تَسْمَعُوا أَنْتُمْ وَلَا آبَاؤُكُمْ فَإِيَّاكُمْ وَإِيَّاهُمْ لَا يُضِلُّونَكُمْ وَلَا يَفْتِنُونَكُمْ رواه أحمد ومسلم عن أبي هريرة دُعَاةٌ عَلَى أَبْوَابِ جَهَنَّمَ مَنْ أَجَابَهُمْ إِلَيْهَا قَذَفُوهُ فِيهَا، قَوْمٌ مِنْ جِلْدَتِنَا وَيَتَكَلَّمُونَ بِأَلْسِنَتِنَا رواه الشيخان عن حذيفة

[1] I.e. replacing *uṣūl al-fiqh* with *maqāṣid al-sharī'a*; doffing hijab; expurgating creed and fiqh of such categories as *kāfir, murtadd, ḥudūd,* etc.; expurgating Qur'ān and its commentaries; reviving Mu'tazilism.

It is noteworthy that both the narrators of the abovementioned hadiths, Abū Hurayra and Ḥudhayfa, are from Yemen.

The writer of these lines consulted with the *Quṭb*s and trusted masters of our time, our beloved teachers Mawlana Shaykh Hisham Kabbani and Mawlana Shaykh Nazim al-Haqqani; the educator and Imam of the Rifā'ī Tariqa Sayyid Yusuf al-Rifa'i; the Imam of the Mosque of Khālid b. al-Walīd in Homs and its *quṭb* Sayyid Muhammad Sa'īd b. Hānī' al-Kaḥīl; the shahid Dr. Muhammad Sa'īd Ramadan al-Buti; the Imam of the *maqām* of Shaykh Arslān al-Dimashqī in Bāb Tūmā Sayyid Muhammad 'Adnan al-Majd al-Hasani; and Sayyid Muhammad Abu al-Huda al-Yaqoubi–may Allah bless them one and all and thank them on behalf of the Umma. They all expressed the duty of publishing these clarifications on the reality of the evidences of the people of the Prophetic Sunna and the Consensus of the Umma—even if they are already clear as the sun—on the issues of *tawassul* (using intermediacy and intercession to Allah), *tabarruk* (getting blessings from blessed ones and their relics), *ziyāra* (visitation of graves of the pious), *kashf* (spiritual unveiling) and more. The book came out in Arabic in Damascus in 2007. Here now, 18 years later, is its expanded English version.

These subheadings of fiqh have long been misrepresented by the Wahhabi sect and their putative model, Aḥmad b. 'Abd al-Ḥalīm al-Ḥarrānī (661-728), who was repeatedly jailed for his heterodox views and died in prison. The division they have inflicted on the Umma endures, as also do the duties of exposing falsehood and demonstrating the evidentiary proofs of the people of truth. We strove to do so in our 2017 denunciation of the substate criminals known as ISIS on the laws of conflict, entitled *The incineration of persons in jihad, criminal penalties and reprisals*, which was published in Malaysia.

May Allah bring us into the fold of His Friends and those who stand in defense of the sacred Law and the Way of the Seal of His Prophets, our liege lord Muhammad–upon him and his Family, Companions and Assembly the blessings and peace of Allah. He is the Grantor of success and the best defender.

I. The claim that Sufis misquote Prophetic Hadiths

The objector said–may Allah guide him: "Shaykh Habib ʿAlī al-Jafrī attributes to al-Bukhārī and Muslim that which is not found in them, and this leads people astray and turns factual realities on their head."

It would have been appropriate to furnish examples of the claim of misattribution so that the latter can be ascertained. Short of it, the above statement remains an unsubstantiated accusation doubling as a calumny. Allah said,

﴿قُلْ هَاتُوا۟ بُرْهَـٰنَكُمْ إِن كُنتُمْ صَـٰدِقِينَ﴾ البقرة ١١١ النمل ٦٤

Say: "Provide your proof if you are truthful" (Baqara 2:111, Naml 27:64).

Second, assuming examples are produced, has the objector ascertained that, by referring to one of the two *Ṣaḥīḥ*s or both—or to the *Sunan* or other authoritative sources—the speaker was not referring to a sound *aṣl* (basis) in the *Ṣaḥīḥ*s or the *Sunan* supporting the meaning of the hadith rather than to its literal wording? This is very far from "turning factual realities on their head." Yet some objector with time on his hands will latch on to inadvertences by the speaker in order to attack him unjustly and calumniate him. Our teacher Dr. Saʿīd al-Buti called this, "blowing out of proportion petty matters and ijtihad-related foibles."

For example, if Habib ʿAlī al-Jafrī ever sourced the report of Ibn ʿUmar's touching of the pommel of the Prophet's pulpit for blessing to Bukhārī's *Ṣaḥīḥ* then it is true that the latter did not narrate it there. Nevertheless he did narrate the Companions' *tabarruk* with the Prophet's hair, his sandals and his utensils. Furthermore the pommel *tabarruk* was related by al-Bukhārī's better, namely his teacher ʿAbd Allāh b. Maslama al-Qaʿnabī—Imam Mālik's companion whom Mālik described as "the best of people on earth"—through whom Ibn Saʿd narrated with a good chain in *al-Ṭabaqāt al-kubrā* from Yazīd b. ʿAbd Allāh b. Qusayṭ that he said, "I saw that several of the Prophet's Companions–upon him the blessings and peace of Allah–when the mosque was empty, would place their right hands on the smooth pommel of the pulpit next to the Grave then they would face the qibla and supplicate." It is also in Ibn Abī Shayba's *Muṣannaf*. Ibn Saʿd also narrated it from the trustworthy *Tābiʿī* Muḥammad b. Ibrāhīm b. al-Ḥārith al-Taymī al-Madanī as the habitual act of Saʿd b. Abī Waqqās and Ibn ʿUmar, as did Ibn ʿAbd al-Barr with his chain in *al-Tamhīd*. Abū Hurayra would habitually place his hand on the pommel before he recited hadith every Jumuʿa as narrated by al-Ḥākim. This *tabarruk* (deriving of blessing) was also practiced by some of the major Successors such as ʿAṭā' b. Abī Rabāḥ. The pommel disappeared in a fire in the time of Ibn ʿAsākir as mentioned by al-Samhūdī in *Khulāṣat al-wafā*. How does any of the above leave any room for the allegation of "turning factual realities on their head"? It is ignorance and calumny.

A Wahhabi website claimed that Habib ʿAlī al-Jafrī had said that "Muslim narrated in his *Ṣaḥīḥ* that some of the Companions of the Messenger of Allah–upon him blessings and peace–asked to bury him at his pulpit, i.e. in his mosque." The Wahhabi commented:

> Thus does al-Jafrī promote his school which permits for the dead to be buried inside mosques and I demand that he show us this unique copy of *Ṣaḥīḥ Muslim* that he owns where this hadith is found. For Muslim did not narrate the hadith but rather Ibn Mājah, Aḥmad, al-Bayhaqī and Abū Yaʿlā narrated it, all of them through Ḥusayn b. ʿAbd Allāh b. ʿUbayd Allāh b. al-ʿAbbās who was accused of being a zindiq. Is this the way of fanaticism for one's own view and school? For us to lie against *Ṣaḥīḥ Muslim* and attribute to it the reports of the zindiqs!!!!!

In reality it is narrated by someone greater and stricter than Muslim, namely Mālik in the *Muwaṭṭā'* (chapter on what was related about the burial of the dead) that it had reached him that "the Messenger of Allah–upon him the blessings and peace of Allah–died on the second day of the week and was buried on the third day, and that people prayed over him individually without anyone leading them, whereupon some people said, 'Let him be buried at the pulpit' while others said, 'Let him be buried in the Baqī'.' Ibn Sa'd cited its chain in his *Ṭabaqāt* and Ibn 'Abd al-Barr rated it sound in *al-Tamhīd*. Bukhārī, furthermore, questioned the accusation of *zandaqa* against Ḥusayn b. 'Abd Allāh. (Unless Mālik, Bukhārī and Ibn 'Abd al-Barr were all fanatics?)

Another example of the Wahhabi obsession with filtering the gnat while letting the camel pass is over Habib 'Alī al-Jafrī's erroneous sourcing of the hadith cited in Ḥujjat al-Islām al-Ghazālī's *Iḥyā' 'ulūm al-dīn*, "The worst of the ulema are those that go to the emirs while the best of the emirs are those that go to the ulema" to Abū Dāwūd whereas what the latter narrated is, "Whoever clings to the sultan is seduced and no servant increases in nearness to the sultan except he increases in remoteness from Allah." The former wording, however, is supported by Ibn Mājah's report, "Of the worst of the readers to Allah are those that visit the emirs." The Wahhabi took this inadvertence as proof that "Habib 'Alī lies against Abū Dāwūd." And if he caught him sourcing a hadith narrated by Dāraquṭnī to Ṭabarānī he would cry out that he lies against al-Ṭabarānī, etc. The Wahhabi nitpicks the sources to no benefit. Worse, he calumniates ulema and he undermines the Prophetic teachings themselves!

Third, has the objector verified what the ulema said of the fiqh and the gist of the discourse that he is objecting to? One of the misguided might claim, for example, that Habib 'Alī al-Jafrī has turned upside-down the meaning of the report of Abū Hurayra's visit to Mount Sinai, whereas in reality he has not turned anything upside-down. Rather he has cited the sound ruling inferred from the transmitted evidence whether the ignoramus likes it or not. Following is the false claim in detail.

He said, "Al-Jafrī said that Abū Hurayra, who relates the hadith, 'One does not travel other than to the three Mosques,' himself undertook travel from Medina to Sinai in order to pray at the Mount where Mūsā–upon him the blessings and peace of Allah–conversed with his nurturing Lord. So al-Jafrī inferred that Abū Hurayra, although he had narrated the hadith, had contravened its manifest wording, namely the prohibition of travel, so that al-Jafrī might thereby promote his position in support of travel to the graves and other than that. See for yourselves the text of the hadith in full, with the passages suppressed by al-Jafrī marked [with underlining]:

> Abū Basrat al-Ghifārī met Abū Hurayra as he was coming from the Mount and said, "From where have you come?" He said, "From the Mount. I prayed there." He said, "Indeed, were I with you before you had travelled to it you would not have travelled. Verily I heard the Messenger of Allah–upon him the blessings and peace of Allah–say, 'One does not travel other than to the three Mosques: the Inviolable Mosque, this Mosque of mine and the farthermost Mosque.'"

"See then how the sense is topsy-turvy and consider how Abū Baṣra disapproved of Abū Hurayra–Allah be well-pleased with him–for going, adducing in support of it this hadith, which confirms the opposite of the sense proclaimed by al-Jafrī. O Umma of Islam! Is there, after this, any bigger lie or fabrication?"

It can be seen that the objector ignored the clear evidence that al-Jafrī had adduced, namely that Abū Hurayra—the narrator of the hadith "One does not travel" and one of the intermediate speakers of fatwa among the Companions, had indeed travelled to visit the Mount for the sake of *tabarruk* (deriving blessing) and *taʿabbud* (offering worship) just as thousands of devotees and worshippers of the righteous predecessors had done with him and after him there, and in Mount Lebanon, and in other than these two places as well. Abū Hurayra knew the fiqh of the matter better than Abū Baṣra al-Ghifārī. Travel is also undertaken to the Quba mosque, and it was recommended by Imam Malik as narrated by Ibn Abī Zayd in his *Jāmiʿ*.

Fourth, established Sufi shaykhs are truthful and trustworthy in their relating of hadiths and reports and they may even be, like Habib ʿAlī al-Jafrī, proficient in hadith and deeply familiar with it and with its sciences, with a strong gift for transmission. Despite that, they cite reports only in the context of practice in order to attract the spiritual and belief-related benefits of excellent acts. It is never only for the sake of narration and verbal teaching. Imam Abū Nuʿaym al-Aṣbahānī and his student al-Mālīnī narrated, as did the latter's two students al-Bayhaqī and al-Khaṭīb with their chains to Bishr b. al-Ḥārith, known as Bish al-Ḥāfi–may Allah have mercy on all of them–that the latter said to the experts of hadith, "Remit the zakat of this Hadith!" They said, "And what is its zakat?" He replied, "Out of every 200 hadiths, put into practice five." Give constructive criticism or say nothing at all!

Fifth, Has any of the masters of the science of hadith concurred with the objector over the accusation of extreme incorrect sourcing so that his claim that Habīb ʿAlī Jafrī "leads people astray and turns factual realities on their head" can be believed? For the matter is relative: there might occur rare mistakes in the writings of even the major ulema that are by general agreement considered knowledgeable in the sciences of narration and the understanding of hadith, and even in the narrations of the hadith masters and scholars, let alone among the great preachers of the Umma in our countries and elsewhere. What then of the discourse of the world-travelled admonisher who excels at the duties of sincere advice in the faith, who is anxious for pointing the Umma in the right direction and fulfills the duty of true *daʿwa* (calling to Allah) in every sense of the word on *a foothold of truth* (Yūnus 10:2) that has been entrusted to him by masters deemed to be friends of Allah such as his principal teachers Habib ʿAbd al-Qādir b. Aḥmad b. ʿAbd al-Raḥmān al-Saqqāf (1331-1431/1913-2010), his maternal great-aunt al-Ḥabbāba Ṣafiyya bint ʿUmar b. Ṣāliḥ b. ʿAbd Allāh al-ʿAṭṭās, al-Ḥabīb Muḥammad b. ʿAbd Allāh al-Haddār (1340-1418/1922-1997) and others?

A Sufi shaykh cites many Quranic verses and Prophetic hadiths but his purpose is to raise and educate. It is not to transmit narrations nor to document them in a specialized way. He cites from memory and he might err in some of the sourcing because he is not infallible. Still, *Ahl al-Sunna* have said, "For us the *ʿadl* (upright one) is he whose excellences outnumber his defects." Not "the one who is faultless." Nor was it ever a precondition for *daʿwa*, or calling people to Allah, or admonishment and preaching to have an infallible memory or to never make mistakes in sourcing to the two *Ṣaḥīḥ*s and the rest of the books of Hadith. So if we suppose that a Sufi shaykh made twenty slips in sourcing hadiths to famous books in the course of 1,000 hours of speech for example, then some ignorant and envious idler tracking the blemishes of Muslims and spying on the ulema to catch them saying something incorrect barks at him, "lies!," "fabrications!," "fanaticism!," "zindiq!," then should the universally-recognized, pious and upright Sufi shaykh be abandoned for what someone of this kind says?

The style of our Sufi guides–may Allah raise their stations in both abodes–is unique and copious because of the copiousness of their knowledge, the purity of their inspiration and orientation, their focus on the hereafter and the miraculous gifts of their spiritual chain of transmission–may Allah reward them abundantly on our behalf! One hour of their speech is like thirty hours of someone else's in quantity of beneficial information. As for the quality of *madad* (spiritual help) contained therein, then no book can match it because it is the embodiment of the Qur'ān and such is rightly deemed rarer than rare even in the holy land of Prophets and Awliya, Syro-Palestine.

The light of rightly-guided wisdom and practical guidance is at the heart of the address of our Sufi teachers and it is the whole point of their activity. They are not about words and references. This is why you have seen tens of thousands of Europeans and Americans flocking to our teacher Mawlana al-Shaykh Nazim al-Haqqani and his caliphs. They did not seek bookish knowledge but emigration to good manners, the way of self-purification and the way of spiritual knowledge and practice. It is for the same reason that people travel from those continents to Yemen with their families in great numbers to study and practice. Is this misguidance? Rather it is the soul of guidance from Allah and its fruit. It suffices as a reply to their detractors and it is enough honor that Allah has consistently brought droves of seekers of guidance to their feet over a half century, and continues to bring them to the feet of their successors.

II. Accusing Sufis of authenticating inauthentic Hadiths

The objector said–may Allah guide him: "He cites the ulema's authentication of a given hadith when in fact they declare it weak and they do not authenticate it."

The objector faults others without doubting himself, like the one whose *self-importance spurs him on to sin* (al-Baqara 2:206). Has he encompassed all that the ulema of hadith have said about the status of those unmentioned inauthentic hadiths? For there might be found one or more strong aspects dictating that a certain hadith that many have declared weak is in fact sound or fair, and verifying experts will come along and declare it authentic. For example the hadith, "**My Companions are like the stars: whichever you take as a leader, you will be rightly guided**."

حديث **أَصْحَابِي كَالنُّجُومِ، بِأَيِّهِمُ اقْتَدَيْتُم، اهْتَدَيْتُمْ** مال إلى تقويته البيهقي في المدخل والاعتقاد وابن عبد البر في جامع بيان العلم والقاضي عياض في الشفا والحافظ ابن حجر في التلخيص الحبير، وعبد الفتاح أبو غدة في حاشية الأجوبة العشرة للَّكْنَوي، وحسّنه الصاغاني وصحّحه اللكنوي مع كونه مشهور الضعف.

Despite its being famously weak, nevertheless Bayhaqī in *al-Madkhal* and *al-Iʿtiqād*, Ibn ʿAbd al-Barr in *Jāmiʿ bayān al-ʿilm*, Qadi ʿIyāḍ in *al-Shifā*, the arch-master Ibn Ḥajar in *al-Talkhīṣ al-ḥabīr* and ʿAbd al-Fattāḥ Abū Ghudda in his marginalia on Laknawī's *al-Ajwibat al-ʿashara* were all inclined to rate it strong while al-Ṣāghānī rated it fair and al-Laknawī rated it sound.

Likewise the hadith, "**I am the city of knowledge and ʿAlī is its door**:" Ibn Maʿīn, Abū Zurʿa, Abū Ḥātim, Yaḥyā b. Saʿīd al-Qaṭṭān, Ibn al-Jawzī, Dhahabī and others such as al-Qurṭubī in his *Tafsīr* all declared it a lie, yet the arch-master Ibn Ḥajar inclined to rate it fair and al-ʿAlāʾī did declare it fair—both of them in their answers to Sirāj al-Dīn Abū Ḥafṣ 'Umar b. 'Alī b. 'Umar al-Qazwīnī's (d. 750/1349) claim that it was a forgery—as did al-Zarkashī in *al-Tadhkira*, al-Sakhāwī in the *Maqāṣid*, al-Suyūṭī in the *La'āli'*, the *Ta'aqqubāt 'alā al-mawḍū'at*, the *Durar* and the *Ḥāwī lil-fatāwā*, Haytamī in *al-Fatāwā al-ḥadīthiyya*, al-Fattanī al-Hindī in *Tadhkirat al-mawḍū'āt*, and Shawkānī in *al-Fawā'id al-majmū'a*. Al-Ḥākim and Aḥmad al-Ghumārī rated it sound.

حديث **أَنَا مَدِينَةُ الْعِلْمِ وَعَلِيٌّ بَابُهَا** كذّبه ابن معين وأبو زرعة وأبو حاتم
ويحيى بن سعيد القطّان وابن الجوزي والذهبي وغيرهم كالقرطبي في تفسيره
لكن مال الحافظ إلى تحسينه وحسّنه العلائي في أجوبتهما على القزويني
لتوضيعه بعض أحاديث مشكاة المصابيح والزركشي في التذكرة، والسخاوي
في المقاصد، والسيوطي في اللآلئ والتعقُّبات والدرر والحاوي للفتاوى،
والهيتمي في الفتاوى الحديثية، والفَتَّني الهندي في تذكرة الموضوعات،
والشوكاني في الفوائد المجموعة، وذهب الحاكم وأحمد الغُماري إلى تصحيحه.

Our Sufi Shaykhs, also, are treasure-troves of hadith even if, like Imam Ghazālī at the end of his *Qānūn al-ta'wīl*, they might humbly disclaim possessing much knowledge therein. The reality is that when they adduce Quranic verses and Prophetic Hadiths in the light of what Allah has opened of lights in their hearts, they are like the rain bringing back life to the dead earth, in illustration of the poet's praise, "every land where you alight comes alive." One will experience this, for example, upon reading the proof-texts Mawlana Shaykh Nazim adduces in his 1970s and 1980s Lebanon Suhbas, as if it were the first time in their life one was hearing Qur'ān and Hadith.

Furthermore, differences of opinion in subsidiary matters are a fact of scholarly life in the mercied Umma, but the ulema have established rules of conduct therein. One of them is that it is impermissible to object to rulings that are derived on the basis of evidences over which there is *khilāf mu'tabar* (a legitimate divergence of views). As for the divergence of groups or individuals who are not qualified or who do not even belong to *Ahl al-Sunna* in the first place (or belong in its periphery), no attention is paid to it.

The upshot of the above points is that Habib 'Alī al-Jafrī might be following the legitimate position of whoever declared such supposedly weak hadiths to be in fact authentic and accepted. What is certain is that the objector gravely errs in passing judgment as if he had encompassed everything that was said about them in the hadith literature. This is not necessarily because of following dubious (or discredited), controverted (if not heterodox) and error-prone authorities. It may just be because he is out of his depth as Hadith is not his field. We have documented some of these divisive figures at length in *Albāni and His Friends* and the introductions to our translations of Ibn Jahbal al-Kilābī's *Refutation of Him* [Aḥmad al-Ḥarrānī] *Who Attributes Direction to Allah* and Mullā 'Alī al-Qarī's *Encyclopedia of Forgeries.*

Finally, there are some among the specialized scholars of hadith that rule a report to be forged or very weak in its wording while, at the same time, ruling its meaning to be authentic and sound because it is supported by mass-transmitted evidence such as the Qur'ān or other authentic sources, among them Zarkashī, al-Suyūṭī, Ibn 'Arrāq in *Tanzīh al-Sharī'at al-marfū'a*, al-Qārī in *al-Asrār al-marfū'a* and 'Ajlūnī in *Kashf al-khafā'*. So the statement might be attributed to the Beloved of Allah–upon him the blessings and peace of Allah–in an informal way, or in consent with someone deemed qualified to be imitated, not as an intentional lie. Rather it is almost always supported by a well-established foundational text, or it is the statement of a Companion or some other eminence of the early authorities. Or are Zarkashī, al-Suyūṭī et al. misguiding the Umma? They are not. May Allah have mercy on them.

III. Sufis follow Consensus in the acceptance of weak hadiths

When a hadith is merely weak and not extremely weak there is no issue in quoting it and for putting it into practice in *faḍā'il al-a'māl* (virtuous acts) by consensus which no one contravenes, as indicated by Ibn 'Abd al-Barr in *al-Tamhīd*, al-Bayhaqī in the introduction of *Dalā'il al-nubuwwa*, Nawawī in *al-Majmū'*, *al-Irshād*, *Sharḥ Ṣaḥīḥ Muslim*, *al-Adhkār* and *Khulāṣat al-aḥkām*, Aḥmad al-Ḥarrānī in *Sharḥ al-'umda*, *Majmū' al-fatāwā* and elsewhere, al-Sakhāwī in *Fatḥ al-Mughīth* and *al-Qawl al-badī'*, 'Alī al-Qārī in *Sharḥ al-Shifā*, *Mirqāt al-mafātīḥ*, *al-Asrār al-marfū'a* and *Sharḥ sharḥ Nukhbat al-fikar*, Ṭāhir al-Jazā'irī in *Tawjīh al-naẓar ilā uṣūl al-athar*, and 'Alawī b. 'Abbās al-Mālikī in *al-Manhal al-laṭīf fī aḥkām al-ḥadīth al-ḍa'īf* to name a few. Some of them have an even more inclusive criterion than what was mentioned, namely "**as long as it is not forged**," such as al-Nawawī in *al-Adhkār*, al-Jazā'irī in the *Tawjīh* and the Hadith master Zayn al-Dīn al-'Irāqī in his *Alfiyya* entitled *al-Tabṣira wal-tadhkira* and its commentaries.

No one to our knowledge has breached this consensus before the Damascene Naqshbandi Jamāl al-Dīn al-Qāsimī–Allah have mercy on him–in his *Qawā'id al-taḥdīth* followed by Nasir the Albanian. Both cited purportedly dissenting positions attributed to al-Bukhārī, Muslim, Yaḥyā b. Ma'īn, Ibn Ḥazm, Qadi Abū Bakr Ibn al-'Arabī al-Mālikī and al-Shawkānī which they never held in reality. Their explicit statements and well-established practice in their works are in complete agreement with the abovementioned consensus as we shall now demonstrate.

Al-Bukhārī patently uses weak hadiths as evidence in his extant multiple-edition books *al-Adab al-mufrad*, *Birr al-wālidayn*, *al-Du'ā'*, *Khalq af'āl al-'ibād*, *al-Qirā'atu khalfa al-imām* and *Raf' al-yadayn*, not to mention his *al-Tārīkh al-kabīr*. He even uses them in the chapter-titles of his magnum opus the *Ṣaḥīḥ* as truncated-chained reports such as, e.g., his statement:

قال البخاري في صحيحه بَاب مَا يُذْكَرُ فِي الْفَخِذِ: قَالَ أَبُو عَبْدِ الله: وَيُرْوَى عَنْ ابْنِ عَبَّاسٍ وَجَرْهَدٍ وَمُحَمَّدِ بْنِ جَحْشٍ عَنِ النَّبِيِّ ﷺ: **الْفَخِذُ عَوْرَةٌ**. وَقَالَ أَنَسُ بْنُ مَالِكٍ: حَسَرَ النَّبِيُّ ﷺ عَنْ فَخِذِهِ. قَالَ أَبُو عَبْد الله: وَحَدِيثُ أَنَسٍ أَسْنَدُ وَحَدِيثُ جَرْهَدٍ أَحْوَطُ.

وقال الترمذي في السنن عن حديث جرهد: مَا أَرَى إِسْنَادَهُ بِمُتَّصِلٍ.

"Chapter: What is mentioned about the thigh. Abū 'Abd Allāh [=Bukhārī] said, 'and it is narrated from Ibn 'Abbās, Jarhad and Muḥammad b. Jaḥsh from the Prophet–upon him the blessings and peace of Allah–*the thigh is nakedness*; while Anas b. Mālik said the Prophet–upon him blessings and peace of Allah–uncovered his thigh.' Abū 'Abd Allāh said, 'now the hadith of Anas is better-chained while the hadith of Jarhad is more precautionary.'" His student Abū 'Īsā al-Tirmidhī said in his *Sunan* about Jarhad's hadith, "I do not think its chain is unbroken at all."

Muslim forbade narrating from arch-liars and arch-forgers, not from weak narrators that are upright and truthful. This is the gist of his discourse in the introduction to his *Ṣaḥīḥ*. This was explicitly stated by Nawawī in *Sharḥ Ṣaḥīḥ Muslim*, al-Zur'ī in *I'lām al-muwaqqi'īn*, al-Sakhāwī in *al-Qawl al-badī'*, and our teacher Nūr al-Dīn 'Itr in his published marginalia on the hadith master Ibn Rajab's commentary on al-Tirmidhī's *'Ilal*. Its internal proof and practical demonstration is Muslim's own chainless citation, in the same introduction, of the broken-chained hadith from 'Ā'isha–Allah be well-pleased with her:

قال مسلم في المقدّمة: وَقَدْ ذُكِرَ عَنْ عَائِشَةَ رَضِيَ اللهُ تَعَالَى عَنْهَا، أَنَّهَا قَالَتْ: **أَمَرَنَا رَسُولُ الله ﷺ أَنْ نُنَزِّلَ النَّاسَ مَنَازِلَهُمْ**. إسناده منقطع كما أفاده البيهقي في الشُعَب. وروى في الصحيح عمن تُكُلّم فيهم: كشدّاد بن

سعيد الراسبي، والوليد بن أبي وليد، ويعقوب بن إسحاق الحضرمي، جميعه
في أحاديث فضائل الأعمال كالأدب والتوبة والبر والصلة وفضائل الصحابة.

"The Prophet–upon him the blessings and peace of Allah–ordered us to give people their due stations." No one narrates this directly from 'Ā'isha as stated by Bayhaqī in *Shu'ab al-īmān* (75: *ruḥm al-ṣaghīr wa-tawqīr al-kabīr*). Muslim also narrated in the body of his *Ṣaḥīḥ* from several controverted narrators such as Shaddād b. Sa'īd al-Rāsibī, al-Walīd b. Abī Walīd and Ya'qūb b. Isḥāq al-Ḥaḍramī, all of them in hadiths about virtuous deeds such as *adab* (high manners), *tawba* (repentance), *birr and ṣila* (piety and family ties) and the merits of the Companions.

As for **Yaḥyā b. Ma'īn** the correct view concerning his position is what is related from him by Ibn Abī Ḥātim in the introduction to his encyclopedia of narrator-commendation and discreditation entitled *al-Jarḥ wal-ta'dīl*, al-Khaṭīb in *al-Kifāya*, Ibn Rajab in *Sharḥ 'Ilal al-Tirmidhī* and Sakhāwī in *Fatḥ al-Mughīth* in complete support of the abovementioned consensus. The claim by Ibn Sayyid al-Nās in the introduction to his *'Uyūn al-athar* that Ibn Ma'īn forbade the narration of weak hadiths in absolute terms is inaccurate. Ibn Ma'īn held the same view as the early authorities among the Hadith experts in his own narrations of weak hadiths and in the practice of them in virtuous deeds and other than that. Ibn 'Adī related in *al-Kāmil* from Ibn Abī Maryam: "I heard Yaḥyā b. Ma'īn say, 'Idrīs b. Sinān: of his hadiths, let the heart-softening ones be written down.'" That is also the basis for his ambivalence towards the Sufi preacher Ṣāliḥ al-Murrī, at times rejecting him and at times retaining him.

As for **Ibn Ḥazm** he adduces the statement of Imam Aḥmad, "Weak hadith is lovelier to us than mere opinion" and he comments, "Aḥmad speaks true" in *al-Iḥkām fī uṣūl al-aḥkām*. Ibn Ḥazm himself states elsewhere in the same work, "weak hadiths are better than *ra'y* (opinion)"—and these statements, both on Aḥmad's part and on Ibn Ḥazm's part, concern hadiths of legal rulings, let alone the hadiths of merits and others! Another proof that Ibn Ḥazm narrated and accepted weak hadiths is that in his *Risāla fil-imāma* (treatise on leading the prayer) he replied the following to a Mālikī's question about praying behind someone who follows a different madhhab:

قال ابن حزم الظاهري في (رسالته في الإمامة): ذكرتَ أنّ هذا الإمام قيل عنه: إنّه يجيز الوضوء بالنبيذ، فاعلم يا أخي أنّ الوضوء بالنبيذ، وإن كنّا لا نقول به لأنّه لم يصحَّ الحديث في ذلك عن النبي ﷺ، فقد رُوِّيناه عن علي بن أبي طالب وعكرمة والأوزاعي، ورُوي عن الحسن ابن حَيّ وحُميد بن عبد الرحمن وغيرهما من الفقهاء. فإن كنتَ لا تجيز الصلاة خلف هؤلاء، فأنت أعلم.

"You mentioned that it was said about this imam that he considers it licit to perform ablution with *nabīdh* (fermented fruit mash). Know, my brother, that although we do not hold this view because the hadith on that is not sound from the Prophet–upon him the blessings and peace of Allah–nevertheless it has been related to us from ʿAlī b. Abī Ṭālib, ʿIkrima and al-Awzāʿī, and it was also related from al-Ḥasan b. Ḥay, Ḥumayd b. ʿAbd al-Raḥmān and others of the jurists. So if you consider it impermissible to pray behind these ones, then you know best."

Consider how Ibn Ḥazm adduced as evidence his narration of hadiths that are *mawqūf* (=statements of a Companion) and *maqṭūʿ* (=statements of a Successor)—i.e. undoubtedly weak reports in his view—to legitimize *ṣalāt* behind an imam with such an ablution as permissible and to suggest it for a Mālikī to imitate the madhhab of the people of Iraq on other than a sound Prophetic foundation in his view. He said "you know best" in the sense of a dismissive rebuke for even considering the premise of the invalidity of such an ablution and prayer.

Ibn al-ʿArabī al-Mālikī also supported the narration and use of weak hadiths since he said in his large work *ʿĀriḍat al-aḥwadhī*, in commentary of the hadith, "The sneezer is blessed thrice" after al-Tirmidhī's commentary that it is an odd-chained hadith and that its chain is unknown: "even if it is unknown, nevertheless it is desirable to put it into practice because it is an invocation of goodness, an affirmation of loving ties with the sitting-companion, and a form of endearment to the latter." The arch-master Ibn Ḥajar cited this comment in *Fatḥ al-Bārī* and added, "Therefore it is more appropriate to put it into practice."

Ibn ʿArrāq al-Dimashqī in his *Tanzīh al-sharīʿa* also related from *Marāqī al-zulaf* which Ibn al-ʿArabī himself authored, that the latter said of the hadith, "When one of you has sex with his wife or his slave girl then let him not look at her pudendum because that leads to blindness:" "I hold it to be disliked to look because, even if the report is not well-established [as a basis] for a legal ruling of dislike, nevertheless a weak report is a more appropriate basis for the ulema than opinion and analogy." Muḥammad ʿAwwāma cited this proof in the first footnote of the conclusion to his edition of Sakhāwī's *al-Qawl al-badīʿ* (p. 472).

Lastly **al-Shawkānī**'s position is that disauthentication is not an exact science. He explicitly states so in the parts on *ṭibb* (medicine) of the book of *ashriba* (beverages) in his *Nayl al-awṭār*—an encyclopedia of the hadiths related to legal rulings which is an expanded commentary on Abū al-Barakāt Majd al-Dīn ʿAbd al-Salām b. al-Khiḍr b. Muḥammad al-Ḥarrānī's (590-653/1194-1255) *al-Muntaqā min akhbār al-Muṣṭafā*, based on the Six Books, the *Musnad* and Dāraquṭnī's *Sunan*—saying:

قال الشوكاني في (نيل الأوطار)، باب ما جاء في الحجامة وأوقاتها: وَالْحَاصِلُ أَنَّ أَحَادِيثَ التَّوْقِيتِ وَإِنْ لَمْ يَكُنْ شَيْءٌ مِنْهَا عَلَى شَرْطِ الصَّحِيحِ إِلَّا أَنَّ الْمَحْكُومَ عَلَيْهِ بِعَدَمِ الصِّحَّةِ إِنَّمَا هُوَ فِي ظَاهِرِ الْأَمْرِ لَا فِي الْوَاقِعِ؛

فَيُمْكِنُ أَنْ يَكُونَ الصَّحِيحُ ضَعِيفًا، وَالضَّعِيفُ صَحِيحًا، لِأَنَّ الْكَذُوبَ قَدْ يَصْدُقُ وَالصَّدُوقُ قَدْ يَكْذِبُ. فَاجْتِنَابُ مَا أَرْشَدَ الْحَدِيثُ الضَّعِيفُ إِلَى اجْتِنَابِهِ، وَاتِّبَاعُ مَا أَرْشَدَ إِلَى اتِّبَاعِهِ مِنْ مِثْلِ هَذِهِ الْأُمُورِ يَنْبَغِي لِكُلِّ عَارِفٍ، وَإِنَّمَا الْمَمْنُوعُ: إِثْبَاتُ الْأَحْكَامِ التَّكْلِيفِيَّةِ أَوِ الْوَضْعِيَّةِ أَوْ نَفْيُهَا بِمَا هُوَ كَذَٰلِكَ.

"Chapter: What has come [to us] as to cupping and its timings: the upshot is that the hadiths of timing, even if none of them meets the criterion of authenticity, nevertheless what is ruled to be inauthentic is only insofar as external appearances, not in actual fact. So it is always possible for the *ṣaḥīḥ* to be *ḍaʿīf* and vice versa, because the inveterate liar might tell the truth and the truthful one might lie. So the avoidance of what the weak hadith directs us to avoid and the pursuance of what it directs us to pursue of the like of such matters imposes itself to every specialist. What is forbidden is only to affirm or negate obligatory or positive rulings on the basis of what has that status."

IV. Even a very weak hadith may convey a sound meaning

The objector said–may Allah guide him: "Or the hadith is inexistent in the books of Hadith—all of them."

Such a sweeping statement requires the kind of encompassing knowledge that is seldom granted to the major Hadith masters of the latter-day righteous memorizers such as Ibn Ḥajar al-ʿAsqalānī and al-Suyūṭī—let alone those that are below their rank by eons! Here is Imam al-Dhahabī—he needs no introduction on this chapter—saying about the nonagenarian Shāfiʿī Hadith master Abū Bakr Aḥmad b. Ibrāhīm al-Ismāʿīlī (277-371 /890-981) the author of a *Mustakhraj* (renarration with shorter chains) of *Ṣaḥīḥ al-Bukhārī*: "I was left speechless by his memorization! And I have categorically concluded that the latter-day scholars can despair of ever hoping to catch up to the earlier ones in memorization and knowledge [of Hadith]." Al-Kattānī mentioned this in *al-Risāla al-mustaṭrafa*. The objector, however, is not know for knowledge of hadith.

Rating a hadith as *munkar* (disclaimed), very *gharīb* (singular), or *lā aṣla lahu* (baseless) is also a relative matter. You might at times find it folded up within copious discourse that is all beneficial if Allah wills. Look at Ḥujjat al-Islām al-Ghazālī's book of *Iḥyā' ʿulūm al-dīn* with its immense benefits, lights and blessings. Look at its precursors Abū Ṭālib al-Makkī's *Qūt al-qulūb*; Abū Naṣr al-Sarrāj's *al-Lumaʿ*; the books of Abū ʿAbd al-Raḥmān al-Sulamī; its epigones al-Jaylānī's *al-Ghunya li-ṭālibī ṭarīq al-Ḥaqq*, the books of Ibn ʿArabī, al-Shaʿrānī and others. They also were not spared the accusation of containing weak hadiths, perhaps even of "leading people astray and turning factual realities on their head" in the objector's extreme view and per his exaggerated terminology. Yet the *Iḥyā'* is without peer among the books of spiritual guidance, to the point one of its paragons, the *Quṭb al-irshād* Abū al-Ḥasan al-Shādhilī, said of it,

قال الإمام أبو الحسن الشاذلي: **تَرْكُ الأمة لمطالعة (إحياء علوم الدين) من أسباب الضَّيم عليها.** وقال: **(الإحياء) يورث العلم و(القوت) يورث النور.** كذا في (لطائف المنن) لابن عطاء الله السكندري.

"For the Umma to stop reading the *Iḥyā'* is of the avenues of its *ḍaym* (injury)." This is his ruling concerning **those who deliberately avoid teaching it, and attack it instead.** He also said, "The *Iḥyā'* fosters knowledge while the *Qūt* fosters light," all as quoted in Ibn 'Aṭā' Allāh's *Laṭā'if al-minan fī manāqib Abī al-'Abbās al-Mursī wa-shaykhih Abī al-Ḥasan* (The kind subtle bestowals on the merits of Abū al-'Abbās al-Mursī and his shaykh Abū al-Ḥasan). The *Iḥyā'*, moreover, has been required reading for generations of teachers and students among the Bā 'Alawī Prophetic descendants as you can ascertain verbatim in the *Fatāwā ṣūfiyya* of the *Quṭb* 'Abd Allāh al-Ḥaddād.

May Allah forgive us. We recognize men by the truth and not vice versa, and we say that these books are practice-bound. Their utility is practical, just as is the case with *taṣawwuf* in general. It is not about discourse. The fruit of deeds is spiritual men and women. A person addresses you with his or her state before doing so with their tongue. This is clear. The Prophet–upon him blessings and peace of Allah–taught his Umma to say, "**O Allah! I seek refuge in You from knowledge that does not benefit**!"[2]

اللَّهُمَّ إِنِّي أَعُوذُ بِكَ مِنْ عِلْمٍ لا يَنْفَعُ رواه الطيالسي وزهير بن حرب وابن أبي شيبة وأحمد ومسلم وابن ماجه وأبو داود والنسائي وغيرهم عن أنس وجابر وزيد ابن أرقم وأبي هريرة وعبد الله بن عمرو مرفوعاً

[2] A Prophetic hadith narrated from Anas, Jābir, Zayd b. Arqam, Abū Hurayra and 'Abd Allāh b. 'Amr by Ṭayālisī, Zuhayr b. Ḥarb, Ibn Abī Shayba, Aḥmad, Muslim, the *Sunan* and others.

We ask Allah to grant them mercy and we affirm them as Imams between us and Allah, accepting their *naṣīḥa* (transparent advice) and the *naṣīḥa* of other than them among the descendants and the spiritual caliphs of the Messenger of Allah–upon him the blessings and peace of Allah–namely the Godwary ulema and righteous Awliya. Furthermore we hope for their intercession just as it is our firm belief concerning our own direct spiritual masters. If the accuser wishes to be accusing them on the Day of Resurrection then let him look forward to his choice.

V. The prohibition of lying about the Prophet is two-edged: do not call a lie a hadith—and do not call a hadith a lie!

The objector said–may Allah guide him: "And we very well know the mass-transmitted hadith, 'Whoever deliberately lies against me, let him from now take his seat in Hellfire.'"

مَنْ كَذَبَ عَلَيَّ مُتَعَمِّدًا فَلْيَتَبَوَّأْ مَقْعَدَهُ مِنَ النَّارِ متواتر

Yes, and many of those that habitually take this magnificent hadith to witness against someone are in fact heedless of its equally grave other sense, namely for one to be rejecting the attribution of something to the Messenger of Allah–upon him blessings and peace of Allah–when it is in fact sound. This is why we also find in one of its wordings from Abū Bakr al-Ṣiddīq–may Allah be well-pleased with him, and in the fact that he is the one narrating it there is a subtle secret–"Whoever deliberately lies against me **or rejects something that I have ordered**, let him from now take his seat in Hellfire."

مَنْ كَذَبَ عَلَيَّ مُتَعَمِّداً أَوْ رَدَّ شَيْئاً أَمَرْتُ بِهِ فَلْيَتَبَوَّأْ مَقْعَدَهُ مِنَ النَّارِ

Furthermore the beginning of that hadith contains an order to convey, an exhortation to call others to Allah and a command and permission to narrate from the Jews and the Christians (i.e. that which is eminently supported and confirmed by the sacred Law): "Convey from me if only a single verse and narrate from the children of Israel without any *ḥaraj* (difficulty / unease / constraint or pressure not to do so), but whoever deliberately lies against me, let him from now take his seat in Hellfire."

بَلِّغُوا عَنِّي وَلَوْ آيَةً وَحَدِّثُوا عَنْ بَنِي إِسْرَائِيلَ وَلَا حَرَجَ وَمَنْ كَذَبَ عَلَيَّ مُتَعَمِّدًا فَلْيَتَبَوَّأْ مَقْعَدَهُ مِنَ النَّارِ

So then, if the narrator slipped or made a statement inadvertently, will he be someone who deliberately lies against the Messenger of Allah–upon him the blessings and peace of Allah? And is it at all probable for any of the pious ulema of *Ahl al-Sunna* to deliberately lie against the Prophet–upon him the blessings and peace of Allah–or for the like of our noble Sufi masters to lie against their grandfather deliberately? If not, then the Prophet–upon him the blessings and peace of Allah–said, as narrated in the *Sunan* and elsewhere:

إِنَّ اللهَ وَضَعَ عَنْ أُمَّتِي الخَطَأَ وَالنِّسْيَانَ وَمَا اسْتُكْرِهُوا عَلَيْهِ رواه

أصحاب السنن وحسّنه الإمام النووي كما في تلخيص الحبير

"Verily Allah has unburdened from my Umma mistakes, forgetfulness, and that over which they have been coerced."

Let us now suppose a mistake did befall as claimed by the talebearer that came bringing fitna to you and, through you, everyone else. How very many of the superlative ulema have been flagged and corrected for their mistakes by scholars who came forward and rectified them in all or nearly all of the disciplines of knowledge including language, history, fiqh and hadith? Among them *Awhām Abū 'Ubayd* (Abū 'Ubayd's delusions) by Ibn Qutayba; *Awhām al-muḥaddithīn* (Delusions of the hadith scholars) by Muslim; *Durrat al-ghawwāṣ fī awhām al-khawāṣṣ* (The diver's pearl on the delusions of the elite) by al-Ḥarīrī; *al-Tanbīh 'alā awhām Abī 'Alī al-Qālī fī amālīh* (Notification of al-Qālī's delusions in his dictations) by al-Bakrī al-Andalusī; *al-Wahm wal-īhām al-wāqi'ān fī kitāb 'Abd al-Ḥaqq al-Ishbīlī al-musammā bil-Aḥkām* (Delusions and false suggestions occurring in 'Abd al-Ḥaqq al-Ishbīlī's *Aḥkām*) by Ibn Qaṭṭān al-Fāsī—this massive book is ranked among the *ṣaḥīḥ* works; al-Khaṭṭābī's *Taṣḥīfāt al-muḥaddithīn* (The textual corruptions of the hadith scholars); Junābidhī's *Tanbīh al-labīb fī taḥqīq awhām al-Khaṭīb* (Notification of the prudent on the ascertainment of al-Khaṭīb's delusions); al-Nājī's *Awhām al-*

Mundhirī fil-Targhīb wal-tarhīb (Mundhirī's delusions in *al-Targhīb wal-tarhīb*); Ibn Nāṣir al-Dīn's *al-I'lām bi-mā waqa'a fī Mushtabah al-Dhahabī min al-awhām* (Announcement of Dhahabī's delusions in his *Mushtabah*); Fayrūzābādī's *Taḥbīr al-mūwashshīn fil-ta'bīr bil-sīn wal-shīn* (Refinement of the adorned on what is pronounced *s* as well as *sh*) in which he gave 90 examples, e.g. the word for chess, *siṭranj* as well as *shiṭranj*—"he flagged in it 1,000 delusions in Ibn Fāris's *al-Mujmal* (an Arabic dictionary), all the while magnifying and praising him" per Burhān al-Dīn al-Ḥalabī; al-Asnawī's *al-Hidāya ilā awhām al-Kifāya* (Guidance to the delusions of al-Suhaylī al-Jājarmī in *al-Kifāya* on Shāfi'ī fiqh); Ibn Fatḥūn and Abū 'Alī al-Ghassānī's *Awhām al-Istī'āb* (Delusions of Ibn 'Abd al-Barr in his encyclopedia of the Companions), also the title of a similar work by the Hadith master Sharaf al-Dīn al-Dimyāṭī; the latter authored another work on the linguistic and historical delusions of Imam Bukhārī in his *Ṣaḥīḥ*; the Hadith master 'Abd al-Ghanī al-Maqdisī authored a work on Abū Nu'aym's delusions in his encyclopedia of the Companions *Ma'rifat al-Ṣaḥāba* while Ibn Ḥajar in his own vaster encyclopedia, *al-Iṣāba fī tamyīz al-Ṣaḥāba*, corrected every single one of those that had preceded him in this branch of knowledge. Finally, when al-Ḥākim saw a copy of the Egyptian Hadith master 'Abd al-Ghanī b. Sa'īd al-Miṣrī's *Awhām al-Ḥākim*, he took to reading it in his classes and he would give thanks to its author and follow his correctives.

The above is a sampling of the calm, qualified and light-filled correctives written on the elite of the ulema by their juniors by far in their specialized fields but without anathema and without discreditation. They provided the evidence in question as a helpful demonstration and exposition of the mistakes without artifice or rudeness in speech, and certainly without falling into misrepresentations and blunders of their own at every turn. As a result these correctives took their place among the Umma's scholarly treasures for which we thank Allah and pride ourselves. They are an illustration for the meaning of the Prophetic hadith of the two *Ṣaḥīḥ*s that forms a magnificent foundation:

إِذَا حَكَمَ الحَاكِمُ فَاجْتَهَدَ ثُمَّ أَصَابَ فَلَهُ أَجْرَانِ، وَإِذَا حَكَمَ فَاجْتَهَدَ ثُمَّ أَخْطَأَ فَلَهُ أَجْرٌ. متفق عليه

"When the maker of a judgment makes his judgment by striving then making the correct judgment then he has two rewards; and when he makes his judgment by striving then making the wrong judgment then he has one reward."

VI. The Messenger of Allah, the Companions and Successors all warned about the Umayyads

The objector said–may Allah guide him: "He [Habib 'Ali al-Jafri] casts aspersions on the Umayyads—a state Allah Most High has made the sword of Islam in its conquests."

All these charges are unsubstantiated and the man is innocent until proven otherwise through careful examination. This is what Allah Most High commanded in His statement,

﴿ يَٰٓأَيُّهَا ٱلَّذِينَ ءَامَنُوٓاْ إِن جَآءَكُمۡ فَاسِقُۢ بِنَبَإٖ فَتَبَيَّنُوٓاْ أَن تُصِيبُواْ قَوۡمَۢا بِجَهَٰلَةٖ فَتُصۡبِحُواْ عَلَىٰ مَا فَعَلۡتُمۡ نَٰدِمِينَ ٦ ﴾ الحجرات وفي قراءة سبعية: ﴿ فَتَثَبَّتُوٓاْ ﴾

O you who believe! If some depraved person has come to you with a piece of news then investigate, lest you should assail a group of people in ignorance then later find yourselves regretting what you have done (al-Ḥujurāt 49:6). Another of the seven Readings also has, *then verify and make sure*. But let us suppose that Shaykh 'Ali al-Jafri spoke about that: should we be forbidding Abū Hurayra's hadith of the Messenger of Allah–upon him blessings and peace–that states, "The ruinous demise of my Umma will take place at the hands of boys of the Quraysh"? It is narrated by Bukhārī who added that 'Amr b. Sa'īd b. al-'Āṣ interpreted it as the Banū Marwān. Another wording in Aḥmad has "little boys."

هَلَكَةُ أُمَّتِي عَلَى يَدَيْ غِلْمَةٍ مِنْ قُرَيْشٍ فقال مروان: لعنة الله عليهم، غِلْمَة!؟ فقال أبو هريرة رضي الله عنه: لو شئت أن أقول: بني فلان وبني فلان لفعلت. فكنت أخرج مع جدي - القائل عمرو بن يحيى بن سعيد بن عمرو بن سعيد بن العاص الأموي - إلى بني مروان حين ملكوا بالشأم، فإذا رآهم غلماناً أحداثاً قال

لنا: عسى هؤلاء أن يكونوا منهم؟ قلنا: أنت أعلم. رواه البخاري. وفي لفظ آخر:
أُغَيْلِمَةٍ سُفَهَاءَ مِنْ قُرَيْشٍ. رواه أحمد.

It is well-known that the caliphate shifted from the Sufyanids after the death of Mu'āwiya b. Yazīd b. Mu'āwiya b. Abī Sufyān to Marwān b. al-Ḥakam b. Abī al-'Āṣ b. Umayya (d. 65/685), whose descendants remained in power for the next 65 years. It is also narrated from Abū Hurayra in the two *Ṣaḥīḥs*, 'Ā'isha in Aḥmad and Ibn 'Abbās in Abū Dāwūd, "Those that will cause the ruinous demise of my Umma will be this sub-tribe of the Quraysh."

وعنه في الصحيحين وعن عائشة في المسند وعن ابن عباس في سنن أبي داود
مرفوعاً: **يُهلِكُ أُمَّتِي هٰذَا الحَيُّ مِنْ قُرَيْشٍ**.

It is also narrated from Abū Hurayra with a sound chain by Ibn Abī Khaythama in his *Tārīkh* and Abū Ya'lā in his *Musnad* that the Prophet–upon him the blessings and peace of Allah–saw the Banū al-Ḥakam sauntering on his pulpit and climbing down of it whereupon he woke up angry and said, "**What ails me that I saw the Banū al-Ḥakam sauntering on my pulpit like monkeys?**" After that he was never seen smiling again until he died. Further down (in chapter XIV) we cite Abū Ayyūb al-Anṣārī's reference of them as "unqualified usurpers."

وعنه أيضاً في التاريخ الكبير لابن أبي خيثمة ومسند أبي يعلى: أَنَّ رَسُولَ الله ﷺ رَأَى فِي المَنَامِ كَأَنَّ بَنِي الحَكَمِ يَنْزُونَ عَلَى مِنْبَرِهِ وَيَنْزِلُونَ، فَأَصْبَحَ كَالْمُتَغَيِّظِ وَقَالَ: **مَا لِي رَأَيْتُ بَنِي الحَكَمِ يَنْزُونَ عَلَى مِنْبَرِي نَزْوَ الْقِرَدَةِ؟** قَالَ: فَمَا رُئِيَ رَسُولُ الله ﷺ مُسْتَجْمِعًا ضَاحِكًا بَعْدَ ذَلِكَ حَتَّى مَاتَ ﷺ. وسيأتي وصف أبي أيّوب الأنصاري لهم بمن ولي ولاية الإسلم وهم غير أهلها.

The Prophet–upon him blessings and peace of Allah–named the Umayyads *imārat al-sufahā'* (governance by fools), *Luka' b. Luka'* (mean fool son of a mean fool), *imārat al-ṣibyān* (governance by boys), the *tāfih* (worthless ones), the *safīh* (impudent fool), the *ruwaybiḍa* (minor scoundrel) and the *fuwaysiq* (ditto) as narrated from Abū Hurayra, Anas, Jābir, Ḥudhayfa b. al-Yamān, 'Abd Allāh b. 'Amr, 'Awf b. Mālik al-Ashja'ī, Mu'ādh b. Jabal and others in the *Muṣannafāt*, *Musnads* and *Sunan*. Abū Hurayra and 'Awf b. Mālik would supplicate to Allah to take them back to Him before the year 60/680, the year Yazīd b. Mu'āwiya b. Abī Sufyān (26-64/647-683) came to power, under whose rule three scandals took place: the Prophet's grandson al-Ḥusayn b. 'Alī was killed; Madīna was ransacked for three days during which the Companions were massacred—after which no survivor of the battle of Badr was left on earth—and a thousand unmarried women gave birth to fatherless children; finally, the Ka'ba was destroyed and burnt, at which time Yazīd died. This is the context of Abū Hurayra's famed statement in Bukhārī:

حَفِظْتُ مِنْ رَسُولِ اللهِ ﷺ وِعَاءَيْنِ فَأَمَّا أَحَدُهُمَا فَبَثَثْتُهُ وَأَمَّا الْآخَرُ
فَلَوْ بَثَثْتُهُ قُطِعَ هَذَا الْبُلْعُومُ رواه ابن سعد والبخاري

"I have memorized two containers from the Messenger of Allah–upon him the blessings and peace of Allah. As for the first one I have disseminated it; and as for the other one, if I had disseminated it this gullet would have been cut."

Abū Hurayra was referring to his knowledge of the heads of fitna among the Umayyads after Mu'āwiya, whose grave at Bāb al-Ṣaghīr was the first one Habib 'Umar b. Ḥafīẓ—one of Habib 'Ali Jafri's teachers—visited on one of his early 2000s visits to Damascus to greet him and recite the Fatiha for him.

If, however, the aspersions the objector is referring to are about Yazīd b. Mu'āwiya for killing al-Ḥusayn, then al-Rūyānī narrated in his *Musnad*, as did Ibn Abī Shayba in *al-Muṣannaf* with a good chain from Abū Dharr:

عن أبي ذر رضي الله عنه قال: سمعت رسول الله ﷺ يقول: **إِنَّ أَوَّلَ مَنْ يُبَدِّلُ سُنَّتِي رَجُلٌ مِنْ بَنِي أُمَيَّةَ**. رواه الروياني في المسند وابن أبي شيبة في المصنف والبيهقي في الدلائل وقال: **يُشْبِهُ أَنْ يَكُونَ هُوَ يَزِيدُ بْنُ مُعَاوِيَةَ.**

"Verily the first of those that will corrupt my Sunna is a man from the Banū Umayya." Bayhaqī said in *Dalā'il al-Nubuwwa*, "It is likely that it is Yazīd b. Muʿāwiya." If you want to see more such predictive reports then look up the chapter entitled "The Prophet's reporting of the state of the Umayyads that come after Muʿāwiya" in Nabhānī's encyclopedia of the Prophet's miracles entitled *Ḥujjat Allāh ʿalā al-ʿālamīn bi-muʿjizāt Sayyid al-Mursalīn* (The conclusive proof of Allah over the worlds with the staggering miracles of the Master of the Prophetic Messengers).

If any Sufi speaks out about this particular aspect of Islamic history he is only saying what none can cover up, by consensus. Many of the authorities have spoken about it and no one criticized them for doing so, which would be *kitmān al-ʿilm* (concealing knowledge), one of the *kabā'ir*. It has been said that the killing of al-Ḥusayn is the greatest crime in human history after the killing of the Prophets–upon them peace–so how could anyone cover it up? Many of the great ulema authored books about it, which can neither be rejected nor denigrated because they were fair and just in castigating some of the un-Islamic acts of the Umayyads. Among the ulema are also those that allowed the cursing of Yazīd and his disparagement such as Imam Aḥmad in Abū Yaʿlā's narration from him in *al-Muʿtamad fīl-uṣūl* as mentioned by Haytamī in *al-Ṣawāʿiq al-muḥriqa* and Taftāzānī in *Sharḥ al-ʿaqā'id al-nasafiyya*. **The rightly-guided Umayyad Caliph ʿUmar b. ʿAbd al-ʿAzīz would have anyone that called Yazīd *amīr al-mu'minīn* (Commander of the believers) lashed twenty times.** Ibn Ḥajar mentioned it in *Lisān al-mīzān*.

To that effect did one of the recent Muslim thinkers—Abū al-Ḥasan al-Nadwī—cite, in his book *al-Murtaḍā*, Imam Aḥmad's statement, "**Does anyone who believes in Allah and the Last Day love Yazīd?**" He also cited Shaykh Ahmad Sirhindi's position that Yazīd was of the *fussāq* (depraved); 'Abd al-Ḥaqq al-Dihlawī's position that Yazīd was *min kibār al-mabghūḍīn* (of the major objects of hatred for the sake of Allah); and Waliyyullah al-Dihlawi's position that Yazīd was one of the major callers to misguidance per the Prophetic hadith on endtimes,

ثُمَّ يَنْشَأُ دُعَاةُ الضَّلَالَةِ رواه معمر وأحمد وغيرهما عن حذيفة مرفوعاً

"**Then the clarion callers to misguidance shall rise.**" Ma'mar b. Rāshid narrated it in his *Jāmi'* and Aḥmad in the *Musnad* among others.

As for what the Umayyads did in obedience of Allah and the Prophet—upon him the blessings and peace of Allah—of good deeds such as the conquests, then no one can deny that and they would be in the balance of the good deeds of whoever of them accomplished them, just as they count Awliya among them such as 'Umar b. 'Abd al-'Azīz and Mu'āwiya b. Yazīd b. Mu'āwiya—may Allah have mercy on them.

VII. Sufism and Sunnism are both defined by the mutual love and respect of *Ahl al-Bayt* and the Companions

From Habib 'Ali Jafri's talk on the Mawlid of our liege lord al-Ḥusayn delivered in Cairo on 28 Rabīʿ II 1423 / 9 July 2002

"The significance of the attachments of hearts, once they love, is immense. It is typical of love, when it enters the heart with force and takes possession of it, for the heart to then attach itself to everything that has to do or is even remotely connected with the object of its love. He–may my soul be his ransom!–affirmed this meaning, or rather he himself certainly instituted it, to the point that he said–upon him the blessings and peace of Allah–about the importance of Medina, '**The *dust* of Medina is a cure from leprosy**!' [Narrated by Zubayr b. Bakkār in *Akhbār al-Madīna* and others. The arch-master Ibn Ḥajar referred to it in his *tawassul* poetry by saying, *its soil's antimony is the essence of remedies.*]

غُبارُ المَدِينَةِ شِفَاءٌ مِنَ الْـجُذَامِ. رواه الزبير بن بكّار في أخبار المدينة عن إبراهيم بلاغاً وابن حبيب في الطب عن الزهري وأبو نعيم في الطب عن ثابت بن قيس بن شماس وابن السني كذلك والرافعي في أخبار قزوين وأبو سعد السمان في مشيخته ورمز السيوطي لضعفه، وللحافظ ابن حجر قصيدة في التوسّل أنشد فيها وهو يذكر المدينة المنوّرة:

فَإِنْ رَمِدَتْ مِنَ التَسْهِيدِ عَيْنٌ ۝ فَإِثْمِدُ تُرْبِهَا عَيْنُ الدَّوَاءِ

"What then is this meaning, O Messenger of Allah? People recognize that Medina, before you bonified it with your sacred self, was called Yathrib (Flayer), and it was a pestilential, noxious land. Whoever entered it would fall ill and become afflicted with fever. You father died there and your mother fell ill there from its baneful, harmful environment. However, when you entered it and alighted in its midst, when you honored it and ennobled it, it rose through your presence to a high level by which it became so passionately beloved to all souls and minds! More than that, its very soil and its very dust became remedies for cure!

"So then, if the very soil and the very dust, for the sake of their attachment to his exalted person–upon him the blessings and peace of Allah–have become remedies by which a cure is sought, then what about him whose connection with his exalted person became strong due to a vestige he left behind? When this is the status of dust that became affiliated to nearness to him, then what about those that are themselves a piece of him–upon him the blessings and peace of Allah? What about those in whose veins runs his noble blood? What about those who have emerged from his very presence? Will not the connection with those beloved ones become a *wasīla* (intermediary) for the good pleasure of the All-Bestowing King?

"It is as part of the above meaning that truthful hearts and minds have readied themselves for the true understanding of **connection with the exalted presence of the Master of lovers through the doors of his *'itra* (close family) and likewise through the doors of his Companions**–may Allah be well-pleased with them and make them pleased. When some took to prattling about the Ṣiddīq, he–upon him the blessings and peace of Allah–turned and said, "**Will you leave alone my Companion for me?**" [Bukhārī narrated it from Abū al-Dardā'.]

فَهَلْ أَنْتُمْ تَارِكُوا لِي صَاحِبِي؟ رواه البخاري عن أبي الدرداء

"Consider well this elevated meaning: are you not going to leave alone **for me**! The Messenger of Allah–upon him the blessings and peace of Allah–did not argue with them about what had happened, who said what and who did what. He only wants to elevate them to the taste of transacting with the meaning of love. And in that there is safety for people from their egos, vested interests and the tricks of their egos.

"He said, 'Will you not leave him alone for me? For my sake? Do I not have some right over you? Am I not of some importance to you? Does not love of me hold some sway over your egos so that those egos will submit? Will you not leave alone my Companion for me?' "He said, '**Verily the one who has rendered me the greatest services among you is Abū Bakr. If I were to take an intimate friend from my Umma I would take Abū Bakr as my intimate friend. Wall up away from me every private access into this Mosque except the private access of Abū Bakr.**' [Narrated by Bukhārī and Muslim.]

إِنَّ أَمَنَّكُمْ عَلَيَّ أَبُو بَكْرٍ. وَلَوْ كُنْتُ مُتَّخِذًا خَلِيلاً مِنْ أُمَّتِي لاتَّخَذْتُ أَبَا بَكْرٍ خَلِيلاً. سُدُّوا عَنِّي كُلَّ خَوْخَةٍ فِي هَذَا الْمَسْجِدِ غَيْرَ خَوْخَةِ أَبِي بَكْرٍ

متفق عليه

He said that so that the hearts would experience a shedding of the attachments of egos and their vested interests. This is why they said that 'the love of 'Uthmān and the love of 'Alī will not be found at the same time other than in a believer's heart' [as spoken by Sufyān al-Thawrī]. Why? They said, because when the hearts fully turn towards love of the Beloved, and when the spirits are truthful in their love of the Beloved, and the egos that incite to evil see that there is no way out from the realization of this meaning, the egos start to preoccupy the hearts with their vested interests away from their love. So the egos want to inject their own interests into the noble presence of love, but love does not accept any vested interests at all! This is why, when the egos that incite to evil find out—and when the devil finds out that the hearts have definitely inclined to the things that Allah loves and have connected themselves to His Elect Beloved, they look around to see from what direction this heart can be accessed so that they can cause interference between the heart and the purity and reality of its love. So when they divert the heart's attention to human affairs and human foibles, it becomes engrossed either with the Companions exclusively or with the *Ahl al-Bayt*

(People of the Prophetic family) exclusively. **This is why you cannot find an innovator who is filled and intoxicated with love of *Ahl al-Bayt* and the Companions at one and the same time—ever.**

"You will find that the one afflicted with illness, the one ruled by the ego's vested interests, if he loves *Ahl al-Bayt* and speaks about them, and praises them, and *tashayyaʿ* (is partial= Shīʿī) to them, his ego will trick him and its vested interests will trick him. Lo and behold, now he shows bad manners to the Messenger of Allah–upon him the blessings and peace of Allah–with regard to his Companions! Why do you love *Ahl al-Bayt* in the first place? He answers, 'Because they are the people of the House of the Prophet!' Oh, so you yourself love them for his sake–upon him blessings and peace of Allah. Now if your love for them is truly for his sake—purely and transparently, and not for some vested interest in yourself, and not out of a certain choice in your ego—then here are his Companions. These ones are 'his *Ahl*' while these ones are 'his *Aṣḥāb*.' The possessive adjective his is one and the same, it goes back to the same referent! His Family, his Companions! Why have you claimed that you love the people of his House 'for his sake,' then, after that, you no longer view that it is 'for his sake' that his Companions are honored and loved?

"The other one also discourses, saying, 'We want the Book and the Sunna. We want what the Messenger of Allah and his Companions were following. The Saved Group are those who will be the same as what he and his Companions were following, and we are on the side of the Companions of the Messenger of Allah.' Very well. What is your problem with *Ahl al-Bayt*? They say, 'No, no, no, no. They are the same as other people. They are the same as other people. *Aḥsin al-aʿmāl takun mithla al-Ḥusayn* (Excel in deeds and you will be like al-Ḥusayn).' O ill-mannered one! O rude one! O ignorant one about the importance of the people of high levels! O untruthful one in his claim that he loves! If you were truthful you would be filled with love for the *ʿitra* (close family of the Prophet).

"Our liege lord Abū Bakr–may Allah be well-pleased with him and make him pleased–is saying,

أُرْقُبُوا مُحَمَّداً ﷺ فِي أَهْلِ بَيْتِهِ رواه البخاري باب مناقب الحسن والحسين

"Keep careful watch of Muhammad with regard to the people of his House," as narrated by al-Bukhārī [in his *Ṣaḥīḥ*, chapter on the virtues of al-Ḥasan and al-Ḥusayn]. It is also transmitted [in it] that when he saw *al-imām al-karrār* (the tactical retreater)—our liege lord 'Alī b. Abī Ṭālib—carrying our liege lord al-Ḥasan on his arm he turned to him and said,

قال أبو بكر رضي الله عنه وهو يحمل الحسن على عاتقه **بِأَبِي شَبِيهٌ بِالنَّبِيِّ لاَ شَبِيهٌ بِعَلِيٍّ وَعَلِيٌّ يَضْحَكُ** رواه البخاري باب مناقب الحسن والحسين

"'My father be his ransom!'—i.e. may Abū Bakr's father be al-Ḥasan's ransom—'he resembles the Prophet, not you O 'Alī!' He is jesting with our liege lord 'Alī to let everyone that hears this feel this taste that the hearts of the Companions were made to absorb, to the point that he [=Abū Bakr al-Ṣiddīq] said, 'I swear that Abū Ṭālib's submission would be dearer to my eyes than my own father's, and that is because Abū Ṭālib's submission would be dearer to his eyes–upon him the blessings and peace of Allah.' [Narrated by 'Umar b. Shabba, Abū Ya'lā, Ibn Sammūyah, al-Ḥākim, Qadi 'Iyāḍ and Ibn Ḥajar who declared its chain sound.]

وقال **لَإِسْلَامُ أَبِي طَالِبٍ كَانَ أَقَرَّ لِعَيْنِي مِنْ إسلام أبي قُحَافَةَ وَذَلِكَ أَنَّ إِسْلَامَ أَبِي طَالِبٍ كَانَ أَقَرَّ لِعَيْنِهِ ﷺ** رواه ابن شَبَّة في كتاب مكّة وأبو يعلى وابن سمُّوْيَه في فوائده وأبو طالب في القوت عن أنس وعياض في الشفا وفي الباب عن ابن عمر وصحح الحافظ إسناده في الإصابة بلفظ: فلمّا مدَّ أبو قحافة يده يبايعه ﷺ بكى أبو بكر فقال النبي ﷺ: **مَا يُبْكِيكَ**؟ قال: **لَأَن تَكونَ**

يَدُ عَمِّكَ مَكَانَ يَدِهِ وَيُسْلِمَ وَيُقِرَّ اللهُ عَيْنَكَ أَحَبُّ إِلَيَّ مِنْ أَنْ يَكُونَ.

"Our liege lord 'Umar–may Allah be well-pleased with him and make him pleased–likewise, when he asked for our liege lord Imam al-Ḥusayn to come to him, the latter came and found Ibn 'Umar returning from his father's door so he asked him, 'What happened?' He said, 'My father did not give me permission to enter.' Hearing this al-Ḥusayn went back. Later, our liege lord 'Umar met him and said, 'What kept you from coming to see me O Ḥusayn, after I had called for you?' He said, 'Commander of the believers, I did come and I saw that you had turned away your son from your door, so I realized that you were busy and that you would turn me away with even better reason.' Our liege lord 'Umar said, 'And is 'Abd Allah the son of 'Umar like you, O Ḥusayn? And has anything grown a single hair on our head [i.e. the crown of honor] except you, the people of the House?' [Narrated by Ibn Sa'd, al-Khaṭīb and others, and Ibn Ḥajar rated its chain sound in *al-Iṣāba*.]

قال عمر للحسين: **أنتَ أحقُّ بالإذنِ من ابْن عُمَر! وإنَّما أَنْبَتَ مَا تَرَى فِي رُؤُوسِنَا اللهُ ثُمَّ أَنْتُمْ.** رواه ابن سعد وابن راهويه والخطيب في التاريخ وابن عساكر والمزي في التهذيب باب الحسن بن علي وصحح إسناده الحافظ في الإصابة

"This is how the Companions were–may Allah be well-pleased with them and make them pleased! So who is this who aims to disparage their good names? Who is this that dares to question their status? Who is the ill-mannered one that wants to harm the Messenger of Allah–upon him the blessings and peace of Allah–in regard to his Companions? He lies, by Allah!–he does not love *Ahl al-Bayt* at all. Does he love *Ahl al-Bayt*? We are *Ahl al-Bayt*. And we know better about what is in our house. We have nothing to do with whoever shows disrespect to our grandfather's Companions. Our House is free and clear of them, and it does not accept their stance.

"The people of the House know best what the House contains. When we say these words, we are saying it on the basis of what we narrate from our masters with a chain of transmission from my Shaykh to the Messenger of Allah–upon him the blessings and peace of Allah–all of them being from *Ahl al-Bayt*. This is our way as the *Ahl al-Bayt*: whoever is loyal to us is loyal to our grandfather's Companions, and whoever loves us loves our grandfather's Companions, and whoever shows him disrespect–upon him the blessings and peace of Allah–concerning his Companions, we certainly wash our hands from such a person.

"This is why it is related that our liege lord Ja'far al-Ṣādiq–upon him peace–when he was on his deathbed, was visited by one of those that are partial to *Ahl al-Bayt* and badmouths our liege lord Abū Bakr and our liege lord 'Umar. Our liege lord Ja'far turned to him and said, 'Do you see my state and what I am in?' The man said yes. Ja'far said, 'May my grandfather's intercession not include me if I am someone who does not have love and loyalty for Abū Bakr and 'Umar!' [See entry on Ja'far b. Muḥammad in *Tahdhīb al-kamāl*, the *Siyar*, *Ṭabaqāt al-ḥuffāẓ*, *Tadhkirat al-ḥuffāẓ*, *al-Tuḥfat al-laṭīfa* and *A'yān al-Shī'a*.]

"This is their way–may Allah be well-pleased with them and make them pleased, and upon them peace. Whoever finds in himself any claim of love for the purified *'itra* then fails to find in himself any good manners towards the Companions—or whoever finds in himself love for the Companions and the claim that he follows the Companions: you have certainly seen the state of the Companions and their love for the people of the House of our liege lord Muhammad–upon him the blessings and peace of Allah. They asked who the saved Group were and he replied, **'Those that follow what I follow and what my Companions follow.'** [Tirmidhī and Ājurrī in his *Arba'īn* from Ibn 'Amr; al-Ṭabarānī from Abū al-Dardā', Abū Umāma, Wāthila and Anas.]

عن عبد الله بن عمرو بن العاص رضي الله عنهما أنّ النبيّ ﷺ قال: **لَيَأْتِيَنَّ عَلَى أُمَّتِي مَا أَتَى عَلَى بَنِي إِسْرَائِيلَ؛ تفرّق بَنُو إِسْرَائِيل عَلَى ثِنْتَيْنِ وَسَبْعِينَ مِلَّةً، وَسَتَفْتَرِقُ أُمَّتِي عَلَى ثَلَاثٍ وَسَبْعِينَ مِلَّةً، تَزِيدُ عَلَيْهِمْ وَاحِدَةً، كُلُّهَا فِي النَّارِ إِلَّا مِلَّةً وَاحِدَةً. قَالُوا: مَنْ هَذِهِ الْمِلَّةُ الْوَاحِدَةُ؟ قَالَ: مَا أَنَا عَلَيْهِ وَأَصْحَابِي** رواه الترمذي والآجُرّي في الأربعين ورواه الطبراني في الكبير عن أبي الدرداء وأبي أمامة وواثلة بن الأسقع وأنس رضي الله عنهم بلفظ **فَإِنَّ بَنِي إِسْرَائِيلَ افْتَرَقُوا عَلَى إِحْدَى وَسَبْعِينَ فِرْقَةً، وَالنَّصَارَى عَلَى ثِنْتَيْنِ وَسَبْعِينَ فِرْقَةً، كُلُّهُمْ عَلَى الضَّلَالَةِ إِلَّا السَّوَادَ الْأَعْظَمَ** وحسّنه الترمذي في نسخة كما أقره العراقي في المغني والسخاوي وصححه البغوي في شرح السنة

"He is the one who said, 'I have left among you that which, if you hold fast to it, you will never ever go astray after me: the Book of Allah—a rope extended from heaven to earth—and my *'itra* (intimate family), the people of my House. I remind you of Allah about the people of my House! I remind you of Allah about the people of my House! I remind you of Allah about the people of my House!' [Narrated in Muslim and the *Sunan*.]

تَرَكْتُ فِيكُمْ مَا إِنْ تَمَسَّكْتُمْ بِهِمَا لَنْ تَضِلُّوا بَعْدِي أَبَداً: كِتَابَ الله حَبْلٌ مَمْدُودٌ مِنَ السَّمَاءِ إِلَى الْأَرْضِ وَعِتْرَتِي أَهْلُ بَيْتِي. أُذَكِّرُكُمُ اللهَ فِي أَهْلِ بَيْتِي! أُذَكِّرُكُمُ اللهَ فِي أَهْلِ بَيْتِي! أُذَكِّرُكُمُ اللهَ فِي أَهْلِ بَيْتِي! رواه مسلم وأصحاب السنن

"An addition is narrated, 'and verily the All-Subtle and All-Aware has told me that the two of them shall never separate until they both come up to the Basin.' [Aḥmad and al-Tirmidhī.]

وفي زيادة وَإِنَّ اللَّطِيفَ الخَبِيرَ أَخْبَرَنِي أَنَّهُمَا لَنْ يَفْتَرِقَا حَتَّى يَرِدَا عَلَيَّ الحَوْضَ رواه أحمد والترمذي الأخير دون لفظ إِنَّ اللَّطِيفَ الخَبِيرَ أَخْبَرَنِي

"'That which, if you hold fast to it, you will never ever go astray after me:' The Prophet–upon him the blessings and peace of Allah–is giving an ironclad guarantee that there shall ensue no misguidance, as narrated in Muslim, Abū Dāwūd, Tirmidhī, Ibn Mājah, al-Ḥākim, al-Bayhaqī and in hadiths that some who work on the Hadith have described as reaching the rank of *tawātur* (mass transmission; see Kattānī five pages down). 'And my *'itra* (intimate family), the people of my House:' whoever wants to be safe from misguidance must hold fast to the Qur'ān and to the Prophet's Family! Whoever wants to be saved must hold fast to the Messenger of Allah and his Companions!

"So whoever well understands this meaning, his ego will surrender and give up its vested interests. It will turn wholly to the Messenger of Allah with love for all that is connected with the Messenger of Allah–upon him the blessings and peace of Allah. It will be loving to his Family and it will be loving to his Companions. Whatever difference of opinion took place between the Companions and the Family is something that takes place between all people. Even between Family and Family there has occurred a difference of opinion, and between Companions and Companions there has occurred a difference of opinion. We neither hold the former to be infallible nor do we hold the latter to be infallible! However, we firmly believe that Allah Most High and Exalted has made him–upon him the blessings and peace of Allah–infallible with respect to them.

"This is the meaning we ought to understand well. This is the reason that when a difference of opinion took place between

Imam al-Ḥusayn–Allah be well-pleased with him and make him pleased–and his paternal half-brother our liege lord Muḥammad b. al-Ḥanafiyya, as happens between brothers, the latter wrote a letter to Imam al-Ḥusayn in which he said, 'O Abū 'Abd Allāh, when this paper of mine reaches you, if you are standing do not sit, and if you are sitting, get up and come to me, and fix what is between us so that I will not precede you in this merit. For you are the son of Fāṭima bint Muḥammad and I am the son of Fāṭima of the Banū Ḥanīfa.' This is the way of the people of the House and the Companions. This is their custom and this is their state. Whoever wants truthful love, this way is right there before you. After that he got up, went, visited him and repaired what was between him and his brother.

"So the meaning of elevation to high levels has become this: you must look for ways to bring your own ego low—for the sake of Allah Almighty—with the people of belief. The meaning of elevation and spiritual progress is not for you to disrespect the people of belief. The Messenger of Allah–upon him the blessings and peace of Allah–says, '**Beware Allah, beware Allah as to my Companions! Beware Allah, beware Allah as to my Companions! Do not take them as targets after me! So whoever loves them, it is with love of me that he loves them, and whoever hates them, it is for hate of me that he hates them, and whoever harms them has certainly harmed me, and whoever harms me has certainly harmed Allah, and whoever harms Allah is on the brink of being seized by Him.**' [Narrated from 'Abd Allāh b. Mughaffal al-Muzanī by Aḥmad, Tirmidhī, Ibn Ḥibbān and others.]

عن عبد الله بن مغفَّل المزني قال: قال رسول الله ﷺ: **اللهَ اللهَ فِي أَصْحَابِي! اللهَ اللهَ فِي أَصْحَابِي! لَا تَتَّخِذُوهُمْ غَرَضًا بَعْدِي، فَمَنْ أَحَبَّهُمْ فَبِحُبِّي أَحَبَّهُمْ، وَمَنْ أَبْغَضَهُمْ فَبِبُغْضِي أَبْغَضَهُمْ، وَمَنْ آذَاهُمْ فَقَدْ آذَانِي، وَمَنْ آذَانِي فَقَدْ آذَى اللهَ وَمَنْ آذَى اللهَ فَيُوشِكُ أَنْ يَأْخُذَهُ** رواه أحمد والترمذي وقال هذا

حديث حسن غريب وابن حبان في صحيحه وحسّنه البغوي في المصابيح
والسيوطي في الجامع الصغير وله شواهد عن ابن عمر وجابر.

"The Beloved is saying this discourse—does it carry no weight for you? Does it have no value in your heart, no sanctity? If a man from this vanishing world were prized by people for his company, no one would stand for anyone harming him. What about our liege lord Muhammad? Our liege lord 'Abd Allāh b. 'Abbās says–may Allah be well-pleased with him and his father–'There is no one dearer to me than he that sits with me. I shudder lest even a fly should fall on him.' [Fasawī, Kharā'iṭī, Bayhaqī.]

قيل لابن عباس: **مَنْ أَكْرَمُ النَّاسِ عَلَيْكَ؟** قَالَ: **جَلِيسِي لَوِ اسْتَطَعْتُ أَنْ لَا يَقَعَ الذُّبَابُ عَلَى وَجْهِهِ لَفَعَلْتُ** رواه يعقوب بن سفيان في المعرفة
والتاريخ والخرائطي في مكارم الأخلاق والبيهقي في الشعب

"Do you think the Master of creation has less self-respect than him? They never drew up any self-respect except from his exalted presence–upon him the blessings and peace of Allah.

"From the above meaning we enter into the pathway of *adab* (high manners). These are the children of the Prophet. Who are you? These are the Companions of the Prophet. Who are you? The latter have the affiliation of *suḥba* (Companionship) while the former have the affiliation of lineage. Tell me, as for yourself, what is your affiliation to him? Where is obedience, where is followership, where is love? If there is anyone that ought to be taken to account here, take yourself to account! If there is anyone that ought to be criticized, criticize yourself, criticize your own state! And learn to practice the utmost high manners with the people of *maḥbūbiyya* (belovedness) from the side of Allah Most High! Try to feel, while you are in this state, with regard to this precious matter, one of the meanings of the breezes of this blessed season [=al-Ḥusayn's mawlid] over you."

These eleven pages are from the discourse of Habib ʿAli al-Jafri on the occasion of the celebration of the mawlid of our liege lord al-Ḥusayn–Allah be well-pleased with him–in Cairo over two decades ago. See, dear reader, the sweetness of the speech of kings and of the king of speeches about the importance of high manners and love that is at the core of the creed of *Ahl al-Sunna wal-Jamāʿa*, foremost among them our Sufi masters, whose discourse is filled with such reminders! Our affiliation is love of the *ʿitra* and the Companions above all other loves, in repudiation of hatred, ignorance and anything that is unsuited for the presence of the Beloved of Allah–upon him the blessings and peace of Allah. Success is from Allah.

VIII. The *Salaf* built structures over graves and visited them

The objector said–may Allah guide him: "And I have seen his fatwa on (i) the building of mosques on top of graves; (ii) magnification of graves and (iii) the undertaking of travel to them, and that he interprets the Messenger's Hadith–upon him blessings and peace of Allah–'May Allah curse the Jews and the Christians, they took the graves of their Prophets as places of prostration' to refer to prostration over the grave. And such speech of his is untrue, and contrary to what the reliable madhhabs follow."

Once again we see how the accusation fails to quote the precise words it claims to refute, as if the Wahhabi objector's attack is unquestionable while the speech of Sufi shaykhs does not deserve to be cited with precision. On this particular issue, the sound legal ruling has already long been stated and expounded extensively in the books of fiqh of the four Schools (i.e. it is valid to pray towards a grave as long as there is a *sitr* or screen, e.g. the Prophet's grave in his mosque), and the heterodox madhhab that contravene them with its laxity disguised as strictness is well-known. There is no benefit in arguing with them. What is strange is that one of the people of Allah and His Book in Syro-Palestine —which is *'uqr dār al-islām* (the heartland of the abode of Islam), the grounding-place of *'amūd al-islām* (the pillar of Islam) and the ultimate home of true belief—should allow himself to become the publicist for such innovated views against which the Sunni shaykhs and schools of Shām had immunized themselves in the last 200 years. His locality should have sufficiently prevented him from endorsing blatant aberrations even if Hadith and Fiqh are not his specialty and even if he has remained uninformed that all four Schools have refuted that heterodox madhhab in decisive fashion.

As for the construction of mosques over the graves, then the enlargement of the Mosque of the Prophet–upon him the blessings and peace of Allah–took place in the preferred earliest centuries, after which the fifth of the rightly-guided caliphs, our liege lord 'Umar b. 'Abd al-'Azīz, ratified it, as have done the *Salaf* and the *Khalaf* through the centuries and down to our time –may Allah be well-pleased with them all–with the sole exception of that heterodox school which alone claimed it was haram!

It is enough that **the noble Prophetic Grave is in fact the purest and noblest of all the spots on earth and in the seven skies including the Kaʿba, the Throne, its Bearers and the eight Paradises**, as stipulated by the consensus mentioned in Ibn 'Aqīl al-Ḥanbalī's *Kitāb al-funūn* as cited by Muḥammad al-Zur'ī in *Badā'i' al-fawā'id*. See also to that effect Qadi 'Iyāḍ's *Shifā* and its commentaries; al-Nawawī's *Majmū'* and *Sharḥ Ṣaḥīḥ Muslim*; Ibn 'Ābidīn in his *Ḥāshiya*, and others.

قال ابن عقيل: **سَأَلَنِي سَائِلٌ أَيُّمَا أَفْضَلُ: حُجْرَةُ النَّبِيِّ ﷺ أَمِ الْكَعْبَةُ؟ فَقُلْتُ: إِنْ أَرَدْتَ مُجَرَّدَ الحُجْرَةِ، فَالْكَعْبَةُ أَفْضَلُ؛ وَإِنْ أَرَدْتَ وَهُوَ فِيهَا، فَلَا - وَاللهِ - وَلَا الْعَرْشُ وَحَمَلَتُهُ وَلَا جَنَّةُ عَدْنٍ وَلَا الْأَفْلَاكُ الدَّائِرَةُ! لِأَنَّ بِالْحُجْرَةِ جَسَداً لَوْ وُزِنَ بِالْكَوْنَيْنِ لَرَجَحَ** ذكره الزُّرعي في بدائع الفوائد.

ونحوه في الشفا لعياض والمجموع وشرح مسلم للنووي وحاشية ابن عابدين

This is the soul of truth and it does not mean that the licit ruling of building over a grave becomes specific and exclusive to his mosque–upon him blessings and peace. Furthermore, there are countless mosques inside which or adjacent to which is found the grave of a pious wali or a virtuous scholar in the Islamic world from the beginning to our time, and, as the Prophet stated in his mass-transmitted Hadith, **the Umma will never concur on misguidance** (Kattānī, *Naẓm al-mutanāthir*).

There are more issues to address as we shall proceed to do at length in the following chapters with Allah's help, especially on the topic of travelling to visit the Holy Prophet and Awliya.

IX. Grave structures for ulema, Awliya and *Ahl al-Bayt*

As for the building of structures over graves which the objector decried as "the magnification of graves," it is subsumed under the established *qāʿida* (axiom) of permitted matters that are not unanimously agreed upon. Review the text of *Tanwīr al-abṣār* and *al-Durr al-mukhtār* in Hanafi fiqh to that effect, their marginalia by Ṭaḥṭāwī and Ibn ʿĀbidīn, and Rāfiʿī's *Taqrīrāt*. Likewise in other madhhabs, there is disagreement over the issue. Even al-Ṣanʿānī in *Subul al-salām* stipulated that the dislike of building over graves was a *tanzīhī* (preferential) one and this is the position of the vast majority. The Shāfiʿī faqih Habib Zayn b. Sumayṭ said in *al-Ajwibat al-ghāliya fī ʿaqīdat al-firqat al-nājiya*:

قال العلامة الفقيه المربي الحبيب زين بن سميط با علوي المدني الشافعي في الأجوبة الغالية في عقيدة الفرقة الناجية: أمّا حديث النهي أن يُجَصَّصَ القبرُ وأن يُبنَى عليه وأن يقعد عليه: فقد اتّفق جمهور العلماء على أن النّهي للتنزيه لا للتحريم. فيُكره ذلك كراهةَ تنزيه.

> "As for the hadith of the prohibition of plastering the grave, building over it and sitting on it, there is definitive agreement of the vast majority of the scholars that the prohibition if for *tanzīh* (preferability), not *taḥrīm* (categorical prohibition). So that is preferably disliked."

Furthermore, "building on top of the graves was said not to be disliked with regard to the graves of the awliya, the ulema and the *Ahl al-Bayt*" as cited by al-Nābulusī from Nāṣir al-Dīn Abū al-Qāsim Muḥammad b. Yūsuf al-Samarqandī's (d. 556/1161) *Jāmiʿ al-fatāwā*[3]—not in "magnification of the grave" as claimed,

[3] See Jāmiʿat al-Riyāḍ ms. 1827 f° 19r lines 11-12 at https://archive.org/download/mishref_gmail_114_20150830/1827.pdf and Muḥ. Muṭīʿ al-Ḥāfiẓ, *Fahras makhṭūṭāt Dār al-kutub al-Ẓāhiriyya: al-fiqh al-Ḥanafī*, 2 vols. (Damascus: Majmaʿ al-Lughat al-ʿArabiyya, 1401/1980) 1:251.

but in magnification of the *dīn* (faith) as stated by the Ḥanafī jurists Mullā 'Alī al-Qārī in *al-Mirqāt*, 'Abd al-Ḥaqq al-Dihlawī in *Sharḥ sifr al-sa'āda*, Ismā'īl Ḥaqqī al-Burūsawī in *Tafsīr rūḥ al-bayān* under the Suras of Barā'a/al-Tawba, 'Abd al-Ghanī al-Nābulusī in *Kashf al-nūr 'an aṣḥāb al-qubūr* (The light unveiling the [stations of the] grave-dwellers) and 'Abd al-Qādir al-Rāfi'ī al-Azharī who cited the latter two in his *Taqrīrāt* (Resolutions) on Ibn 'Ābidīn's *Radd al-muḥtār* as translated thus:

> *Only they maintain the mosques of the One God that believe in the One God and the Last Day, establish the prayer and remit the zakat, and never fear other than the One God. Then it may well be that they shall be among the well-guided* (Barā'a/Tawba 9:18): Shaykh 'Abd al-Ghanī al-Nābulusī said in *Kashf al-nūr 'an aṣḥāb al-qubūr* in sum, that the excellent innovation that conforms with the intent of the sacred Law is called a sunna. Thus, building domes over the graves of scholars, Awliya and the righteous, and placing covers, turbans and cloth over their graves is a permissible matter when the objective thereby is magnification in the eyes of the general public so that they will not disdain the occupant of this grave. Likewise, lighting lanterns and candles at their graves is also from showing magnification and reverence to the Awliya, so the objective therein is an excellent objective. The vowing of oil and candles to Awliya that must be ignited at their graves in magnification of them and out of love for them is also permissible and ought not to be forbidden.[4]

The hadith of our liege lord 'Alī–Allah ennoble his countenance–on the demolishing of magnified graves in the two *Ṣaḥīḥs* is understood to mean what the people of Jahiliyya would habitually do in heightening the graves through elaborate tall superstructures as Ibn al-Jawzī stated in *al-Taḥqīq fī aḥādīth al-khilāf* (The verification on the hadiths that support divergent views). Al-Zayla'ī mentioned it in *Naṣb al-rāya*. It never applies to Muslim practice except at the hands of the neo-Khawārij who show the Umma the same impiety their impious predecessors showed the Companions.

[4] al-Nābulusī, *Kashf al-nūr* (pp. 44-46); İsmail Hakkı, *Rūḥ al-bayān* (10:400); Rāfi'ī, *Taqrīrāt al-Rāfi'ī 'alā Radd al-muḥtār*, ed. 'Ādil Aḥmad 'Abd al-Mawjūd and 'Alī Muḥammad Mu'awwaḍ, 2 vols. (Riyadh: Dār 'Ālam al-Kutub, 1423/2003) 1:166; cf. https://web.archive.org/web/20020812011700/http://66.34.131.5/ISLAM/misc/nabulsi.htm

X. Travel to visit graves for *duʿā*, *tabarruk* and *tawassul* is a Sunna among the *Salaf* and the *Khalaf*

As for travelling to visit graves we have already seen—in the very first section—that Abū Hurayra, who relates the hadith, "One does not travel other than to the three Mosques," himself undertook travel from Medina to Sinai in order to pray at the Mount where Mūsā–upon him the blessings and peace of Allah–conversed with his nurturing Lord. He did so for no other reason than to supplicate there, derive blessing and remember the hereafter, which are among the very reasons why Muslims travel to visit the graves of the Prophets and the pious.

Our liege lord Bilāl b. Rabāḥ al-Ḥabashī (d. 20/641) set out to travel to Medina—after he had taken up residence in Dārayyā (Syria)—to visit the noble Prophetic Grave when he saw the Prophet in dream telling him to come and visit him. This is narrated by Ibn ʿAsākir in the seventh volume of his great history, *Tārīkh Dimashq* (Dār al-Fikr ed. p. 136), with a chain which al-Shawkānī rated *ḥasan* (fair) at the end of the section on Hajj in *Nayl al-awṭār.* Ibn ʿAsākir narrates, "so he came to the grave of the Prophet–upon him the blessings and peace of Allah–and he started to weep and rub his face over it."

عن أبي الدرداء قال: لَمَّا دَخَلَ عُمَرُ بْنُ الخَطَّابِ الجَابِيَةَ سَأَلَ بِلالاً أَنْ يَقْدَمَ الشَّامَ فَفَعَلَ وَنَزَلَ دَارَيَّا وَتَزَوَّجَ فِيهَا ثُمَّ إِنَّ بِلَالاً رَأَى فِي مَنَامِهِ النَّبِيَّ ﷺ وَهُوَ يَقُولُ لَهُ: مَا هٰذِهِ الجَفْوَةُ يا بِلَالُ؟ أَمَا آنَ لَكَ أَنْ تَزُورَنِي يَا بِلَالُ؟ فَانْتَبَهَ حَزِيناً وَجِلاً خَائِفاً فَرَكِبَ رَاحِلَتَهُ وَقَصَدَ المَدِينَةَ فَأَتَى قَبْرَ النَّبِيِّ ﷺ فَجَعَلَ يَبْكِي عِنْدَهُ وَيُمَرِّغُ وَجْهَهُ عَلَيْهِ رواه ابن عساكر في التاريخ وحسّن الشوكاني سنده آخر باب الحج من نيل الأوطار

The Imam and Hadith master Zayn al-Dīn al-ʿIrāqī travelled from Egypt to al-Khalīl to visit the grave of the Friend of the All-Merciful, our liege lord Ibrāhīm–upon him peace–in Palestine. His son Walī al-Dīn al-ʿIrāqī narrated it in the chapter on vows of his large work on the hadiths pertaining to legal rulings entitled *Ṭarḥ al-tathrīb* (6:43), in illustration of the sound and orthodox explanation of the hadith "One does not travel other than to the three Mosques." He said, "My father–may Allah have mercy on him–would tell us how he had been the travel mate of the Ḥanbalī Shaykh Zayn al-Dīn ʿAbd al-Raḥīm Ibn Rajab as they headed for the land of al-Khalīl–upon him peace. He said that when they approached the region, the latter [=Ibn Rajab] said, 'I have made the intention of visiting al-Khalīl's Mosque' in order to clear himself of having set out to travel in order to visit al-Khalīl himself [=the Prophet Ibrāhīm–upon him the blessings and peace of Allah], per the way of the Shaykh of the Ḥanbalīs, [Aḥmad al-Ḥarrānī]. My father said, 'I have made the intention of visiting the grave of al-Khalīl–upon him peace. Now, as for you, you have contravened the Prophet–upon him the blessings and peace of Allah–who said, *One does not travel other than to the three Mosques*. Yet you have travelled to a fourth mosque. As for myself I have followed the Prophet–upon him the blessings and peace of Allah–because he said *Visit the graves*. Did he ever say, *except the graves of the Prophets*?' My father said that the Shaykh could not reply anything."

Note that the Imam's final rhetorical question is an implied rejection of the fatwa "the Shaykh of the Ḥanbalīs" Aḥmad al-Ḥarrānī had given to the effect that "travelling to visit the grave of the Prophet–upon him the blessings and peace of Allah–is a *maʿṣiya* (rebellious sin)." No one gave such a fatwa before him whether in his school or in the other three. More importantly, the more authoritative masters of the Ḥanbalī school such as al-Mardāwī, Ibn Hubayra, Ibn Qudāma and others have stated that the entirety of the early and late authorities in that school stipulate the high desirability of visiting the grave of the Prophet–upon blessings and peace–in Medina, most especially after Hajj, and travelling to do so. This is stipulated in Muwaffaq al-Dīn b. Qudāma's *Mughnī*; his *Muqni'* and his *Kāfī*; Burhān al-Dīn Ibn Mufliḥ's *Mubdi' fī sharḥ al-Muqni'*; al-Buhūtī's *Kashshāf al-qinā'* and *Rawḍ al-Murba'*; Ibn Dawyān's *Manār al-sabīl*; Shams al-Dīn ibn Mufliḥ's *Furū'*; Ḥajjāwī's *Iqnā'*; 'Abd al-Raḥmān Ba'lī's *Kashf al-mukhaddarāt*; Mar'ī's *Ghāyat al-muntahā* and *Dalīl al-ṭālib*; Ibn al-Jawzī's *al-Madhhab al-aḥmad*; Aḥmad al-Ba'lī's *al-Rawḍ al-nadīy*; Bahā' al-Dīn al-Maqdisī's *Sharḥ al-Muqni'*; Ibn al-Najjār's *Muntahā al-irādāt*; Shams al-Dīn b. Qudāma's *Sharḥ al-kabīr*; Ibn Hubayra's *Ifṣāḥ*; Kawladhānī's *Hidāya*; Mardāwī's *Inṣāf* and others. All of Ibn Mufliḥ, Mardāwī and Mar'ī b. Yūsuf in *Ghāyat al-muntahā* stated the **Sunnī character of visiting the graves of the Muslims and the permissibility of travelling to do so**. Mar'ī reiterated the ruling in his monograph on the visitation of graves, *Shifā' al-ṣudūr fī ziyārat al-mashāhid wal-qubūr*.

The Turkish then Syrian erudite scholar Shihāb al-Dīn Yāqūt b. 'Abd Allāh al-Rūmī al-Ḥamawī (575-626/1179-1229) wrote in his geographical encyclopedia *Mu'jam al-buldān*: "Tibn, pronounced like the *tibn* (hay) animals eat, is the name of a vast area that was in Baghdad by the moat, in the vicinity of Qaṭī'at Umm Ja'far. It is now desolate and is used for planting. The grave of 'Abd Allāh b. Aḥmad b. Ḥanbal is found there. He was buried there by his last will." He then quoted what al-Khaṭīb al-Baghdādī in his vast history of the city, Abū Isḥāq al-Shīrāzī in *Ṭabaqāt al-fuqahā'*, Ibn Abī Ya'lā in *Ṭabaqāt al-Ḥanābila* and others narrated whereby 'Abd Allāh said, "I have authentic proof that there is a Prophet buried in al-Qaṭī'a and it is more beloved for me to be near a Prophet than being near my father." We ask, what is the benefit of this Prophetic grave that he intended to be placed near to? And, what is more, after death? There is no doubt something deeply meaningful driving him to make such a request and giving such an explanation, as 'Abd Allah is the most advanced of the sons of Imam Aḥmad in fiqh as well as narration of hadith. Will they say that this qualifies as *shirk* (polytheism) with Allah Most High, *bid'a* (reprehensible innovation), *qubūriyya* (grave-worship) and what not?

XI. Visiting the Prophet's Grave is a pious act by consensus, unrelated to the hadith "One does not travel other than to the three Mosques"

The Syrian Hadith master al-Dhahabī–Allah have mercy on him –formally stipulated that it is "of the best of *qurab* (acts of piety to draw near to Allah)" to visit the grave of the Messenger–upon him blessings and peace–even if it involves the intention of travelling to visit him, because the latter intention is inseparable from the intention of visiting his mosque. He wrote this fatwa in conformity with the consensus and in firm rejection of the innovative claim of his teacher Aḥmad al-Ḥarrānī that whoever travels to visit the Prophet's grave commits an act of *fisq* (depravation)—"an extraordinarily ugly statement" according to the Hadith master Walī al-Dīn al-'Irāqī as cited below. Al-Dhahabī was therefore keen to distance himself from that major error and rejected it in no uncertain terms:

> Whoever stands at the sanctified Chamber, humble, submitting, invoking blessings on his Prophet, then O blessing for him! For he has made the visit excellent and he has done expertly well in showing humbleness and love, and he has offered worship in addition to the worship of whoever invoked prayers in his own land or in his prayer. For **the visitor has the reward of the visit and the reward of invoking blessings on him while the one invoking blessing in all other lands has the reward of invocation only**. But whoever visits him and shows bad manners in the visit or prostrates to the grave or does something that is not allowed in the Law—such a person has dome something beautiful and something bad at the same time. So he must be educated gently and Allah is Most Forgiving, Most Merciful. For–by Allah!–a Muslim never gets disquieted and starts shouting and kissing the walls and weeping profusely except he is a true lover of Allah and His Messenger! **Thus his love is the criterion of difference between the people of Paradise and the people of Hellfire. So the visit to his grave is of the best of *qurab*!** As for the act of travelling to the graves of the Prophets and the Awliya, even if we were to concede that it is not allowed due to the general sense of his statement–upon him the blessings and

peace of Allah–'**Do not saddle up except to go to the Three Mosques,' nevertheless the saddling up to go to our Prophet–upon him the blessings and peace of Allah–is inseparable from the saddling up to go to his mosque**. So let one begin with the mosque-greeting prayer and, after that, the greeting of the Master of the mosque—may Allah grant us and you that grant!"[5]

قال الذهبي في ترجمة الحسن المثَنَّى رضي الله عنه من سير أعلام النبلاء: مَنْ وَقَفَ عِنْدَ الحُجْرَةِ المُقَدَّسَةِ ذَلِيْلاً، مُسْلِماً، مُصَلِيّاً عَلَى نَبِيِّهِ، فَيَا طُوْبَى لَهُ، فَقَدْ أَحْسَنَ الزِّيَارَةَ، وَأَجْمَلَ فِي التَّذَلُّلِ وَالحُبِّ، وَقَدْ أَتَى بِعِبَادَةٍ زَائِدَةٍ عَلَى مَنْ صَلَّى عَلَيْهِ فِي أَرْضِهِ، أَوْ فِي صَلاَتِهِ، إِذِ الزَّائِرُ لَهُ أَجْرُ الزِّيَارَةِ، وَأَجْرُ الصَّلاَةِ عَلَيْهِ، وَالمُصَلِّي عَلَيْهِ فِي سَائِرِ البِلاَدِ لَهُ أَجْرُ الصَّلاَةِ فَقَطْ... وَلَكِنْ مَنْ زَارَهُ - صَلَوَاتُ اللهِ عَلَيْهِ - وَأَسَاءَ أَدَبَ الزِّيَارَةِ، أَوْ سَجَدَ لِلْقَبْرِ، أَوْ فَعَلَ مَا لاَ يُشْرَعُ، فَهَذَا فَعَلَ حَسَناً وَسَيِّئاً، فَيُعَلَّمُ بِرِفْقٍ، وَاللهُ غَفُوْرٌ رَحِيْمٌ. فَوَاللهِ مَا يَحْصُلُ الانْزِعَاجُ لِمُسْلِمٍ، وَالصِّيَاحُ وَتَقْبِيْلُ الجُدْرَانِ، وَكَثْرَةِ البُكَاءِ، إِلاَّ وَهُوَ مُحِبٌّ للهِ وَلِرَسُوْلِهِ، فَحُبُّهُ المِعْيَارُ وَالفَارِقُ بَيْنَ أَهْلِ الجَنَّةِ وَأَهْلِ النَّارِ. فَزِيَارَةُ قَبْرِهِ مِنْ أَفْضَلِ القُرَبِ، وَشَدُّ الرِّحَالِ إِلَى قُبُوْرِ الأَنْبِيَاءِ وَالأَوْلِيَاءِ، لَئِنْ سَلَّمْنَا أَنَّهُ غَيْرُ مَأْذُوْنٍ فِيْهِ لِعُمُوْمِ قَوْلِهِ - صَلَوَاتُ اللهُ عَلَيْهِ - **لَا تَشُدُّوا الرِّحَالَ إِلاَّ إِلَى ثَلاَثَةِ مَسَاجِدَ**، فَشَدُّ الرِّحَالِ إِلَى نَبِيِّنَا ﷺ مُسْتَلْزِمٌ لِشَدِّ الرَّحْلِ إِلَى مَسْجِدِهِ، وَذَلِكَ مَشْرُوْعٌ بِلاَ نِزَاعٍ، إِذْ لاَ وُصُوْلَ إِلَى حُجْرَتِهِ إِلاَّ بَعْدَ الدُّخُوْلِ إِلَى مَسْجِدِهِ. فَلْيَبْدَأْ بِتَحِيَّةِ المَسْجِدِ، ثُمَّ بِتَحِيَّةِ صَاحِبِ المَسْجِدِ. رَزَقَنَا اللهُ وَإِيَّاكُمْ ذَلِكَ آمِيْنَ. اهـ.

[5] Al-Dhahabī, *Siyar a'lām al-nubalā'*, entry on al-Ḥasan b. al-Ḥasan b. 'Alī b. Abī Ṭālib–Allah be well-pleased with them.

Al-Dhahabī's statement that "even if we were to concede that it [=travel to visit the grave of the Prophet] is not allowed due to the general sense of the hadith '**Do not saddle up except to go to the Three Mosques**'" is a hypothetical concession of a flimsy, innovative and misguided premise which is rejected by the people of knowledge as demonstrated by the Hadith master Zayn al-Dīn al-'Irāqī's rebuke of Ibn Rajab cited in the previous chapter and Taqī al-Dīn al-Subkī al-Kabīr in his landmark book *Shifā' al-saqām fī ziyārat Khayri al-anām* (The healing of the sick in visiting the Best of creation) which is cited below. As 'Irāqī said, any supposed prohibition not to travel to visit the Prophet's grave is pre-empted by his hadith ***Visit the graves!***.[6] Al-'Irāqī added, "Did he ever say, *except the graves of the Prophets*??"

'Irāqī's son the Hadith master Walī al-Dīn al-'Irāqī began the abovementioned report in *Ṭarḥ al-tathrīb* saying, "[Al-Ḥarrānī] here said something extremely ugly [in his *Fatāwā*] whose gist is the prohibition of travelling to visit [the Prophet], and that such was not of the *qurab* (acts that draw near to Allah) but the contrary. Shaykh Taqī al-Dīn al-Subkī rebutted him in *Shifā' al-saqām*, whereby he healed the breasts of the believers." The same is expressed by the Hadith master 'Izz al-Dīn Ibn Jamā'a in his *Hidāyat al-sālik*(4:1518-1521), a Hajj encyclopedia according to the four Schools, in which he mentioned the famous report of the desert Arab who visits the Prophet's grave, recites the verse, *and if only they, when they wronged themselves, came to you and asked forgiveness of the One God, and the Messenger asked forgiveness for them, they would certainly realize that the One God is Oft-Relenting, Most Merciful* (Nisā' 4:64) and then says, "I have wronged myself and I have come to you so that you will ask forgiveness for me!" Al-Ḥarrānī in his ill-titled *Qā'ida fil-maḥabba* went so far as to describe the above request as the act of an ignorant *munāfiq*. Ibn Jamā'a commented, "What a far cry this desert Arab is from him whom Allah has led astray so that

[6] Mass-transmitted from 'Alī b. Abī Ṭālib, Burayda, Umm Salama, Ibn 'Abbās, Zayd b. al-Khaṭṭāb, 'Ā'isha, Thawbān, Ibn Mas'ūd, Anas, Abū Sa'īd al-Khudrī, Wāsi' al-Anṣārī, Abū Dharr and Abū Hurayra.

he ended up declaring the visitation of the Prophet haram! Whereas it is in fact one of the most magnificent of the *qurubāt* as we have already said."

The report of the Arab is related with many different chains respectively from (i) our liege lord ʿAlī b. Abī Ṭālib by al-Thaʿlabī in his *Tafsīr* under that verse with a good chain; (ii) Abū Ḥarb Muḥammad b. Ḥarb al-Hilālī by Bayhaqī in *Shuʿab al-īmān* (25: *Manāsik, faḍl al-ḥajj wal-ʿumra*), Abū Saʿd Aḥmad b. Muḥ. b. Aḥm. al-Baghdādī al-Aṣbahānī in *Majlisān li-Abī Saʿd al-Baghdādī*, Ibn ʿAsākir in *Muʿjam al-shuyūkh* in the entry on ʿAbd al-Ghālib b. Thābit b. Māhān and Ibn al-Jawzī in *Muthīr al-gharām al-sākin ilā ashrafi al-amākin*; and (iii) al-ʿUtbī[7] by Ibn ʿAsākir in the same entry in *Muʿjam al-shuyūkh*. In the first version a voice replies from the grave, "**You have certainly been forgiven**" and in the third version al-ʿUtbī dozes off and sees the Prophet–upon him blessings and peace–in his dream telling him to run after the desert Arab and tell him he has been forgiven. In the second and third version the Bedouin also recites this poetry:

O best of those whose bones are buried in the mound,
scenting the sites and hills with his perfume!
May my life be the ransom for a grave you dwell,
where virtue lives, and open-handed generous bounty!

قال الإمام أبو إسحاق الثعلبي في تفسير الكشف والبيان: أخبرني أبو القاسم عبد الخالق بن علي بن محمد بن عبد الخالق (ثقة)، أنبأ أبو الحسن علي بن إبراهيم الكرخي (هو الجرجاني ت ٣٥١، روى عن يحيى بن محمد بن صاعد وهناد بن السري وأبي سعيد الأشج وسفيان بن وكيع وطبقتهم وروى عنه الإسماعيلي وابن عدي وجماعة)، أخبرنا علي بن محمد بن خالد (هو المطرِّز الشهيد ت ٢٩٤، لا بأس به)، ثنا محمد بن أحمد بن الهيثم الطائي (هو أبو جعفر الدوري المصري ت ٣٠٤، ثقة، سمع أباه وهارون بن إسحاق الهمداني وأحمد

[7] Al-ʿUtbī is the arch-eloquent hadith scholar and linguist Abū ʿAbd al-Raḥmān Muḥammad b. ʿUbayd Allah b. ʿAmr b. Muʿāwiya b. ʿAmr b. ʿUtba b. Abī Sufyān Sakhr b. Ḥarb (d. 228/843) per Taqī al-Dīn al-Subkī al-Kabīr in *Shifā' al-saqām*.

ابن منصور المعروف بزاج ومحمد بن عبد الملك الدقيقي وعبد الرحمن بن الحسن ابن القاسم العلاف وعبيد الله بن محمد بن سليمان وروى عنه أبو بكر الشافعي وأحمد بن عبد الله الذارع النهرواني ومحمد بن الحسن اليقطيني وأبو الفتح الأزدي ومحمد بن المظفَّر)، ثنا أبي (هو أحمد بن الهيثم قاضي الثَّغْر، ثقة، من مشايخ البزار والنسائي وأبي عوانة)، عن أبيه (هو الهيثم بن حفص، روى له البيهقي حديثاً عن أبيه في السنن الكبرى)، عن سلمة بن كهيل (ثقة)، عن أبي صادق (عبد الله بن ناجذ، وقيل اسمه مسلم بن يزيد، الأزدي الكوفي التابعي، وُثِّق، ويروي عن علي مرسلاً)، عن علي بن أبي طالب رضي الله عنه، قال:

قَدِمَ علينا أعرابيٌّ بَعْدَمَا دَفَنَّا رسولَ الله ﷺ بثلاثةِ أيّامٍ، فرمى بنفسه على قبر النبي ﷺ وحَثَا على رأسه من ترابه، وقال: **يَا رَسُولَ الله، قُلْتَ فَسَمِعْنَا قَوْلَكَ وَوَعَيْتَ عَنِ الله فِيمَا وَعَيْنَا عَنْكَ، وَكَانَ فِيمَا أَنْزَلَ اللهُ عَلَيْكَ ﴿وَلَوْ أَنَّهُمْ إِذ ظَّلَمُوٓاْ أَنفُسَهُمْ جَآءُوكَ فَٱسْتَغْفَرُواْ ٱللَّهَ وَٱسْتَغْفَرَ لَهُمُ ٱلرَّسُولُ لَوَجَدُواْ ٱللَّهَ تَوَّابًا رَّحِيمًا﴾، وَقَدْ ظَلَمْتُ نَفْسِي وَجِئْتُكَ لِتَسْتَغْفِرَ لِي فَنُودِيَ مِنَ الْقَبْرِ: أَنَّهُ قَدْ غُفِرَ لَكَ.** ورواه البيهقي عن أبي حرب محمد بن حرب الهلالي في شعب الإيمان وأبو سعد البغدادي الأصبهاني في مجالسه وابن عساكر في معجم الشيوخ وابن الجوزي في مثير الغرام بأسانيدهم، و ابن عساكر في المعجم عن محمد بن عبيد الله العُتْبي (ت ٢٢٨)، جميعهم بزيادة شعر الأعرابي المشهور:

يَا خَيْرَ مَنْ دُفِنَتْ بِالْقَاعِ أَعْظُمُهُ فَطَابَ مِنْ طِيبِهِنَّ الْقَاعُ وَالْأَكَمُ
نَفْسِي الْفِدَاءُ لِقَبْرٍ أَنْتَ سَاكِنُهُ فِيهِ الْعَفَافُ وَفِيهِ الْجُودُ وَالْكَرَمُ

Shaykh ʻAbd al-Ghanī al-Nābulusī wrote in his travelogue to al-Quds entitled *al-Ḥaḍrat al-unsiyya fīl-riḥlat al-Qudsiyya* (pp. 34-36): "There is no reference in these hadiths [i.e. the various wordings of the hadith *One does not travel other than to the three Mosques*] to the visit of Prophets or Awliya or other than that.... So **whoever has construed travel to visit the righteous to be a *maʿṣiya* (rebellious sin)** and has based on that the impermissibility of one's freedom to travel—according to his position—**has in fact committed a gross error.**"

Then al-Nābulusī cited Akmal al-Dīn al-Bābartī's (710-786/1310-1384) statement in *Tuḥfat al-abrār*—a commentary on al-Ṣaghānī's *Mashāriq al-anwār*—regarding this hadith:

> There is evidence in it for the superlative merit of these three mosques and the great merit of travelling there because they were built by the Prophets–upon them peace–and many hadiths have emerged on the merit of prayer in them.... This is why the jurists have said that when one vows to pray in one of these three mosques he is bound to go to it and pray in it. If he prays in any other mosque he has not fulfilled his vow. However, if one vows to pray in a mosque other than the three, then he does not have to pray in it. He only has to pray wherever he wishes. **So its prevalent implied meaning is, *One does not* [*have to*] *travel to any mosque <u>for the sake of praying therein</u>* [subsequent to a vow] *except to three mosques.* Thereby becomes null and void the claim of him** [=Aḥmad al-Ḥarrānī] **who said that to travel to visit the Prophet–upon him peace–and to visit the Intimate Friend of the All-Merciful** [in al-Khalīl, Palestine]–upon him peace–**and others of the Prophets and righteous are categorically forbidden. We seek refuge in Allah Most High from deviant misguidance after guidance!**[8]

The Maliki Shaykh Aḥmad Zarrūq said in the introduction to his commentary on *Ḥizb al-Baḥr*, "[Aḥmad al-Ḥarrānī] is a Muslim who had a talent for memorization and proficiency but

[8] "So its prevalent implied meaning..." → "deviant misguidance after guidance." Ms. of Akmal al-Dīn al-Bābartī's *Tuḥfat al-abrār* posted at https://archive.org/details/shmashariq, folio 137, verso, lines 9-11.

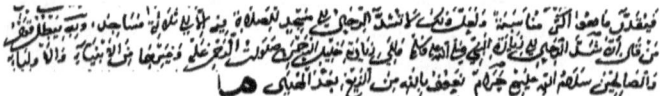

who was impugned and questioned in credal doctrines... The upshot of that is that his quotations may be taken into consideration but not his stances in sacred knowledge." Shaykh Yūsuf al-Nabhānī cited the above towards the end of his encyclopedia of *tawassul* entitled *Shawāhid al-ḥaqq fil-istighātha bi-Sayyid al-khalq* (The proof-texts of the truth on using the help of the Master of creation) and commented, "His words, 'may be taken into consideration' **exclude** whatever [al-Ḥarrānī] adduced in support of his misguided innovations by which he contravened the vast majority of the Imams of the Muslims, especially all that is connected to travelling for the purpose of visiting and using his help and that of the rest of the Prophets and the righteous. Anything he quotes in this respect is not given any consideration unless the trustworthy ulema happen to agree with him as has been resolved. This is indicated by the words of the Shāfi'ī Hadith master al-'Irāqī, the Mālikī Imam al-Zurqānī and the Ḥanafī al-Shihāb al-Khafājī that are mentioned in this book [=*Shawāhid al-ḥaqq*], not to mention the two Imams al-Subkī and al-Haytamī among others."

As for the ruling on traveling to visit the graves of the Prophet and the Awliya in the Ḥanbalī school it is in conformity with the massive majority as evidenced by the words of their Imams such as the Damascene Muwaffaq al-Dīn Ibn Qudāma in *al-Muqni'*, *al-Mughnī* and *al-Kāfī* to the effect that "Once one has finished with Hajj it is desirable for him to visit the grave of the Prophet–upon him the blessings and peace of Allah–and his two Companions," which obviously presupposes travel and the intention to do so. More than that, 'Awn al-Dīn Ibn Hubayra asserted agreement to that effect: "**They have agreed upon the desirability of visiting the Elect Prophet–upon him the blessings and peace of Allah–and his two Companions and have recommended it.**" The same was stated by al-Burhān Ibn Mufliḥ in *al-Mubdi'*, Shams al-Dīn Ibn Mufliḥ *al-Furū'*, Buhūtī in *al-Rawḍ al-murbi'* and *Kashshāf al-qinā'*, al-Ḥajjāwī in *al-Iqnā'*, Mar'ī b. Yūsuf in *Ghāyat al-muntahā* and *Dalīl al-ṭālib*, 'Abd al-Raḥmān al-Ba'lī in *Kashf al-mukhaddarāt*, Ibn al-Najjār, Kalwadhānī and others.

All of them disregarded Aḥmad al-Ḥarrānī's innovated prohibition of travel, let alone his false claim that there was consensus over that position. All of them also cited the abovementioned story of the desert Arab as an additional proof-text for the desirable and recommended visit of the Prophetic grave, again in rejection of al-Ḥarrānī's false claim.

Yet the false claim was reduplicated by al-Ḥarrānī's asp-tongued defender Muḥammad b. Aḥmad b. ʿAbd al-Hādī in his attack on Shaykh al-Islām Taqī al-Dīn al-Subkī al-Kabīr entitled *al-Ṣārim al-munkī fī naḥr al-Subkī* (The painful sword in the throat of al-Subkī) [!]: "None of the Imams viewed the desert-Arab report [also known as al-ʿUtbī's report] as something of probative value in the case." In reality **the Ḥanbalī Imams have endorsed the desert-Arab report as probative in their discussions on post-Hajj and ʿUmra *ziyāra*, and all four Schools have concurred on the desirability of *ziyāra* from their inception**. Al-Ḥakīm al-Tirmidhī even made it one of his foundations in *Nawādir al-uṣūl*. Al-Ājurrī in *al-Sharīʿa* said that all the learned scholars had ordered it for the Umma, and most of the jurists and pilgrimologists since the early fourth century have adduced the desert-Arab report in support and encouragement of its practice including the Ḥanbalīs such as Ibn al-Jawzī, Ibn al-Munajjā, Ibn Qudāma and others.

XII. The hadiths "Do not make my grave a *'īd*" and "Whoever visits my grave, my intercession must take place for him"

The Hadith master al-Sakhāwī said in the fifth benefit at the end of the fourth chapter of his celebrated book *al-Qawl al-badī' fil-ṣalāt 'alā al-Ḥabīb al-Shafi'* (The magnificent statement concerning the invocation of blessings on the Beloved Intercessor) that the author of *Silāḥ al-mu'min* [The weapon of the believer, a book on dhikr and *du'ā'* by Muḥammad b. Muḥ. b. 'Alī b. Humām al-Shāfi'ī (682-745/1283-1344)] said of the hadith, "**Do not make my grave a *'īd*:**" "It is possible that what is meant is the exhortation to visit him abundantly and not to make it like a festival that only occurs twice a year. This is supported by his saying, '**Do not make your houses graves,**' i.e. do not quit praying in your houses to the point you make them like graves where there is no prayer."

Al-Sakhāwī then cited one of the commentators of Baghawī's *Maṣābīḥ al-Sunna* as saying, "There is ellipsis in the style. Its subaudition is, '**Do not make the visit to my grave a *'īd*.**' Its meaning is the prohibition of gathering to visit him the way they gather for *'īd*. The Jews and the Christians used to gather for the visit to the graves of their Prophets and become engrossed in entertainment and music, so the Prophet–upon him blessings and peace–forbade his Umma from doing that. It was also said that it is possible his prohibition was in order to ward off hardship for his Umma; or—lastly—in dislike that they might exceed the proper bounds and magnify his grave with the greatest excess." Sakhāwī comments, "**The exhortation to visit his noble grave has come in a number of hadiths** if it were not already amply sufficient to have among them only the promise of the Truthful and Confirmed One–upon him blessings and peace–of the necessity of his intercession and other than that for his visitor. And **the Imams have concurred from the time after his demise–upon him the blessings and peace of Allah–to our own present time over the fact that such** [visit] **is one of best *qurubāt*** (acts that draw one near to Allah). And from Allah is all success."

He is referring to the Prophetic hadith narrated from Ibn 'Umar, "**Whoever visits my grave, my intercession has become certain** [*wajabat*] **for him**" or "**has taken place** [*ḥallat*] **for him**" or "**I am certainly an intercessor for him.**"[9] Dhahabī said this hadith has many chains which altogether yield a rank of "mutual strengthening because none of them contains anyone accused of lying." It also has many witness narrations which are weak but likewise have the same effect, "among the best of which is the report, '**Whoever visits me after my death then it is as if he has visited me in my life.**'"[10] Lastly, these reports are about excellent deeds and Prophetic merits. For all the above reasons the former hadith was deemed *ṣaḥīḥ* (sound) or *ḥasan* (fair) by Ibn al-Sakan in his *Ṣiḥāḥ*; 'Abd al-Ḥaqq al-Ishbīlī, *Aḥkām al-Ṣughrā* and *al-Wusṭā*; Shaykh al-Islām al-Taqī al-Subkī, *Shifā' al-saqām*; Ḍiyā' al-Dīn al-Maqdisī, *Faḍā'il al-a'māl*; Ibn al-Mulaqqin, *al-Badr al-munīr*; Ibn Ḥajar, *al-Ināra bi-ṭuruq ḥadīth al-ziyāra* and *Talkhīṣ al-ḥabīr*; his student al-Sakhāwī in *al-Qawl al-badī'*; al-Samhūdī, *Wafā al-wafā*; Laknawī, *al-Ajwibat al-fāḍila*, *Ẓafr al-amānī* and *Sharḥ Muwaṭṭa' Muḥammad*; and Shaykh Aḥmad al-Ghumārī, *al-Mudāwī*. None of the thirty Hadith masters who addressed it—all named on this page—called it a forgery. Only those who were led astray by ignorance and whim did so.

[9] Narrated through I. the *Tābi'ī* 'Ubayd Allāh b. 'Umar al-'Umarī who is trustworthy by al-Dāraquṭnī, *Sunan*; al-Sakan b. Jumay', *Ḥadīth al-Sakan b. Jumay'*; al-Khila'ī, *al-Fawā'id al-ḥisān*; Qawwām al-Sunna, *al-Targhīb*; Abū Ṭāhir al-Silafī, *Mashyakha Baghdādiyya*; Abū al-Yumn Ibn 'Asākir, *Itḥāf al-zā'ir*; II. his younger brother 'Abd Allāh b. 'Umar b. Ḥafṣ al-'Umarī who is weak by Abū Dāwūd al-Ṭayālisī, *Musnad*; Ibn Abī al-Dunyā, *al-Qubūr*; Dūlābī, *al-Kunā wal-asmā'*; Ibn Khuzayma, *Mukhtaṣar al-mukhtaṣar*; Ḥakīm al-Tirmidhī, *Nawādir al-uṣūl*; 'Uqaylī, *al-Ḍu'afā'*; al-Dīnawarī, *al-Mujālasa*; Ibn 'Adī, *al-Kāmil fil-Ḍu'afā'*; al-Bayhaqī, *Shu'ab*; al-Khaṭīb, *Tālī talkhīṣ al-mutashābih*; and III. (with *ḥallat*) 'Abd Allāh b. Ibrāhīm al-Ghifārī who is very weak by Bazzār per Haythamī, *Kashf al-astār* and Ibn Ḥajar, *Mukhtaṣar zawā'id al-Bazzar*.

[10] Narrated from Ibn 'Umar by al-Janadī, *Faḍā'il al-Madīna*; Ṭabarānī, *Awsaṭ* and *Kabīr*; Ibn 'Adī, *Kāmil*; Dāraquṭnī, *Sunan*; Bayhaqī, *Sunan kubrā* and *Shu'ab*; Qawwām al-Sunna, *Targhīb*; and others. Dhahabī's words are in Sakhāwī, *al-Maqāṣid al-ḥasana* (*Man zāra qabrī wajabat*).

XIII. The hadith "They have taken their Prophets' graves as places of prostration" has a mainstream explanation as well as a misleading explanation

The objector said–may Allah guide him: "Al-Jafrī interprets figuratively the hadith of the Messenger of Allah–upon him blessings and peace–'Allah curse the Jews and the Christians! They have taken the graves of their Prophets as places of prostration' to mean 'prostrating on top of the grave,' and this claim of his is untrue and contravenes what the relied-upon schools follow."

The above objection is itself based on the ill-interpretive presumption of *shirk* for whoever prays even near the grave of one of the righteous. Only *lā-madhhabīs*, Wahhabis and similar peripheral sectarians fall into that presumption in order to accuse other Muslims of the greatest of all *kabā'ir*, in the process assimilating themselves with the Kharijites of old who, in the words of Ibn 'Umar, "took the verses revealed about the polytheists and applied them to the Muslims." It is on the basis of that view that the rankest among them have even advocated for the grave of the Prophet–upon him the blessings and peace of Allah–to be brought out of his Mosque in recent times. Such a view is a combination of ignorance with Kharijism and it has nothing to do with the Prophetic Sunna and "the relied-upon schools."

In reality Habib 'Alī al-Jafrī's understanding of the abovementioned hadith as meaning "prostrating on top of the grave" is nothing but the understanding of *Ahl al-Sunna wal-Jamā'a*. The hadith is referring to a prostration of magnification that is specifically directed to the grave as the qibla and its purported dweller as the recipient. To prevent even the appearance of such magnification with respect to the worshippers' prayer in the Prophetic Mosque in Medina, the Companions walled up the room of 'Ā'isha within a triangular structure that prevents worshippers from facing it squarely when praying towards the qibla. This was stated by al-Nawawī in *Sharḥ Ṣaḥīḥ Muslim* followed by Shaykh

'Abd Allāh al-Ghumārī in the chapter entitled "The building of masjids on top of graves" in his book *Itqān al-ṣan'a fī taḥqīq ma'nā al-bid'a* (Perfect handiwork in ascertaining the meaning of *bid'a*) and our teacher Shaykh Nūr al-Dīn 'Itr in *I'lām al-anām sharḥ Bulūgh al-marām*. It was further documented at length by Maḥmūd Sa'īd Mamdūḥ in his 350-page *Kashf al-sutūr 'ammā ushkila min aḥkām al-qubūr* (Clarification of what was obscure of the rulings pertaining to the graves).

Imam Ibn Ḥajar al-Haytamī said in his encyclopedia of grave sins entitled *al-Zawājir 'an iqtirāf al-kabā'ir* (§93-98), "Our [Shāfi'ī] colleagues said that it is categorically prohibited for one to pray towards the graves of Prophets and Awliya *tabarrukan* (for the sake of deriving blessing) or *i'ẓāman* (for magnification). So they stipulated two conditions: one, for the grave to belong to someone considered important, and two, for the aim of praying towards it—**and likewise praying on top of it**—to be the derivation of blessing and the expression of magnification." In other words **the prohibition of praying towards or on top of the graves of Prophets and Awliya**—which are usually in prominent spots and sometimes near, inside or under places or edifices of worship—**is not absolute but relative**. If the act is missing the above two conditions it is allowed in the *dīn*. **To make the prohibition absolute is an innovation of misguidance** because it would result in prohibiting people from praying in the Ka'ba, the Meccan sanctuary, the Mosque of al-Khayf, and other places under which the Prophet–upon him the blessings and peace of Allah–or the Companions and the later historians said that Prophets and Awliya were buried.[11]

Ibn 'Abd al-Barr said in *al-Tamhīd*, "There is in this hadith [='They have taken the graves of their Prophets as places of prostration'] the **categorical prohibition of prostration on top of**

[11] A most thorough survey of the proof-texts to that effect is found in Mamdūḥ, *Kashf al-sutūr* (pp. 111-136, ch. 5, §4: *qubūr al-Anbiyā' fil Masjid al-Ḥarām*; §5: *qubūr al-Anbiyā' al-latī bi-Masjid al-Khayf*). He wrote this book in rebuttal of the arch-innovator Nasir the Albanian's denial of the early Muslims' abundant documentation to that effect.

the graves of the Prophets, and in the same sense, that it is not lawful to prostrate to other than Allah Almighty. The hadith can also be explained to mean that the graves of the Prophets must not be made a qibla towards which one prays." Ibn Qudāma construed it in the latter sense in *al-Mughnī*. So did al-Zurqānī in *Sharḥ al-Muwaṭṭa'*. They said, "I.e. **they took them [=the graves of their Prophets] as the direction of their qibla**." Al-Sakhāwī cited all the above meanings in *al-Qawl al-badī'*.

Ibn Ḥajar 'Asqalānī in the *Fatḥ* and *Taghlīq al-ta'līq* clarified that when 'Umar saw Anas praying and shouted at him, "The grave! The grave!" (Bukhārī) the continuations of the reports say that Anas simply shifted away and continued to pray, i.e. he made sure he was not facing it. Aḥmad b. Ismā'īl al-Gūrānī (d. 893/ 1488) supported it in his commentary on Bukhārī in light of the Prophetic hadith narrated from Abū Marthad in Muslim,

عن أبي مَرثَدٍ الغَنَوِي مرفوعاً **لَا تُصَلُّوا إِلَى الْقُبُورِ** رواه مسلم

Do not pray towards the graves.

Muḥammad b. 'Abd al-Wahhāb in his book of *Tawḥīd* and his followers are clueless (or heedless) of this clarification, which was cited in full by Muḥammad al-Amīn al-Shinqīṭī (1905-1973) in *Aḍwā' al-bayān fī īḍāḥ al-Qur'ān bil-Qur'ān* (Ḥijr 15:80). Another clarification is that the dislike has to do with possible filth. The Mālikī faqih and qadi of Medina Muḥammad Khaḍir al-Shinqīṭī (1868-1935) said in his commentary on Bukhārī's *Ṣaḥīḥ* (9:118) after citing 'Umar's report: **"Mālik's madhhab is that prayer in the graveyard is permissible without dislike** if it is safe from filth, whether it is a functional cemetery or disused, whether one is sure it has been freshly dug or unsure, whether there is a barrier between him and it or not, whether it is that of a Muslim or that of a non-Muslim, and even if the grave is right in front of him, and there is no need to repeat it in any of the above cases per the *mashhūr* (well-known) view." The same is found in Ibn Rushd's (d. 520/1126) *al-Bayān wal-taḥṣīl* (18:131) citing Ibn al-Qāsim's *Mudawwana* and Ibn Ḥabīb's *al-Wāḍiḥa*.

قال الفقيه محمّد الخَضِر بن عبد الله بن أحمد الشنقيطي في شرحه الكبير على البخاري: **مذهب مالك أن الصلاة في المقبرة جائزة بدون كراهة إن أمِنَت من النَجَس، عامرةً كانت أو دارسة، تيقّن نبشَها أو شك فيه، جُعل بينه وبينها حائل أم لا، كانت لمسلم أو لمشرك، ولو كان القبر بين يديه، ولا إعادة عليه على المشهور في الجميع.** اهـ. ومثله في البيان والتحصيل لابن رشد عن المدونة والواضحة.

The Imam and renewer of *tafsīr* Abū Sa'īd 'Abd Allāh b. 'Umar b. Muḥammad al-Bayḍāwī (d. 691/1292) said in his commentary on Baghawī's *Maṣābīḥ al-Sunna* titled *Tuḥfat al-abrār*:

> Since the Jews and Christians were prostrating to the graves of the Prophets in magnification of their status, making them a qibla and turning towards them in prayer—whereby they took them as idols—he cursed them and categorically forbade the Muslims to do the same. As for him that takes for himself a place of prostration [or: a mosque] in the vicinity of a righteous person or prays in his burial-place, his purpose in that being to use the latter's spiritual help, or for some *athar* (blessed relic) of the effects of his worship to reach him—not in magnification of him and in turning to him—then there is nothing wrong in that. Do you not see that the resting-place of Ismā'īl–upon him peace–in the Inviolable Mosque is at the Ḥaṭīm (Chamber of Ismā'īl) and, what is more, that that Mosque is the very best spot the worshipper is pursuing for his prayer? As for the prohibition of praying in cemeteries, it is specific to the freshly dug graves because of what they contain of filth.

قال الإمام المجدد المفسر اللغوي ناصر الدين أبو الخير عبد الله بن عمر البيضاوي في تحفة الأبرار شرح مصابيح السنة: **لمّاَ كانت اليهود والنصارى يسجدون لقبور الأنبياء تعظيما لشأنهم ويجعلونها قبلةً ويتوجهون في الصلاة نحوها فاتخذوها أوثاناً، لعنهم ومنع المسلمين عن مثل ذلك ونهاهم عنه. أمّا من**

اتخذ مسجداً في جوارِ صالحٍ، أو صلَّى في مقبرته، وقصد به الاستظهار بروحه، أو وصولَ أثرٍ من آثار عبادته إليه - لا التعظيمَ له والتَوَجُّهَ نحوه - فلا حَرَجَ عليه. ألا ترى أن مرقد إسماعيل - عليه السلام - في المسجد الحرام عند الحطيم، ثمّ إن ذلك المسجد أفضل مكان يتحرّى المصلّي لصلاته؟ والنهيُ عن الصلاة في المقابر مختصٌّ بالمقابر المنبوشة لِمَا فيها من النجاسة. واستشهد به الحافظ في فتح الباري (قوله: باب: هل تُنبَش قبور مشركي الجاهلية) والسيوطي في حاشيته على سنن النسائي في كتاب المساجد واللّاعي المغربي في البدر التمام شرح بلوغ المرام في باب المساجد من كتاب الصلاة. ثم جائت ظاهرية الزيدية كالأمير الصنعاني والشوكاني والقِنَّوجي البهوبالي فنسبوا قول البيضاوي واستشهاد أئمّة السّنّة به إلى (التشبيه بعبدة الأوثان الذين يعظِّمون الجمادات) وعدّه بعض أتباعهم الوهابيّة من (المخالفات العقدية في فتح الباري) على حدّ زعمه.

Bayḍāwī's clarification was cited and endorsed by al-Ṭībī in *Sharḥ al-Mishkāt*, Ibn Ḥajar in the *Fatḥ*, al-'Aynī in the *'Umda*, Suyūṭī on Nasā'ī and Ibn Mājah's *Sunan*, al-Qārī and al-Zurqānī among others. Then came the no-madhhab neo-Ẓāhirīs such as al-Amīr al-Ṣan'ānī, Shawkānī and Ṣiddiq Ḥasan Khān of Bhopal —among others—who wrote that Bayḍāwī's words are "an invitation to resemble idolaters who magnify **inanimate objects**" (by which these writers mean the Prophets and the Awliya in *Barzakh*), one of them including it in his defamation of *Fatḥ al-Bārī* which he entitled "Ibn Ḥajar's contraventions of the Creed."

The above objectors are all ardent admirers and followers of Muḥammad b. 'Abd al-Wahhāb rather than any of the four Sunni Schools. However, Ibn 'Abd al-Wahhāb construed the hadith to mean "proximity to the grave"–even if there is a *sitr* (screen) between the worshipper and the grave–and not just "prostration to" or "on the grave." This is expressed in his tract *al-Tawḥīd al-*

ladhī huwa ḥaqq Allāh 'alā al-'abīd (The monotheism that is the right of Allah over the slaves). This is why you will not see those that affiliate themselves to him praying in a mosque that contains a grave, such as the Mosque of the Prophet–upon him the blessings and peace of Allah–in Medina or the Umawi Mosques in Damascus and Homs for example—**even when they patently know that the Companions prayed in them and other of the blessed ancient mosques**, such as the Masjid of al-Khayf in Mina, about which the Messenger–upon him the blessings and peace of Allah–said, "**In the Masjid of al-Khayf there is the grave of seventy Prophets.**"[12]

Do you see how the Shaykh from Najd and his imitators have attributed polytheism to the near-totality of the Muslims? Their *takfīr* includes the giants of the *Salaf* such as Ibn Jurayj and his teacher 'Aṭā' b. Abī Rabāḥ the Imam of Mecca who named Ibn Jurayj "the Sayyid of the people of Hijaz" and to whom he said, "Do not pray with a grave between you and the qibla, but **if there is between you and the grave a cubit-high *sitra* (screen), then pray!**" ('Abd al-Razzāq's *Muṣannaf* and Ibn Ḥazm's *Muḥallā*).

قال إمام أهل مكة عطاء بن أبي رباح التابعي لتلميذه ابن جريج سيد أهل الحجاز: **لَا تُصَلِّ وَبَيْنَكَ وَبَيْنَ الْقِبْلَةِ قَبْرٌ، فَإِنْ كَانَ بَيْنَكَ وَبَيْنَهُ سِتْرَةُ ذِرَاعٍ، فَصَلِّ**. رواه عبد الرزاق في المصنّف وذكره ابن حزم في المُحَلَّى بالآثار

Let then the objector choose for himself what path he wishes to follow and have others follow, after he decides in good conscience who among the abovementioned authorities are the true representatives of what he calls "the relied-upon schools."

[12] Narrated from Ibn 'Umar by al-Fākihī in *Akhbār Makka*; Ṭabarānī in *al-Mu'jam al-kabīr*; al-Bazzār with a sound chain per Ibn Ḥajar in *Mukhtaṣar zawā'id al-Bazzār* and others such as al-Haythamī in *Majma' al-zawā'id* and Taqī al-Dīn al-Fāsī in *Shifā' al-gharām bi-akhbār al-balad al-ḥarām*, also al-Dāraquṭnī in *al-Afrād* and Abū Ṭāhir al-Silafī in *al-Mashyakhat al-Baghdādiyya*.

XIV. Touching and kissing the grave out of love and for blessing is desirable according to Imam Aḥmad b. Ḥanbal

The objector said–may Allah guide him–"and one of his teachers would touch the grave and prostrate over it, and I have seen this with my own eyes in the computer."

The noble sacred Law counts any testimony that states "with my own eyes in the computer" as a lie and a self-contradiction. For the honor of a Muslim deserves better than to be assailed on the basis of something heard or seen by way of a machine unless it is ascertained and verified through accountable human witnesses. It is too well-known that electronic devices are the easiest means by which an illusion can be constructed to appear in the form of truth. So even if an reputable eyewitness of a *ḥadd*-punishable offense adduces a video showing image and sound, he still has to support his accusation with the testimonies of other reliable eyewitnesses, otherwise he is flogged and never again to be trusted as a witness.

Moreover, the objector himself has precluded the claim that Shaykh 'Alī al-Jafrī's teacher prostrated over the grave when he claimed that he "interprets figuratively" the prohibitive hadith **They have taken the graves of their Prophets as places of prostration** to mean prostration over the grave, i.e. that al-Jafrī does curse whoever does that. How then could he or his teacher condone its doing? Al-Jafrī even took care to sign an explicit written statement disowning what the objector claimed in which he said, "I declare that I am innocent before Allah of what was attributed to me or to any of my teachers with regard to any prostration over the grave." The objector has been fully informed of that written statement. Yet he did not retract his false accusation—which the enemies of the truth have manipulated him to endorse and propagate on their behalf so that they could defame Ḥabīb 'Alī al-Jafrī—just as he did not exonerate the latter of what he called "his errors." On the contrary, he said, "I do not count as deceptive the website of So and so [the libelous Wahhabi site], nor do I exonerate al-Jafrī from his errors." But this taking of sides on the side of error is exoneration enough.

As for the purported prostration, it might not be a prostration at all in reality, but only an act that is unfairly described as such, for example bowing down to kiss someone's hand or foot out of respect for the possessors of merit in the faith or for one's parents. Someone looking from afar—or someone who is ignorant of the Sunna proof-texts of such an act or who is ignorant of the excuses the Sharia gives to someone who does something strange out of emotion—might harbor an ill opinion and rush to condemnation, even someone high-placed who ought to have known better as in the following example.

Majd al-Dīn Abū al-Barakāt 'Abd al-Salām b. 'Abd Allāh al-Ḥarrānī the Grandfather (590-653/1194-1255) in *al-Muntaqā min akhbār al-Muṣṭafā* and Shaykh al-Islām al-Taqī al-Subkī al-Kabīr in *Shifā' al-saqām* mentioned that Marwān[13] came over one day and found a man with his face pressed against the Grave [of the Prophet], so he seized him roughly by the neck and shouted, "Do you know what you are doing!" The man said yes and turned to him. Behold, it was Abū Ayyūb al-Anṣārī–Allah be well-pleased with him. He said, "I came to the Messenger of

[13] Abū 'Abd al-Malik Marwān b. al-Ḥakām b. Abī al-'Āṣ b. Umayya (2-65/624-685 was eight at the time of the Prophet's demise. He remained in Medina with his father until the latter's death, after which he became 'Uthmān's secretary until the latter was killed. He went to Basra with Ṭalḥa and al-Zubayr then back to Medina. When Mu'āwiya became caliph he made him governor of Medina in the year 42, then replaced him with Sa'īd b. al-'Āṣ and al-Walīd b. 'Utba b. Abī Sufyān successively, then brought him back then replaced him again. He remained in Medina until its dwellers expelled him in the time of Yazīd b. Mu'āwiya in the year 63/683. The Umayyads and some of the Syrians gave him their pledge when the pious 23-year-old caliph Mu'āwiya b. Yazīd died and he ruled from 64/684 to 65/685, taking over the rest of Syria and wresting Egypt from Ibn al-Zubayr's authority. He died suffocated by his wife and her maids before achieving full power. He narrated from 'Umar, 'Uthmān, 'Alī, Zayd b. Thābit, 'Abd al-Raḥmān b. al-Aswad b. Yaghūth and Busra bint Ṣafwān (al-Dhahabī, *Siyar a'lām al-nubalā'*).

Allah–upon him blessings and peace of Allah–and I did not come to a stone! I heard the Messenger of Allah say, 'Do not weep over the faith when its people are put in charge of it; but weep over it when other than its people are put in charge of it.'"[14]

Al-Dhahabī in the *Siyar* and *Tārīkh al-Islām* cites the same act as the habit of the arch-trustworthy *Tābi'ī* Muḥammad b. al-Munkadir, whom Mālik called the Sayyid of the Qur'ān-reciters: "He would suddenly fall into a deep silence then he would get up, go and place his cheek on the Prophet's grave, after which he would come back. He was rebuked about that, so he said, 'Verily a fleeting thought might smite me and whenever I find myself in that state I go and seek help (*istaghathtu*) with the grave of the Prophet–upon him the blessings and peace of Allah.' And he would go in the pre-dawn to a spot in the mosque then rub his face on it and lie down. Asked about it he replied, 'Verily I saw the Prophet–upon him the blessings and peace of Allah–in this spot. I see him in my sleep.'"[15]

We already cited in chapter XI Dhahabī's excellent defense of those that kiss the walls and prostrate to the Prophetic grave out of love and emotion. He also said, in his major encyclopedia of his teachers (*Mu'jam al-shuyūkh* 1:73 of the Saudi edition), in the entry on his teacher Rukn al-Dīn Abū al-'Abbās Aḥmad b. 'Abd al-Mun'im al-Qazwīnī, that the latter narrated to him with his chain to Ibn 'Umar–Allah be well-pleased with him and his father–that he disliked to touch the grave of the Prophet–upon him blessings and peace of Allah. Al-Dhahabī then commented, "The only reason he disliked it is because he considered it *min tark al-adab* (a breach of manners). Aḥmad b. Ḥanbal was asked about one who would touch the grave of the Prophet–upon him

[14] It is narrated from (i) Ibn Abī Ṣāliḥ by Aḥmad (38:558 §23585); Ḥākim (4:515, *ṣaḥīḥ*); and (ii) Muṭṭalib b. 'Abd Allāh b. Ḥanṭab al-Makhzūmī [*thiqa thiqa*, Marwān's sororal nephew] by Ibn Abī Khaythama, *al-Tārīkh al-kabīr* (2:76-77 §1801); Ibn 'Asākir, *Tārīkh* (57:250).

[15] Narrated from Ismā'īl b. Ya'qūb al-Taymī by Ibn Abī Khaythama, *al-Tārīkh al-kabīr* (2:258-259 §2777); Ibn 'Asākir, *Tārīkh* (56:50-51).

the blessings and peace of Allah–and kiss it, and he considered it harmless. His son 'Abd Allāh narrated it from him." He is referring to the narration in *al-'Ilal wa-ma'rifat al-rijāl li-Aḥmad riwāyat Ib nihi 'Abd Allah* in which 'Abd Allāh says, "I asked him about **the man that touches the Prophet's pulpit and derives blessing by touching it and kissing it, and does the same with the grave** or something like it, seeking thereby to draw near to Allah Almighty. **He said, 'There is no harm in that.'"**

Al-Dhahabī goes on to say in the long entry on the biography of Imam Aḥmad in *Siyar a'lām al-nubile* (Risāla ed. 11:212 = Fikr ed. 9:457):

> Also part of his habitual high manners is that his son 'Abd Allah said, "I saw my father take a hair of the Holy Prophet–upon him blessings and peace–and put it on his mouth to kiss it. I reckon I also saw him put it on his eyes, and he would also dip it in water and drink the water to derive healing from it. I also saw him taking the bowl of the Prophet, wash it in well water and then drink from it. I also saw him drink Zamzam water for healing and wiping his hands and face with it." I say, where is the pseudo-strict one that would find fault with Aḥmad, when it is firmly established that 'Abd Allāh asked his father about the one that touches the pommel of the Prophet's pulpit and touches the Prophet's chamber, and he said, "I do not see any harm in that"? May Allah grant us and you protection from the opinions of the Kharijites and from misguided innovations!

قال الذهبي في سيرة الإمام أحمد في باب آدابه رضي الله عنه من سير أعلام النبلاء:

ومن آدابه: قال عبد الله بن أحمد: رَأَيْتُ أَبِي يَأْخُذُ شَعْرَةً مِنْ شَعْرِ النَّبِيِّ ﷺ فَيَضَعُهَا عَلَى فِيهِ يُقَبِّلُهَا وَأَحْسَبُ أَنِّي رَأَيْتُهُ يَضَعُهَا عَلَى عَيْنِهِ وَيَغْمِسُهَا فِي الْمَاءِ وَيَشْرَبُهُ يَسْتَشْفِي بِهِ. وَرَأَيْتُهُ أَخَذَ قَصْعَةَ النَّبِيِّ ﷺ فَغَسَلَهَا فِي حُبِّ الْمَاءِ ثُمَّ شَرِبَ فِيهَا. قُلْتُ: أَيْنَ الْمُتَنَطِّعُ الْمُنْكِرُ عَلَى أَحْمَدَ؟ وَقَدْ ثَبَتَ أَنَّ عَبْدَ

الله سَأَلَ أَبَاهُ عَمَّنْ يَلْمَسُ رُمَّانَةَ مِنْبَرِ النَّبِيِّ ﷺ وَيَمَسُّ الْحُجْرَةَ النَّبَوِيَّةَ، فَقَالَ لاَ أَرَى بِذَلِكَ بَأْساً. أَعَاذَنَا اللهُ وَإِيَّاكُم مِنْ رَأْيِ الْخَوَارِجِ وَمِنَ الْبِدَعِ!

Burhān al-Dīn Ibn Mufliḥ said in *al-Mubdi'*, a reference of fiqh in the Hanbali School:

> It is desirable for the visitor to stand in front of the grave he visits. It is also narrated from him—i.e. Imam Aḥmad—"wherever he wishes." It is also narrated from him, "and his sitting is the same as his standing." He must be near it just as if he were visiting him in his lifetime. **It is permissible to touch the grave with the hand.... It is also related from him that it is desirable—Abū al-Ḥusayn [i.e. Qadi Ibn Abī Ya'lā al-Farrā'] declared it sound—because it resembles the handshake of the living, especially from someone whose blessing is hoped for.**

The same phrase is also found in Shams al-Dīn Ibn Mufliḥ's *al-Furū'* while Mar'ī b. Yūsuf al-Karmī in *Ghāyat al-muntahā* contents himself with saying "**There is no harm in touching the grave with the hand, especially that of someone whose blessing is hoped for.**"

قال برهان الدين ابن مفلح في (المُبْدِع شرح المُقْنِع) في فروع الحنابلة ٢/ ٢٨١:

يُسْتَحَبُّ لِلزَّائِرِ أَنْ يَقِفَ أَمَامَ الْقَبْرِ، وَعَنْهُ ـ أي: الإمام أحمد ـ: **حَيْثُ شَاءَ، وَعَنْهُ: قُعُودُهُ كَقِيَامِهِ، ذَكَرَهُ أَبُو الْمَعَالِي** ـ هو القاضي وجيه الدين أسعد بن المُنَجَّى بن أبي البركات التَّنُوخِي المعَرِّي الدمشقي (ت ٦٠٦) صاحب الخلاصة والنهاية في شرح الهداية ـ **وَيَنْبَغِي قُرْبُهُ، كَزِيَارَتِهِ فِي حَيَاتِهِ، وَيَجُوزُ لَمْسُ الْقَبْرِ بِالْيَدِ... وَعَنْهُ** ـ أي: الإمام أحمد ـ **يُسْتَحَبُّ، صَحَّحَهَا أَبُو الْحُسَيْنِ فِي التَّمَامِ** ـ وهو القاضي ابن أبي يعلى الفرّاء ـ **لِأَنَّهُ يُشْبِهُ مُصَافَحَةَ**

الحَيِّ، وَلَا سِيَّمَا مِمَّنْ تُرْجَى بَرَكَتُهُ والعبارة أيضاً في (الفروع) ٢/ ٣٠٠ للشمس ابن مفلح. وقال مَرعي بن يوسف الكَرمي في (غاية المنتهى) ١/ ٢٥٩: **وَلَا بَأْسَ بِلَمْسِ قَبْرٍ بِيَدٍ لَا سِيَّمَا مَنْ تُرْجَى بَرَكَتُهُ.**

Kissing the grave of parents is allowed in the Hanafi School per the *Fatāwā Hindiyya* (*karāhiya*) and Shaykh 'Abd al-Ghanī al-Dihlawī's commentary on the *Mishkāt* entitled *Shī'at al-lama at* (*darn*). Imam al-Nawawī compared a person's shaykhs to his spiritual parents, so they are more even deserving of love and respect yet. And Allah knows best.

XV. The life of Prophets in their graves and the Prophet's awareness of his Umma are categorical knowledge in Islam

The objector said–may Allah guide him–"He [=Ḥabīb ʿAlī al-Jafrī] also says that the Prophet–upon him the blessings and peace of Allah–is alive in his grave! And that he is cognizant of us! And that we go to him in times of need!"

Objecting to the Prophet being alive and cognizant is an enormity since the firm belief of the people of the Sunna and the Congregation of the Muslims is that **the Prophets are alive in their graves with a real and full life in their graves on top of the life of all the believers in the *Barzakh* (Interlife)**. Imam al-Suyuṭī stipulated that this is mass-transmitted in his *Mirqāt al-ṣuʿūd sharḥ Sunan Abī Dāwūd* and in his fatwa entitled *Inbāʾ al-adhkiyāʾ bi-ḥayāt al-Anbiyāʾ* where he said, "the life of the Prophet –upon him blessings and peace–in his grave and that of the rest of the Prophets is known to us categorically due to the amount of evidence and the mass-transmitted reports to that effect."

Shaykh al-Islam Taqī al-Dīn al-Subkī al-Kabīr said, "The fact that their life is real does not make it necessary for the bodies to accompany it the way they were in this world in the need for food and drink and other of the attributes of bodies that we witness. Rather, they have a different status." Suyūṭī mentioned it in *Zahr al-rubā ʿalā al-Mujtabā* (*Qiyām al-layl, ṣalāt Nabiyyu-l-Lāhi Mūsā*). At the same time, as the author of *Kitāb al-Rūḥ* (The book of the soul) said in the sixth *masʾala* (question) of his book, "**It is categorically-obligatory knowledge to know that the body of the Prophet is, in the earth, tender and humid** [as in life], and when the Companions asked him, 'How will our invocation of blessing be presented to you when you have turned to dust?,' he replied, '**Verily Allah has made it categorically forbidden for the earth to consume the bodies of the Prophets.**'"[16]

[16] Narrated from Aws b. Aws by Aḥmad in the *Musnad*, al-Dārimī, Ibn Mājah, Abū Dāwūd and al-Nasāʾī in their *Sunan* and Ibn Khuzayma, Ibn Ḥibbān and al-Ḥākim in their *Ṣaḥīḥ*s.

The same author cited in his *Jilā' al-afhām fil-ṣalāt wal-salām 'alā khayri al-anām* Imam al-Qurṭubī's statement:

> It is authentically related from the Prophet–upon him blessings and peace–that (i) the earth does not consume the bodies of the Prophets; that (ii) he–upon him blessings and peace–met with the Prophets on the night of the heavenly Ascent in Jerusalem and (iii) in the sky, and (iv) especially Mūsā, and that (v) no Muslim greets him but Allah has returned his life to him so that he will answer, and more of that whose upshot is the **categorical definitive knowledge that the death of Prophets only refers to the fact that they have been veiled from us whereby we no longer perceive them**, even though they are still existing and alive. That is just like the state of the angels, for they exist and live but we cannot see them.

The quote ends here but Qurṭubī's original text continues, "and none of our species sees them [=angels] except whoever Allah has given a special miraculous gift among His Awliya."[17]

Imam al-Qushayrī said in *Shikāyat Ahl al-Sunna bi-ḥikāyat mā nālahum min al-miḥna* (Complaint of the Sunnis with the account of the tribulation they have faced)—the epistle he wrote in defense of the Ash'arīs of Nishapur against the enviers, false accusers and innovators that are rampant to this day:

> According to them—i.e. Ash'arīs—Muḥammad–upon him the blessings and peace of Allah–is alive in his grave. Allah Most High said, *and never count those who were killed in the way of the One God as dead. Rather they are alive with their nurturing Lord, receiving provision* (Āl 'Imrān 3:169), so He recounted that the shahids are alive in the presence of their nurturing Lord—and the Prophets are even more deserving of that since the rank of shahid falls short of the rank of Prophethood.... Sound reports were also transmitted to that effect such as what was narrated to us from Ibn Mas'ūd that

[17] Al-Qurṭubī, *al-Tadhkira bi-aḥwāl al-mawtā wa-umūr al-ākhira* (*mā jā'a fī inqirāḍi hādhā al-khalq wa-dhikr al-nafkhi wal-ṣa'q, faṣl*), ed. al-Ṣādiq Muḥ. Ibrāhīm, 3 vols. (Riyadh: Dār al-Minhāj, 1425/2004) 1:460.

the Messenger of Allah–upon him the blessings and peace of Allah–said, "**Verily Allah has angels roaming the earth and conveying to me the greeting of my Community**."[18] And **the greeting cannot be conveyed to him unless he is alive**. It was also narrated to us from Anas b. Mālik that the Prophet–upon him the blessings and peace of Allah–said, "**No Prophet dies and resides in his grave for forty mornings except his soul is given back to him**."[19] It was also narrated to us from Abū Hurayra that the Messenger of Allah–upon him the blessings and peace of Allah–said, "**None greets me except Allah has returned to me my soul** [i.e. once and for all] **so that I may answer**."[20]

عن أبي هريرة رضي الله عنه أن رسول الله ﷺ قال **مَا مِنْ أَحَدٍ يُسَلِّمُ عَلَيَّ إِلَّا رَدَّ اللهُ عَلَيَّ رُوحِي حَتَّى أَرُدَّ عَلَيْهِ السَّلَامَ** رواه أحمد وأبو داود وصححه البيهقي والنووي والحافظ وغيرهم

Sakhāwī said in *al-Qawl al-badī'*, "Shaykh al-Islām Abū al-Ḥasan al-Subkī said in his *Shifā' al-saqām* that a group of Imams adduced the latter hadith as a foundational proof for the desirability of visiting the grave of the Prophet–upon him blessings and peace –[among them al-Dhahabī as we have shown in chapter XI], and it is certainly a sound basis, for when the visitor gives salam the reply takes place for him from near, and this is a much sought-after merit. May Allah facilitate it for us again and again!" Qadi Yūsuf al-Nabhānī adduced more texts on the Prophet's

[18] Narrated by 'Abd al-Razzāq, Ibn Abī Shayba, Aḥmad, al-Dārimī, al-Nasā'ī with six chains, Ṭabarānī, Abū Ya'lā, Ibn Ḥibbān, Ḥākim (*ṣaḥīḥ*) and al-Bayhaqī, and declared sound by the author of *Jilā' al-afhām*.

[19] Narrated from Anas by Ḥākim in his *Tārīkh*, al-Bayhaqī in *Ḥayāt al-Anbiyā'*, Ṭabarānī in *Musnad al-Shāmiyyīn* and Abū Nu'aym in *Ḥilyat al-awliyā*. Ibn Ḥajar in the *Fatḥ* and *Talkhīṣ al-ḥabīr* suggests that its rank is *ḥasan* based on corroborative narrations adduced by al-Bayhaqī. Al-Suyūṭī explicitly declares it *ḥasan* in *al-La'ālī' al-maṣnū'a*.

[20] Narrated by Aḥmad and Abū Dāwūd. It was rated sound by Bayhaqī, Nawawī, Ibn Ḥajar and others. See also four notes up.

hearing in the grave in *Shawāhid al-Ḥaqq* (pp. 283-285).

Then Qushayrī said:

> The report indicates that the deceased does not know until the soul is returned to him and it indicates that the Prophet–upon him the blessings and peace of Allah–is alive in his grave. It was narrated to us from Abū Hurayra that the Messenger of Allah–upon him blessings and peace–said, "**Whoever invokes blessings upon me at my grave I hear him, and whoever invokes blessings on me from afar I am informed of it.**"[21] It was also narrated to us from Anas b. Mālik that the Messenger of Allah–upon him blessings and peace–said, "**On my night Journey I passed by Mūsā at the red dune as he was standing in prayer in his grave.**'"[22] [He went on narrating the long hadith of the heavenly Ascent mentioning the Prophet's sighting of the various Prophets.] So this report indicates that they are all alive–upon them peace. Al-Ḥasan b. Qutayba narrated with his chain from Anas that the Messenger of Allah–upon him blessings and peace–said, "**The Prophets are alive in their graves, praying.**"[23]

Shaykh al-Islām Tāj al-Dīn al-Subkī likewise said in *Ṭabaqāt al-Shāfi'iyyat al-kubrā* (3:384), "It is part of our [=Asharis'] firm beliefs that the Prophets–upon them peace–are alive in their graves." The *Ḥāfiẓ* said in *Fatḥ al-Bārī* (7:29), "**his life**–upon him the blessings and peace of Allah–**in the grave is not followed by**

[21] Narrated by Abū al-Shaykh in *Thawāb al-ṣalāt 'alā al-Nabīy* with a chain rated strong by Ibn Ḥajar in the *Fatḥ*, al-Sakhāwī, al-Suyūṭī, Ibn 'Arrāq, Shawkānī, 'Abd Allāh Sirāj al-Dīn, Aḥmad Ghumārī and others.

[22] Narrated by Ibn Abī Shayba, Aḥmad, 'Abd b. Ḥumayd, Muslim, al-Nasā'ī, Abū Ya'lā, and Ibn Khuzayma and Ibn Ḥibbān in their *Ṣaḥīḥs*.

[23] Narrated by Abū Ya'lā through trustworthy narrators per Haythamī in *Majma' al-zawā'id* and Bayhaqī in *al-Risālat al-Ash'ariyya* and *Ḥayāt al-Anbiyā' fī qubūrihim*. Ibn Ḥajar rated its chain sound in the *Fatḥ* as did al-Zurqānī in *Sharḥ al-Muwaṭṭa'* and al-Suyūṭī in *Inbā' al-adhkiyā'*. Al-Qushayrī, *Shikāyat Ahl al-Sunna* in al-Rasā'il al-Qushayriyya, ed. Pir Muḥammad Ḥasan (Karachi: Islamic Research Academy, 1964; rept. Sidon: al-Maktabat al-'Aṣriyya, 1970) pp. 10-23.

death but rather he is perpetually alive, and the Prophets are alive in their graves." We remind you of the words of Imam al-Suyūṭī and of the author of *Kitāb al-Rūḥ* which we cited on the first page of this chapter to the effect that **all of the above is obligatory knowledge in Islam**, but the objector has gone the way of the neo-Ẓāhirīs exposed in Chapter XIII and Nasir the Albanian who proclaimed in his footnotes on Nuʿmān al-Ālūsī's book *al-Āyāt al-bayyināt fī ʿadam samāʿ al-amwāt*, "I have found no evidence for the Prophet's hearing of the salam of those who greet him at his grave." This is one of that man's enormities and the essence of innovation and deviation.

XVI. Belief in the life of Prophets in *Barzakh* explained from the book *Methodology of the Salaf in understanding texts*

The Shaykh al-Islam of the Holy Meccan sanctuary, our teacher and the educator of the Umma Shaykh Muḥammad Ḥasan b. ʿAlawī b. ʿAbbās b. ʿAbd al-ʿAzīz b. ʿAbbās al-Ḥasanī al-Idrīsī al-Mālikī (1367-1425/1948-2004) wrote the following lines in his 600-page book *Manhaj al-Salaf fī fahm al-nuṣūṣ* which this writer received from his blessed hands in his house in al-Ruṣayfa in Mecca the Ennobled the year of the *Ḥajj al-akbar* (1419/1999), at which time he said to me that the latter work was meant as a follow-up on his landmark book *Mafāhīm yajib an tuṣaḥḥaḥ* (Misconceptions in need of correction). These lines contain an apt reminder that **whoever finds the Sunni belief that the Prophet–upon him the blessings and peace of Allah–is alive in his grave and cognizant of the Umma objectionable, has left the pale of Islam and taken the way of the Jahiliyya** in its materialistic denial of the unseen and the life of the hereafter.

Shaykh Muḥammad b. ʿAlawī al-Mālikī said:

"We often hear certain people repeat the Quranic verse, *verily you are dying and verily they are dying* (Zumar 39:30) and other verses of similar import, as proofs for denying the human perfections and Prophetic characteristics whereby our Master and liege lord Muḥammad–upon him the blessings and peace of Allah–is distinguished from the remainder of human beings. Also among those verses is the saying of Allah, *and We never appointed for any human being before you immortality. Is it that if you die, then they are the immortal ones?* (Anbiyāʾ 21:34).

"But who denies those explicit verses? Who claims that the Prophet–upon him the blessings and peace of Allah–is still alive exactly in the same way as he was alive in the world? Surely no one makes such claims except a dull-witted, ignorant person who has not the least acquaintance with the Qurʾān and Sunna.

But he who cites these verses has overlooked—either by design or through ignorance—to warn people that such verses have come to show that our master Muḥammad–upon him the blessings and peace of Allah–is subject to the same death to which all human beings are subject, and that it is Allah alone Who is the Eternally Remaining, the Living One Who Does Not Die.

"The fact seems hidden from the minds of these would-be objectors that the noble verses that declare this important truth —whereby the Prophet–upon him the blessings and peace of Allah–is a human being and that he shall die just as human beings die—were only revealed for a specific reason: to correct a widespread misconception and aberration that prevailed in the mindsets of the Jahiliyya, the time of Ignorance. This aberration consisted in linking together, on the one hand, human perfections and merits by which a man was known, and, on the other hand, life. They believed that when a man died, his merit ended and so did his perfection, as well as anything for which he was held to be special. By dying, he lost all value and all merit, and his values and qualities died with him. Those verses came to show the falsehood and complete invalidity of this position.

"The verses came to tell Abū Jahl, Abū Lahab, the masses of idol-worshippers and all **those that are cut from the same cloth** that our master Muḥammad–upon him the blessings and peace of Allah–is a human being and that he is not an immortal walking on the face of the earth. Rather, he will be subject to whatever human beings undergo in their totality—but that does not diminish his perfections nor lower his level. For he is a human being, not an immortal, and the day of his death shall come—since death is forewritten for every human being as Allah Most High said, *every soul shall taste death* (Āl 'Imrān 3:185). However, such death never changes his high station and merit! It is as if He were saying to them, "beware lest one of you thinks of the Prophet's station in disparaging terms at the time he dies and imagines, at that time, that he no longer benefits nor serves a purpose nor hears nor replies nor supplicates nor intercedes!"

"These verses came to show these truths explicitly. People were in denial of Resurrection and Judgment. Their speakers would say, 'It is nothing more than wombs that thrust and earth that swallows. Nothing but time causes us to die.' The Qur'ān is replete with verses that show us such positions of theirs, which entail the denial of the life of the *barzakh* between death and Resurrection and the attending Paradise-life of the grave or torture of the grave, as in His statements:

Verily these ones indeed do say, 'There is nothing but our first and only death and we are never going to be risen. Bring back our ancestors then, if you are telling the truth!' Are they better, or the people of Tubba' and those that were before them? We obliterated them. Verily they were criminals. And We never created the heavens and the earth and what is between the two in jest. We never created them but in truth, but most of them do not know. Verily the Day of the Determination is their appointment one and all (al-Dukhān 44:34-40).

And the human being says, 'What! When I am dead, shall I indeed then be brought forth alive?' What! And does the human being not heed that We created him before, when he was nothing at all? (Maryam 19:66-67).

And they said, 'It is nothing but our life of this world; we die and we live; and nothing but time destroys us.' But they have no knowledge of that at all. They do nothing but presume. And whenever are recited to them Our manifest signs, their conclusive proof is never but that they say, 'Bring forth our forefathers if you are telling the truth.' Say, 'The One God, He gives you life, after which He causes you to die, after which He gathers you unto the Day of Resurrection—there is no doubt in it. But most people do not know' (al-Jāthiya/al-Sharī'a 45:24-26).

And he has struck a similitude for Us while forgetting his own creation: he said, 'Who shall revive bones when they are decayed?' Say, 'He shall revive them Who produced them in the first place, and He is, of every kind of creation, All-Knowing' (Yā Sīn 35:78-79).

"That is why the truthful and trusting one—al-Ṣiddīq—announced this truth saying, 'Whoever worshipped Muḥammad–upon him the blessings and peace of Allah–let him know that Muḥammad has died, and whoever worshipped Allah Most High, let him know that He is the Living One Who Never Dies.'[24] At this point one of those whom Allah has forsaken comes and cites the verse, *verily you are dying and verily they are dying* (Zumar 39:30) together with other Quranic texts and Prophetic hadiths of related meaning, attempting to use them as proofs for their own corrupt designs and ill intentions. This is in order to cast aspersions on the perfections of the Prophet Muḥammad–upon him the blessings and peace of Allah–and so as to assert for him ordinary humanity as well as parity between the noblest of all Prophetic Messengers and all other human beings.

"How much have we heard and read on the part of one of them who blackened many a page saying that the Prophet–upon him blessings and peace of Allah–neither hears nor benefits anyone! Impudence and lack of manners have reached such a point in one of them that he says, 'If you were to come to the Prophet's grave and ask of him the smallest worldly service such as a dirham or a cup of water, he will be incapable of giving it to you.' I ask, what does the dim-witted writer of the above words know of those who seek a *wasīla* (means) in the Prophet–upon him the blessings and peace of Allah–or ask him something? They are only asking him to ask Allah for them. This is due to the Prophet's immense rank and pre-eminence in the Divine presence.

"Furthermore, one does not ask for lowly matters which do not come to mind except to those that worship this lowly world and run after money and property. Those ones will not earn anything more than this worldly race and competition in the accumulation of wealth. The Prophet–upon him the blessings and peace of Allah–told us about this kind of people when he said: 'He has perished and failed!'[25] This is actually an imprecation

[24] Narrated from 'Ā'isha and Ibn 'Abbās by al-Bukhārī.

[25] "Perish the worshipper of gold and silver and silk, who agrees when

against them that Allah make them perish and fail, as well as a report that this is their actual condition. We seek refuge in Allāh!

"This is our answer to those who want a knowledge-based examination of the question, without passion, partisanship or obduracy, and who want to tread the path of the People of Truth —meaning the people of high manners, refinement and true knowledge. Upon such it is incumbent to let discourse reflect the understanding of the following truths:

- that the Prophet's perfections–upon him the blessings and peace of Allah–endure and remain entirely preserved without the slightest doubt;
- that he hears spoken words, replies to the salam given, praises Allah for the good deeds of his *Umma* that are shown to him, and asks forgiveness for the evil ones;
- that showing excellent manners with him at his *maqām* (high station) upon visiting him, greeting him with our salam at his grave, in his mosque and in his *Rawḍa*, are all among the most stringent obligations and the most binding of duties;
- that 'his sanctity after he died is exactly as his sanctity when he was alive [in the world],' as stated by the Imam of the Abode of Emigration to the Abbasid Caliph [in the narration where he tells the latter to supplicate to Allah without turning his back away from the Prophet and reminds him that the Prophet–upon him the blessings and peace of Allah–'is your *wasīla* (intermediary) to Allah and that of your father Adam–upon him peace'];[26]

given and, if he does not get anything, becomes angry. He has perished and failed! [Or: Perish, and failure to him!] If adversity come to him, may it not go away." Narrated as part of a longer Prophetic hadith from Abū Hurayra by al-Bukhārī and Ibn Mājah and, first half only, Tirmidhī.

[26] Narrated from Mālik by Ibn Fihr al-Mālikī al-Miṣrī (fl. 440) in his *Faḍā'il Mālik*; Qadi 'Iyāḍ in *al-Shifā* "with a good or rather sound chain" per Zurqānī in his commentary on *al-Mawāhib al-ladunniyya* and al-Khafājī in *Nasīm al-riyāḍ* (3:398), his commentary on the *Shifā'*; *Tartīb al-madārik*; Ibn Qunfudh in *Wasīlat al-Islām*; Nabhānī, *Shawāhid al-ḥaqq* (pp. 186-188); also—without attribution to Mālik—by al-'Abdarī,

- and that even though he–upon him blessings and peace of Allah–died, and his body has undoubtedly disappeared from our sights—for none eternally remains except the One Alone, the Living, the Self-Sustaining Who never tires nor sleeps—nevertheless, he is alive with a complete *ḥayāt barzakhiyya* (interlife) that is greater and better and more perfect than the life of this world—indeed, higher, dearer, sweeter, more perfect and more beneficial than worldly life.

"It is enough that those who enjoy this interlife are described as possessing three magnificent attributes related to perfection: *ḥayāt* (life), *rizq* (provision), and *'indiyya* (being-with-Allah). These attributes are expressed in the saying of Allah, *they are alive with their nurturing Lord, receiving provision* (Āl 'Imrān 3:169). If this was said about the shahids, who have a lesser rank than the Prophets, then what about the latter? The blessings and peace of Allah be upon them."

al-Tāj wal-iklīl; al-Ḥaṭṭāb, *Mawāhib al-Jalīl*; al-Buhūtī, *Kashshāf al-qinā'*; and al-Shirwānī, *Ḥawāshī Tuḥfat al-muḥtāj* (2:164). Al-Zurqānī in *Sharḥ al-Mawāhib* rejected the claim of forgery as "stemming either from ignorance or arrogance" and stated that the books of the Mālikīs are replete with the stipulation that *du'ā'* be made while facing the grave cf. al-Qābisī; Abū Bakr b. 'Abd al-Raḥmān; Khalīl, *Mansak*; al-'Abdarī; al-Ḥaṭṭāb and others. Similarly rejected is Dr. Muḥ. Sa'īd al-Būṭī's claim in his *Fiqh al-Sīra* that *du'ā'* facing the Grave is an ignorant innovation. Ibn Jamā'a said in *Hidāyat al-sālik* (4:1514-1517): "The report [of Mālik allowing for the Grave to be faced during *du'ā'*] is related by the two Hadith masters Ibn Bashkuwāl and Qadi 'Iyāḍ, and no attention is paid to the words of those who claim that it is forged purely on the basis of their whims," by which he refers to Aḥmad al-Ḥarrānī.

XVII. The sound hadith "Your works are shown to me" and the Prophet's witnessing of the Umma from *Barzakh*

As for the second of the three objections mentioned at the beginning of chapter XV, namely that "he [Ḥabīb 'Alī al-Jafrī] says that the Prophet is cognizant of us!"—then such cognizance is firmly established by the Quranic and Sunna proofs and the scholarly inferences already brought up by Qushayrī, Bayhaqī, al-Subkī father and son, Ibn Ḥajar, Sakhāwī, Suyūṭī and others.

More explicitly, it is also firmly established by the sound report that the Prophet–upon him the blessings and peace of Allah–said:

عن زاذان، عن عبد الله، عن النبي ﷺ قال **إِنَّ لله مَلَائِكَةً سَيَّاحِينَ يُبَلِّغُونِي عَنْ أُمَّتِي السَّلَامَ.** قال: وقال رسول الله ﷺ **حَيَاتِي خَيْرٌ لَكُمْ تُحَدِّثُونَ وَيُحَدَّثُ لَكُمْ، وَوَفَاتِي خَيْرٌ لَكُمْ تُعْرَضُ عَلَيَّ أَعْمَالُكُمْ، فَمَا رَأَيْتُ مِنَ خَيْرٍ حَمِدْتُ اللهَ عَلَيْهِ وَمَا رَأَيْتُ مِنَ شَرٍّ اسْتَغْفَرْتُ اللهَ لَكُمْ** رواه البزار قال في مجمع الزوائد ورجاله رجال الصحيح وصحح إسناده العراقي في طرح التثريب والسيوطي في الخصائص و المناهل والقسطلاني في المواهب والزرقاني في شرح الموطأ وشرح المواهب وغيرهم كمحمد ابن عبد الهادي فيما أسماه الصارم ورواه ابن سعد والقاضي إسماعيل في فضل الصلاة وابن أبي أسامة في مسند الحارث عن بكر بن عبد الله بسند مرسل صحيح كما في شفاء السَّقام للتقي السبكي وشرح الشفا لعلي القاري

Allah has angels roaming the earth who convey to me salams from my Umma. My life is an immense good for you. You will converse and you will be conversed with;[27] and my death is a greater good for you! Your deeds will be

[27] *Tuḥaddithūna wa-yuḥaddathu lakum*, i.e. with the Prophet and one another. It is also read *tuḥdithūna wa-yuḥdathu lakum*, "you will bring about new things and new things will be brought about for you," such as answers, knowledge, revelation and practice.

displayed to me, so whatever goodness I see, I give praise to Allah over it, and whatever evil I see, I ask Allah forgiveness for it.[28]

Our teacher the scholar of Qur'ān and Hadith Dr. Samer al-Nass mentioned in his landmark book *al-Wasīla ilā fahmi ḥaqīqat al-tawassul* (The means to the understanding of the reality of seeking intermediacy)—one the most comprehensive and succinct works on the topic—that al-Bayhaqī narrated in *Dalā'il al-Nubuwwa* from Ibn 'Abbās:

> When 'Umar b. al-Khaṭṭāb–Allah be well-pleased with him–was asked what prompted him to say what he said at the time the Prophet died–upon him the blessings and peace of Allah–(i.e. when he proclaimed it forbidden to say that the Prophet had died) he replied, "I was interpreting the verse, *and thus have We made you a just Umma so that you would be witnesses against people and that the Messenger would be, over you, a witness* (al-Baqara 2:143). For, by Allah! I verily had thought that he would indeed abide in his Umma until he would bear witness over it to the last of its deeds. Verily that is what drove me to say what I said."

Shaykh Samer commented:

> His interpretation—as one of the experts in the Arabic language—was entirely correct even if it did not make it neces-

[28] It is narrated from (i) Ibn Mas'ūd in Bazzār's *Musnad* with a chain of trustworthy narrators per Haythamī in *Majma' al-zawā'id*. Many Hadith masters declared its chain sound: 'Irāqī in *Ṭarḥ al-tathrīb*; Haythamī as stated; Qasṭallānī in the *Mawāhib*; al-Suyūṭī in the *Khaṣā'iṣ al-kubrā* and *Manāhil al-ṣafā*; Zurqānī in *Sharḥ al-Muwaṭṭa'* and *Sharḥ al-Mawāhib*; even Muḥammad b. 'Abd al-Hādī in *al-Ṣārim al-munkī* despite his fanatic partiality. It was rated sound by 'Abd Allāh al-Ghumārī in *Nihāyat al-āmāl fī sharḥ wa-taṣḥīḥ ḥadīth 'arḍ al-a'māl* and his students Maḥmūd Mamdūḥ in *Raf' al-mināra li-takhrīj aḥādīth al-tawassul wal-ziyāra* and 'Abd Allāh al-Talīdī in *Tahdhīb al-Khaṣā'iṣ al-kubrā*. It is also narrated from (ii) Bakr b. 'Abd Allāh al-Muzanī by Ibn Sa'd in his *Ṭabaqāt*, Qadi Ismā'īl al-Mālikī in *Faḍl al-ṣalāt 'alā al-Nabīy* and al-Ḥārith b. Abī Usāma in his *Musnad* with a sound *mursal* chain per al-Subkī in *Shifā' al-saqām* and al-Qārī in *Sharḥ al-Shifā*.

sary for the Prophet to remain in our physical presence. However, **our deeds are displayed to him and by this token he will be a witness over us.**

قال الأستاذ العلامة القارئ المقرئ الدكتور محمد سامر النصّ الدمشقي في كتابه (الوسيلة إلى فهم حقيقة التوسّل) مِن أجمع وأتقن المختصرات في الباب: روى البيهقي في الدلائل عن ابن عباس رضي الله عنهما: أن عمر بن الخطاب ذُكِر له: ما حَمَلَهُ على مقالته التي قال حين تُوُفِّيَ النبي ﷺ؟ قال: **كُنْتُ أَتَأَوَّلُ هَذِهِ الآيَةَ: ﴿ وَكَذَٰلِكَ جَعَلْنَٰكُمْ أُمَّةً وَسَطًا لِّتَكُونُواْ شُهَدَآءَ عَلَى ٱلنَّاسِ وَيَكُونَ ٱلرَّسُولُ عَلَيْكُمْ شَهِيدًا ﴾** البقرة من آيه ١٤٣. **فَوَاللهِ إِنْ كُنْتُ لأَظُنُّ أَنَّهُ سَيَبْقَى فِي أُمَّتِهِ حَتَّى يَشْهَدَ عَلَيْهَا بِآخِرِ أَعْمَالِهَا وَإِنَّهُ الَّذِي حَمَلَنِي عَلَى أَنْ قُلْتُ مَا قُلْتُ.** قال النصّ: وتأوُّله ـ رضي الله عنه، وهو من أهل اللسان ـ صحيح، وإن كان لا يَستوجِبُ بَقاءَه ﷺ بين أظهرنا، ولكن تُعْرَضُ عليه أعمالُنا، وبهذا يكون شهيداً علينا. اهـ.

There are other narrations that mention I. the display of the deeds of the Umma (i) to the Prophet–upon him the blessings and peace of Allah–as well as (ii) to one's relatives, and II. the display of the Umma in person to the Prophet. Among them:

- The report narrated by Ibn Mājah in his *Sunan* from Abū al-Dardā' and rated sound by Būṣīrī in *Miṣbāḥ al-zujāja* whereby the Prophet–upon him blessings and peace of Allah –said, "**Verily, no one invokes blessings upon me except his invocation is shown to me until he finishes it**."
- The sound report narrated by Aḥmad in his *Musnad*, Dārimī, Ibn Mājah, Abū Dāwūd and al-Nasā'ī in their *Sunan*, and Ibn Khuzayma, Ibn Ḥibbān and al-Ḥākim in their *Ṣaḥīḥ*s from Aws b. Aws whereby the Prophet–upon him the blessings and

peace of Allah–said, "**Invoke blessings upon me abundantly on that day** [=Jumuʿa]**, for your invocation is shown to me.**"

- The report narrated by ʿAbd al-Razzāq in his *Muṣannaf* from Mujāhid with a sound *mursal* chain that the Prophet–upon him the blessings and peace of Allah–said, "**Verily you are displayed to me together with your names and your traits, so beautify** (*fa-aḥsinū*) **the invocation of blessing on me.**"[29]
- The report narrated in closely-similar wordings by al-Ṭayālisī in his *Musnad* from (i) Jābir; Aḥmad in his *Musnad* and others from (ii) Anas; al-Ṭabarānī in *al-Muʿjam al-awsaṭ*, *al-Muʿjam al-kabīr* and *Musnad al-Shāmiyyīn* from (iii) Abū Ayyūb al-Anṣārī; Abū Dāwūd in *al-Zuhd* from (iv) Abū al-Dardā' (in *mawqūf* form); Ibn al-Jawzī in *al-Thabāt ʿinda al-mawt* from (v) Abū Hurayra; and al-Ḥakīm al-Tirmidhī in *Nawādir al-uṣūl* from (vi) ʿAbd al-Ghafūr b. ʿAbd al-ʿAzīz b. Saʿīd al-Shāmī, from his father, from his grandfather, whereby the Prophet–upon him the blessings and peace of Allah–said, **"Verily your deeds are shown to your relatives and your kin among the dead, so if it is goodness they rejoice, and if it is otherwise they say, 'O Allah! Do not cause them to die before You first guide them just as You guided us.'"**

إِنَّ أَعْمَالَكُمْ تُعْرَضُ عَلَى أَقَارِبِكُمْ وَعَشَائِرِكُمْ مِنَ الأَمْوَاتِ فَإِنْ كَانَ خَيْراً اِسْتَبْشَرُوا وَإِنْ كَانَ غَيْرَ ذَلِكَ قَالُوا: اللهُمَّ لا تُمِتْهُمْ حَتَّى تَهْدِيَهُمْ كَمَا هَدَيْتَنَا. رواه بألفاظ متقاربة الطيالسي عن جابر وأحمد عن أنس والطبراني عن أبي أيوب والحكيم الترمذي عن سعيد الشامي وابن الجوزي عن أبي هريرة في الثبات عند الموت وأبو داود عن أبي الدرداء في الزهد، جميعهم مرفوعاً إلا الأخير

[29] See the Arabic texts and documentation for these reports in Sayyid Muhammad b. ʿAlawī al-Mālikī, *The Life of the Prophets in Their Graves*, transl. Gibril Fouad Haddad (Birmingham and New York: AQSA Publications and IGI, 2021), esp. pp. 20-28, 42.

The latter hadith applies to our spiritual parents even more. Their supplication that Allah raise their murids just as He has raised them endures in the world of *barzakh* as it had been before, or rather more, since their world is all dhikr and *du'ā'*.

Shaykh 'Abd Allāh al-Ghumārī said in the first volume of his *Khawāṭir dīniyya* (Faith-related meditations): "His statement–Exalted is He–*O you who believe, beware the One God and relinquish once and for all whatever remains of usury if you are indeed believers. If you will not do that, then hear the declaration of war from the One God and His Messenger!* (al-Baqara 2:278-279) imparts that the Prophet–upon him the blessings and peace of Allah–is alive in his noble grave, fighting the usurers by supplicating against them or with whatever suits his *Barzakh* life. I have no knowledge of anyone making this inference before me."

قال العلامة عبد الله الغُماري في الجزء الأول من (خواطره الدينية) ص ١٩:

قوله تعالى ﴿ يَـٰٓأَيُّهَا ٱلَّذِينَ ءَامَنُوا۟ ٱتَّقُوا۟ ٱللَّهَ وَذَرُوا۟ مَا بَقِىَ مِنَ ٱلرِّبَوٰٓا۟ إِن كُنتُم مُّؤْمِنِينَ ﴿٢٧٨﴾ فَإِن لَّمْ تَفْعَلُوا۟ فَأْذَنُوا۟ بِحَرْبٍ مِّنَ ٱللَّهِ وَرَسُولِهِۦ ﴾ البقرة.

يفيد أن النبي ﷺ حي في قبره الشريف يحارب المرابين بالدعاء عليهم، أو بما يناسب حياته البرزخية. ولم أر من سبقني إلى هذا الاستنباط. اهـ.

XVIII. Visiting the Messenger of Allah–upon him blessings and peace–and his grave for the fulfillment of needs

As for the last of the three objections mentioned at the beginning of chapter XV, namely that "he [=Ḥabīb ʿAlī al-Jafrī] says that we go to him [=the Prophet–upon him the blessings and peace of Allah] in times of need!" then the Prophet himself said, "**Allah is the Giver and I am the distributor.**" It is part of a tremendous hadith which folds the knowledge of these lofty Attributes within fiqh—i.e. profound understanding—of the faith-system as part of the divine gift to whomever Allah wants goodness for, and they are the spiritual elite of this Umma until the day of Resurrection:

عن حميد بن عبد الرحمن أنه سمع معاوية يقول: قال رسول الله ﷺ: مَنْ يُرِدِ اللهُ بِهِ خَيْرًا يُفَقِّهْهُ فِي الدِّينِ، وَاللهُ الْمُعْطِي وَأَنَا الْقَاسِمُ، وَلاَ تَزَالُ هَٰذِهِ الأُمَّةُ ظَاهِرِينَ عَلَى مَنْ خَالَفَهُمْ حَتَّى يَأْتِيَ أَمْرُ اللهِ وَهُمْ ظَاهِرُونَ البخاري

Ḥumayd b. ʿAbd al-Raḥmān said he heard Muʿāwiya say the Messenger of Allah–upon him blessings and peace of Allah–said,"**They for whom Allah wants immense goodness, He shall grant them deep understanding in the faith-system. And Allah is the Giver while I am the distributor. And this Umma shall never cease to prevail over whoever contravenes them until the command of Allah comes while they are prevailing.**" Al-Bukhārī narrated it in his *Ṣaḥīḥ*.

By "this Umma" in the hadith are meant the abovementioned section of the Umma that are granted "deep understanding in the faith-system," i.e. the knowers of Allah in the verse, *only do fear the One God, of His servants, the possessors of knowledge* (Fāṭir 35:28). This is confirmed by al-Ṭabarānī and al-Bayhaqī's wording of the hadith in *Musnad al-Shāmiyyīn* and *al-Madkhal*:

يَا أَيُّهَا النَّاسُ إِنَّمَا الْعِلْمُ بِالتَّعَلُّمِ وَالْفِقْهُ بِالتَّفَقُّهِ، وَمَنْ يُرِدِ اللهُ بِهِ خَيْرًا
يُفَقِّهْهُ فِي الدِّينِ، وَ﴿إِنَّمَا يَخْشَى ٱللَّهَ مِنْ عِبَادِهِ ٱلْعُلَمَـٰٓؤُاْ﴾، وَلَنْ تَزَالَ
أُمَّتِي عَلَى الْحَقِّ ظَاهِرِينَ عَلَى النَّاسِ، لَا يُبَالُونَ مَنْ خَالَفَهُمْ حَتَّى يَأْتِيَ
أَمْرُ اللهِ وَهُمْ كَارِهُونَ الطبراني في مسند الشاميين والبيهقي في المدخل

O people! Knowledge comes only through learning and fiqh only through learning fiqh, and **they for whom Allah wants immense goodness, He shall grant them deep understanding in the faith-system, and** *only do fear the One God, of His servants, the possessors of knowledge* (Fāṭir 35:28), and my Umma **shall never cease to stand on the truth, prevailing over people, not caring who contravenes them, until the command of Allah comes while they are reluctant.**

May Allah grants us the *ṣuḥba* of the Umma of true understanding of His faith-system and of the meanings and practices of the beliefs that guarantee victory. Amin!

Furthermore the Prophet–upon him the blessings and peace of Allah–said, "**I am the one who can do it**!" (*anā lahā*) in reference to the major Intercession on the Day that humankind shall come to all of the Prophets one after another for the fulfillment of their needs, but only the Seal of Prophets is able to respond. This is narrated in the books of *tawḥīd* and *īmān* of *Ṣaḥīḥ al-Bukhārī* and *Ṣaḥīḥ Muslim* respectively.

Indeed **the Companions all came to the Prophet–upon him blessings and peace–after he left this world as commanded by the Mother of the Believers ʿĀʾisha** when she told them to open a skylight above his noble grave so that they would be granted rain at a time of drought. This is narrated by al-Dārimī in his *Sunan* and it is a strong hadith as established by the author of its largest commentary entitled *Fatḥ al-Mannān sharḥ al-musnad al-jāmiʿ lil-Dārimī ʿAbd Allāh b. ʿAbd al-Raḥmān.*

قَالَ أَبُو الجَوْزَاءِ أَوْسُ بْنُ عَبْدِ الله **قُحِطَ أَهْلُ المَدِينَةِ قَحْطاً شَدِيداً فَشَكَوْا إِلَى عَائِشَةَ رَضِيَ اللهُ عَنْهَا فَقَالَتْ: اُنْظُرُوا قَبْرَ النَّبِيِّ ﷺ فَاجْعَلُوا مِنْهُ كِوًى إِلَى السَّمَاءِ حَتَّى لاَ يَكُونَ بَيْنَهُ وَبَيْنَ السَّمَاءِ سَقْفٌ قَالَ فَفَعَلُوا فَمُطِرْنَا مَطَراً حَتَّى نَبَتَ الْعُشْبُ وَسَمِنَتِ الإِبِلُ حَتَّى تَفَتَّقَتْ مِنَ الشَّحْمِ فَسُمِّيَ عَامَ الْفَتْقِ** رواه الدارمي في سننه بسند حسن.

Likewise the report that in the year of the drought called al-Ramāda (17-18/638-639) during 'Umar's caliphate, the Companion Bilāl b. al-Ḥārith al-Muzanī, while slaughtering a sheep for his kin, noticed that the sheep's bones had turned red because the dry flesh clung to them. He cried out "Yā Muḥammadāh!" Then he came to the grave of the Prophet and said, "Messenger of Allāh, *istasqi li-ummatik* (ask for rain for your Community) for verily they have but perished!" After that he saw the Prophet in a dream telling him: "**Go to 'Umar and give him my greeting then tell him, 'You are going to have rain.' Tell him, 'Be wise, be wise!'**" Another version has, "**Tell him, I have always known you to fulfill your trust and be staunch, so—wisdom, wisdom, O 'Umar!**" The man went and told 'Umar. The latter wept and said, "O my nurturing Lord! I spare no effort except in what escapes my power!"[30]

[30] Narrated from Mālik al-Dār by Ibn Abī Shayba, *Muṣannaf* (17:63-65 §32665); Ibn Abī Khaythama, *al-Tārīkh al-kabīr* (2:80 §1818); Bayhaqī, *Dalā'il al-Nubuwwa* (7:47); Ibn 'Abd al-Barr, *Istī'āb* (Mālik al-Dār); Ibn 'Asākir, *Tārīkh* (44:345). It was rated sound-chained by Ibn Ḥajar, *Fatḥ al-Bārī* (2:495, *Istisqā'*) and *Iṣāba* (Mālik al-Dār) and Ibn Kathīr, *Bidāya* (Year 18) and *Jāmi' al-asānīd*. The Companion Mālik b. 'Iyāḍ al-Madanī al-Jabalānī was known as Mālik al-Dār (Mālik of the house) because 'Umar had put him in charge of the food. "'Umar b. al-Khaṭṭāb's freedman, he narrated from Abū Bakr and 'Umar. He was known" per Ibn Sa'd. "A senior *Tābi'ī*, he is agreed upon (as reliable) and the Successors approved highly of him" per Abū Ya'lā al-Khalīl b. 'Abd Allāh al-Khalīlī al-Qazwīnī, *al-Irshād fī ma'rifat 'ulamā' al-ḥadīth*, ed. Muḥ. Sa'īd 'Umar

Then 'Umar assembled the people and recounted the dream to them. They told him, "He [=the Messenger of Allah–upon him the blessings and peace of Allah] found you too slow in praying for rain."[31] Thereupon 'Umar came out to pray for rain through al-'Abbās, the uncle of the Prophet.[32]

عن مالك الدّار ـ وكان خازن عمر على الطعام ـ قال: **أَصَابَ النَّاسَ قَحْطٌ فِي زَمَنِ عُمَرَ، فَجَاءَ رَجُلٌ إِلَى قَبْرِ النَّبِيِّ ﷺ فَقَالَ: يَا رَسُولَ اللهِ اسْتَسْقِ لِأُمَّتِكَ فَإِنَّهُمْ قَدْ هَلَكُوا، فَأَتَى الرَّجُلَ فِي الْمَنَامِ فَقِيلَ لَهُ: ائْتِ عُمَرَ فَأَقْرِئْهُ السَّلَامَ، وَأَخْبِرْهُ أَنَّكُمْ مَسْقِيُّونَ وَقُلْ لَهُ: عَلَيْكَ الْكَيْسُ، عَلَيْكَ الْكَيْسُ، فَأَتَى عُمَرَ فَأَخْبَرَهُ فَبَكَى عُمَرُ ثُمَّ قَالَ: يَا رَبِّ لَا آلُو إِلَّا مَا عَجَزْتُ عَنْهُ** رواه ش في المصنف وابن أبي خيثمة في التاريخ والبيهقي في الدلائل وابن عبد البر في الاستيعاب وابن عساكر في التاريخ وصحح اسناده ابن كثير في البداية وجامع الأسانيد والحافظ في الفتح والإصابة وأورده جر وابن كثير في تاريخهما من رواية سيف بن عمر التميمي بسنده إلى عاصم بن عمر بن الخطاب **أَنَّ رَجُلًا مِنْ مُزَيْنَةَ عَامَ الرَّمَادَةِ سَأَلَهُ أَهْلُهُ أَنْ يَذْبَحَ لَهُمْ شَاةً، فَقَالَ: لَيْسَ فِيهِنَّ شَيْءٌ. فَأَلَحُّوا عَلَيْهِ فَذَبَحَ شَاةً، فَإِذَا عِظَامُهَا حُمْرٌ، فَقَالَ: يَا مُحَمَّدَاهْ! فَلَمَّا أَمْسَى أُرِيَ فِي الْمَنَامِ أَنَّ رَسُولَ اللهِ ﷺ**

Idrīs, 3 vols. (Riyadh: Maktabat al-Rushd,1989) in 'Abd Allāh Ghumārī, *Irghām al-mubtadi' al-ghabī bi-jawāz al-tawassul bil-Nabī*, ed. Ḥasan Saqqāf, 2nd ed. (Amman: Dār al-Imām al-Nawawī, 1992) p. 9. "Mālik b. 'Iyāḍ: 'Umar's freedman. He is the one named Mālik al-Dār. He saw the Prophet–upon him blessings and peace of Allah–and heard narrations from Abū Bakr al-Ṣiddīq. He narrated from Abū Bakr and 'Umar, Mu'ādh and Abū 'Ubayda. From him narrated Dhakwān Abū Ṣāliḥ al-Sammān and Mālik's two sons 'Awn and 'Abd Allāh" (Ibn Ḥajar, *Iṣāba*).

[31] Ṭabarī, *Tārīkh* (4:99); Ibn Kathīr, *al-Bidāya wal-nihāya* (Year 18).

[32] See full documentation in the section entitled, "'Umar's *tawassul* (using means) through al-'Abbās as intercessor" in Haddad, *The Rightly-Guided Caliphs* (Fenton, MI: Institute for Spiritual & Cultural Advancement, 2023) pp. 149-157.

يَقُولُ لَهُ: أَبْشِرْ بِالْحَيَا، اِئْتِ عُمَرَ فَأَقْرِئْهُ مِنِّي السَّلَامَ وَقُلْ لَهُ: إِنَّ عَهْدِي بِكَ وَفِيَّ الْعَهْدِ، شَدِيدَ الْعَقْدِ، فَالْكَيْسَ الْكَيْسَ يَا عُمَرُ. فَجَاءَ حَتَّى أَتَى بَابَ عُمَرَ فَقَالَ لِغُلَامِهِ: اسْتَأْذِنْ لِرَسُولِ رَسُولِ اللهِ ﷺ. فَأَتَى عُمَرَ فَأَخْبَرَهُ فَفَزِعَ، ثُمَّ صَعِدَ عُمَرُ الْمِنْبَرَ فَقَالَ لِلنَّاسِ: أَنْشُدُكُمْ بِالَّذِي هَدَاكُمْ لِلْإِسْلَامِ، هَلْ رَأَيْتُمْ مِنِّي شَيْئًا تَكْرَهُونَهُ؟ فَقَالُوا: اللَّهُمَّ لَا، وَعَمَّ ذَاكَ؟ فَأَخْبَرَهُمْ بِقَوْلِ الْمُزَنِيِّ - وَهُوَ بِلَالُ بْنُ الْحَارِثِ - فَفَطِنُوا وَلَمْ يَفْطَنْ فَقَالُوا: إِنَّمَا اسْتَبْطَأَكَ فِي الِاسْتِسْقَاءِ فَاسْتَسْقِ بِنَا. فاستسقى لهم كما في الروايات المشهورة.

Likewise the saying of the supercentenarian Companion-poet and *Mu'allaqāt* author Labīd b. Rabī'at al-'Āmirī (d. 40?/661) in the long poem that he declaimed when he came to the Prophet–upon him the blessings and peace of Allah –as part of the delegation of Qays to ask for his supplication for relief from a drought that raged in Muḍar, and which begins with the lines:

أَتَيْنَاكَ يَا خَيْرَ الْبَرِيَّةِ كُلِّهَا   لِتَرْحَمَنَا مِمَّا لَقِينَا مِنَ الْأَزْلِ

We've come to you, best of all creatures,
so that you'll show us mercy in our encounter with woe.

وَلَيْسَ لَنَا إِلَّا إِلَيْكَ فِرَارُنَا   وَأَيْنَ فِرَارُ النَّاسِ إِلَّا إِلَى الرُّسْلِ

And we have none but you to flee to,
for where can people flee other than to the Messengers?

Hearing this the Prophet stood up, dragging his garment, climbed up the pulpit and supplicated, whereupon it rained.[33]

[33] Narrated from Anas b. Mālik by al-Ṭabarānī, *al-Aḥādīth al-ṭiwāl* (p. 62-64 §28), *Du'ā'* (3:1775-1777 §2180), *Kabīr* (25:243-245 §28); Qiwām al-Sunna, *Dalā'il al-Nubuwwa* (p. 184 §238); Bayhaqī, *Dalā'il* (6:141); Maqrīzī, *Imtā' al-asmā'* (12:74-76); cf. Labīd, *Dīwān Labīd b. Rabī'a*, ed. Ḥamdū Ṭammās (Beirut: Dār al-Ma'rifa, 1425/2004); Ibn 'Abd al-Barr, *Tamhīd* (22:63-67); Ibn Ḥajar, *Fatḥ* (2:495 *isnād ṣāliḥ*) and *Iṣāba*.

Likewise the saying of the arch-faqih of the Companions, 'Abd Allāh b. Mas'ūd, "There are five verses in the Sura of al-Nisā' which I would not give away even for the whole world and what is in it," the first four focusing on the Attributes of justice (4:40), forgiveness of enormities (4:31), forgiveness of all other than *shirk* (4:48), forgiveness and mercy (4:111), and the fifth highlighting the Prophet's intermediacy in the above (4:64).[34]

قَالَ عَبْدُ اللهِ بْنُ مَسْعُودٍ: إِنَّ فِي النِّسَاءِ لَخَمْسُ آيَاتٍ، مَا يَسُرُّنِي أَنَّ لِي بِهَا الدُّنْيَا وَمَا فِيهَا، وَلَقَدْ عَلِمْتُ أَنَّ الْعُلَمَاءَ إِذَا مَرُّوا بِهَا يَعْرِفُونَهَا. قَوْلُهُ عَزَّ وَجَلَّ ﴿ إِن تَجْتَنِبُوا۟ كَبَآئِرَ مَا تُنْهَوْنَ عَنْهُ نُكَفِّرْ عَنكُمْ سَيِّـَٔاتِكُمْ وَنُدْخِلْكُم مُّدْخَلًا كَرِيمًا ﴿٣١﴾ ﴾ وَقَوْلُهُ ﴿ إِنَّ ٱللَّهَ لَا يَظْلِمُ مِثْقَالَ ذَرَّةٍ ۖ وَإِن تَكُ حَسَنَةً يُضَٰعِفْهَا وَيُؤْتِ مِن لَّدُنْهُ أَجْرًا عَظِيمًا ﴿٤٠﴾ ﴾ وَقَوْلُهُ ﴿ إِنَّ ٱللَّهَ لَا يَغْفِرُ أَن يُشْرَكَ بِهِۦ وَيَغْفِرُ مَا دُونَ ذَٰلِكَ لِمَن يَشَآءُ ۚ وَمَن يُشْرِكْ بِٱللَّهِ فَقَدِ ٱفْتَرَىٰٓ إِثْمًا عَظِيمًا ﴿٤٨﴾ ﴾ وَقَوْلُهُ ﴿ وَلَوْ أَنَّهُمْ إِذ ظَّلَمُوٓا۟ أَنفُسَهُمْ جَآءُوكَ فَٱسْتَغْفَرُوا۟ ٱللَّهَ وَٱسْتَغْفَرَ لَهُمُ ٱلرَّسُولُ لَوَجَدُوا۟ ٱللَّهَ تَوَّابًا رَّحِيمًا ﴿٦٤﴾ ﴾ وَقَوْلُهُ

[34] An overall fair report narrated from (i) 'Abd al-Raḥmān b. 'Abd Allāh by Qāsim b. Sallām, *Faḍā'il al-Qur'ān (faḍl āyāt al-Qur'ān)*; Sa'īd b. Manṣūr, *Sunan* (4:1297 §659); Ibn al-Mundhir, *Tafsīr* (Nisā' 4:31, 4:40, 4:64); Ṭabarānī, *Kabīr* (9:220 §9069) through a chain of *Ṣaḥīḥ* narrators per Haythamī, *Majma' al-zawā'id* (7:11); al-Ḥākim, *Mustadrak* (2:305); Bayhaqī, *Shu'ab* (19: *Ta'ẓīm al-Qur'ān, faḍā'il al-Suwar wal-āyāt, dhikr al-sab' al-ṭiwāl*); (ii) Mu'āwiya b. Qurra by Kalābādhī, *Baḥr al-fawā'id* p. 237); (iii) an unknown man by 'Abd al-Razzāq, *Tafsīr* (Nisā' 4:31); Qāḍī Ismā'īl, *Aḥkām al-Qur'ān* (ditto); al-Ṭabarī, *Tafsīr* (ditto). It is further confirmed by Ṭabarī's report from Ibn 'Abbās citing eight verses including the above five as mentioned by Ibn Kathīr, *Tafsīr* (Nisā' 4:1).

﴿ وَمَن يَعْمَلْ سُوٓءًا أَوْ يَظْلِمْ نَفْسَهُۥ ثُمَّ يَسْتَغْفِرِ ٱللَّهَ يَجِدِ ٱللَّهَ غَفُورًا رَّحِيمًا ﴿١١٠﴾ ﴾. قَالَ: قَالَ عَبْدُ الله: مَا يَسُرُّنِي أَنَّ لِي بِهَا الدُّنْيَا وَمَا فِيهَا.

رواه أبو عبيد في فضائل القرآن وسبعد بن منصور في السنن وابن المنذر في التفسير والطبراني في الكبير ورجاله رجال الصحيح وغيرهم وجاء من طرق أخرى وله شاهد عن ابن عباس رواه الطبري وأورده ابن كثير في التفسير

Shaykh Samer al-Nass pointed out in *al-Wasīla* that the first four verses serve to show that **the fifth verse, *and if only they, when they wronged themselves, came to you and asked forgiveness of the One God, and the Messenger asked forgiveness for them, they would certainly realize that the One God is Oft-Relenting, Most Merciful* (Nisā' 4:64), is meant for all time until the Day of Judgment, and not only in the time of the Companions** as the Wahhabis have claimed.

Likewise the saying of another poet of the Companions, Sawād b. Qārib,

وَأَنَّكَ أَدْنَى الْمُرْسَلِينَ وَسِيلَةً إِلَى الله يَا ابْنَ الأَكْرَمِينَ الأَطَايِبِ

And that you are the nearest means to Allah,
O son of the most honorable, purest ones![35]

The above proofs from the Qur'ān, the hadiths "**I am the distributor**" and "**I am the one who can intercede,**" and the understanding of the masters of Arabic and fiqh among the Companions such as 'Ā'isha, 'Umar, Ibn Mas'ūd, Labīd b. Rabī'a and Sawād b. Qārib of **the meaning of the *wasīla* (intermediacy) mentioned in the Quranic verse *O you who believe! Beware the***

[35] From Muḥammad b. Ka'b al-Quraẓī by Abū Ya'lā, *Mu'jam* (p. 263 §309); Ṭabarānī, *al-Aḥādīth al-ṭiwāl* and *al-Mu'jam al-kabīr*; al-Ḥākim; Abū Nu'aym, *Dalā'il al-Nubuwwa* and *Mu'jam al-Ṣaḥāba*; and others. It is also cited by Abū Zayd al-Qurashī, *Jamharat ash'ār al-'Arab*; Ibn Dāwūd al-Ẓāhirī, *al-Zahra*; and others.

***One God and seek the* wasīla *unto Him* (Māʾida 5:35) is the person of the Prophet**–upon him blessings and peace of Allah–**as an accessible source of blessing in this world and the next.**

This is why the Companions would continue to seek and derive blessings from the vestiges of the Prophet–upon him the blessings and peace of Allah–after he had left this world. Ibn Saʿd narrates in the *Ṭabaqāt*, Ibn Abī Shayba in the *Muṣannaf*, in the chapter entitled, "Touching the pulpit of the Prophet," Ibn Ḥibbān in *al-Thiqāt*, and Qadi ʿIyāḍ in the *Shifā* (chapter entitled: "Concerning the visit to the Prophet's grave, the excellence of those who visit it and how he should be greeted"):

> Ibrāhīm b. ʿAbd al-Raḥmān b. ʿAbd al-Qārī said **he beheld Ibn ʿUmar putting his hand on the seat of the Prophet's pulpit then placing it on his face.** Yazīd b. ʿAbd Allāh b. Qusayṭ and al-ʿUtbī narrated that **it was the practice of the Companions in the mosque of the Prophet to place their hands on the smooth *rummāna* (pommel) of the pulpit where the Prophet used to place his hand. Then they would face the qibla and supplicate.** Abū Mawdūd said: "And I saw Yazīd b. ʿAbd Allāh do the same." Ibn Saʿd also names Saʿd b. Abī Waqqāṣ and Ibn ʿUmar among them.[36]

روى ابن سعد في الطبقات بإسناده عن إبراهيم بن عبد الرحمن بن عبد القاري أنه **نَظَرَ إِلَى ابْنِ عُمَرَ وَضَعَ يَدَهُ عَلَى مَقْعَدِ النَّبِيِّ ﷺ مِنَ المِنْبَرِ ثُمَّ وَضَعَهَا عَلَى وَجْهِهِ** ـ ذكره ابن حبان في الثقات ـ وعن أبي مودود عبد العزيز مولى لهذيل، عن يزيد بن عبد الله بن قسيط قال: **رَأَيْتُ نَاساً مِنْ أَصْحَابِ النَّبِيِّ ﷺ إِذَا خَلَا المَسْجِدُ أَخَذُوا بِرُمَّانَةِ المِنْبَرِ الصَّلْعَاءَ الَّتِي تَلِي الْقَبْرَ بِمَيَامِنِهِمْ ثُمَّ اسْتَقْبَلُوا الْقِبْلَةَ يَدْعُونَ**. وذكر ابن سعد في رواية أخرى أن منهم سعد بن أبي وقاص وابن عمر. وفي مصنف ابن أبي شيبة نا زيد بن الحباب قال: حدثني أبو مودودة

[36] It was also cited by Ibn Qudāma, *Mughnī*; Buhūtī, *Kashshāf*; Mardāwī, *Inṣāf*, Ibn Mufliḥ, *Furūʿ*.

قال: حدثني يزيد بن عبد الملك [كذا] بن قسيط قال رَأَيْتُ نَفَرًا مِنْ أَصْحَابِ النَّبِيِّ ﷺ إِذَا خَلَا لَهُمُ الْمَسْجِدُ قَامُوا إِلَى رُمَّانَةِ الْمِنْبَرِ الْقَرْعَاءَ فَمَسَحُوهَا وَدَعَوْا. قال: وَرَأَيْتُ يَزِيدَ يَفْعَلُ ذَلِكَ.

The above is similar to the act of Abū Ayyūb al-Anṣārī resting his face on the Prophet's grave already cited in chapter XIV. Ibn 'Umar and Ḥafṣa would use the Prophet's *jubba* for medication as mentioned in Muslim's *Ṣaḥīḥ*. Anas would use the cup of the Prophet for blessing, etc.[37] All of the above examples of the practice of the Companions illustrate two facts. The first is the permissibility of asking Allah for good things through the *wasīla* (intermediacy) of the Prophet–upon him blessings and peace–after his death since, by their acts, the Companions were truly making *tawassul*. (Likewise it is permitted to ask Allah for things by means of other pious Muslims.) The second is the permissibility of *tabarruk* (deriving blessing), for the same beneficial purpose, from objects the Prophet had touched, or used, or owned.

The Shāfi'ī faqih, linguist, historian of the *Sīra*, heresiologist, and Mufti of Mecca Sayyid Aḥmad b. Zaynī Daḥlān said in the second volume of *Khulāṣat al-kalām fi bayān umarā' al-balad al-ḥarām* (Summary of the exposition of the rulers of the inviolable country) and in *al-Durar al-saniyya fīl-raddi 'alā al-Wahhābiyya* (The shining pearls in refuting the Wahhabis) and the Qadi of Quds, *muḥaddith*, poet of the Prophet–upon him the blessings and peace of Allah–and heresiologist Yūsuf al-Nabhānī in *Shawāhid al-ḥaqq* (The proof-texts of the truth) both cited Imam Ibn Ḥajar al-Haytamī's book *al-Jawhar al-munaẓẓam fī ziyārat al-qabri al-mukarram* (The refined jewel on the visit to the honored Grave, ch. 6, Benefit 13) to that effect:

There is no difference in *tawassul* (using means) between the terms

[37] See Shaykh Muhammad Hisham Kabbani, *Encyclopedia of Islamic Doctrine* (4:135-156).

tawassul, tashaffu' (using intercession), *istighātha* (asking help) and *tawajjuh* (turning to someone). For *tawajjuh* is derived from *jāh*, "high standing"—and one may use someone as an intermediary to someone who has a higher standing yet—while *istighātha* means the request of *ghawth* (help), whereby the *mustaghīth* (asker for help) requests from the *mustaghāth bihi* (one sought for help) that he obtain *ghawth* for him from someone else, even if the latter is higher than him. So *tawajjuh* and *istighātha* by him–upon him blessings and peace–and through other than him have no other meaning, in the hearts of the Muslims, than the request for help from Allah Most High in reality, and from other than Him in figurative terms through normal *tasabbub* (everyday causality). **No Muslim means anything other than that meaning**. But he whose breast has not expanded for that [understanding]—let him weep over himself! We ask Allah for safety.[38]

So the one that is being asked for help in reality is Allah Most High. As for the Prophet–upon him the blessings and peace of Allah –then he is a *wāsiṭa* (intermediary) between Him and the one asking help. For it is Allah Who is being asked for help *ḥaqīqatan* (in reality), and help is from Him by His creating and bringing something into being, whereas the Prophet–upon him the blessings and peace of Allah–is being sought for help *majāzan* (figuratively), and help is from him through *kasb* (earning) and customary *tasabbub* in consideration of his *tawajjuh* and *tashaffu'* in the presence of Allah because of his high standing and great worth. Thus he is exactly as when Allah Most High said, *and you did not throw when you threw, but rather the One God threw* (al-Anfāl 8:17), i.e. "and you did not throw by creating and by bringing something into being, since you threw through *tasabbub* and *kasb*, but Allah threw by creating and by bringing something into being. Likewise His statement, *so you did not kill them but rather the One God killed them* (Anfāl 8:17), and his statement–upon him the blessings and peace of Allah–"It is not I that have furnished you with mounts but Allah has furnished you" [narrated from Abū Mūsā in the *Ṣaḥīḥayn* and *Sunan*].

قال فقيه الشافعية الإمام أحمد بن حجر الهيتمي في كتاب الجوهر المنظَّم في زيارة القبر المكرَّم كما ذكره عنه مفتي الشافعية بكمة المكرَّمة قامع أهل البدعة السيد أحمد بن زيني دحلان في كتاب خلاصة الكلام في بيان أمراء البلد الحرام وكتاب الدرر السَّنِيّة في الردّ

[38] I.e. from deviant belief, spiritual disease, fitna and punishment.

على الوهّابيّة وكذلك القاضي يوسف النبهاني في شواهد الحق في الاستغاثة بسيد الخلق

لا فرقَ في التَّوَسُّل بين أنْ يكونَ بلفظ التوسُّل أو التَّشَفُّع أو الإسْتِغَاثَة أو التَّوَجُّهِ لأنّ التَوَجُّهَ من الجَاهِ، وهو عُلُوُّ المَنزِلَة وقد يُتَوَسَّلُ بذي الجاه إلى من هو أعلى منه جاهاً، والاستغاثة مَعناها طلبُ الغَوث والمستغيثُ يطلب من المستغاث به أن يحصِّلَ له الغوثَ من غيره وإن كان أعلى منه. فالتَّوَجُّهُ والاستغاثةُ به ﷺ وبغيره ليس لهما معنى في قلوب المسلمين إلا طلبُ الغوثِ حقيقةً من الله تعالى، ومجازاً بالتسبُّبِ العادِي من غيره، ولا يَقصِدُ أحدٌ من المسلمين غيرَ ذلك المعنى. فمن لم يَنشرحْ لذلك صدرُه فَلْيَبْكِ على نفسه! نسأل الله العافية. فالمستغاثُ به في الحقيقة هو الله تعالى، وأما النبيُّ ﷺ فهو واسطةٌ بينه وبين المستغيث. **فهو ـ سبحانه وتعالى ـ مستغاثٌ به حقيقةً، والغوثُ منه بالخَلْق والإيجاد، والنبي ﷺ مستغاثٌ به مجازاً، والغوثُ منه بالكَسْبِ والتَسَبُّب العادِيِّ باعتبار توجُّهِهِ وتشفُّعِهِ عند الله لعلوِّ مَنزِلته وقدْرِه.** فهو على حد قوله تعالى **وَمَا رَمَيْتَ إِذْ رَمَيْتَ وَلَٰكِنَّ ٱللَّهَ رَمَىٰ** الأنفال ١٧ أي وما رَميتَ خَلْقاً وإيجاداً، إذ رميتَ تسبُّباً وكَسباً، ولكنَّ اللهَ رمى خَلْقاً وإيجاداً. وكذا قوله تعالى **فَلَمْ تَقْتُلُوهُمْ وَلَٰكِنَّ ٱللَّهَ قَتَلَهُمْ** الأنفال ١٧ وقوله ﷺ **مَا أَنَا حَمَلْتُكُمْ وَلٰكِنَّ اللهَ حَمَلَكُمْ** رواه الطيالسي وأحمد والبخاري ومسلم وهذا لفظه وابن ماجه والنسائي وغيرهم عن أبي موسى الأشعري.

More importantly yet, **if the objector to such *tawassul* and *tabarruk* bases his objection purely on the criterion of the absence of life, he has committed *shirk* (polytheism) because, by ascribing to the deceased the incapacity of benefitting merely**

because they are deceased, he has attributed to the living the power to benefit which belongs to Allah alone. This was pointed out by our teachers such as Shaykh Muḥammad Sa'īd al-Būṭī in his Damascus public lectures and Shaykh Samer al-Nass in his book *al-Wasīla* which I read with him from beginning to end.

Nor was the practice of using the Prophet for the fulfillment of needs only the practice of the Companions. It was also that of the pious *Salaf* as seen in the following examples:

> Al-Dhahabī in three of his biographical encyclopedias, *Tārīkh al-Islām*, *Siyar a'lām al-nubalā'* and *Tadhkirat al-ḥuffāẓ*, cites Abū Ṭāhir Ibn Salamat al-Hamadhānī's report from the Hadith master Ibn Abī 'Alī al-Ḥīrī al-Naysābūrī that the major Hadith master Ibn al-Muqri' Ibn Zādhān al-Aṣbahānī (285-381/898-991) would relate,
>
> "I was in Medina with Ṭabarānī (260-360/874-971) and Abū al-Shaykh (274-369/887-980) with nothing [to eat] so we had to fast for two consecutive days. When time for *'ishā* came I stood at the Grave and said, **'Messenger of Allah! Hunger!'** [Back in our quarters that night] al-Ṭabarānī said to me, 'Sit. Either provision will come, or death.' I and Abū al-Shaykh got up and opened the door and there was a descendant of 'Alī standing with two boys carrying baskets full of food. He said, 'Did you complain to the Prophet about me? I saw him in my dream and he ordered me to bring you something.'"
> The report is also in Ibn al-Jawzī's *al-Wafā bi-aḥwāl al-Muṣṭafā*.

في تاريخ الإسلام وتذكرة الحفاظ وسِيَر أعلام النبلاء للذهبي وهو في الوفا بأحوال المصطفى لابن الجوزي: روى الإمام المحدث ـ شيخ هَمَذان ـ أبو طاهر الحسين بن علي بن الحسن بن محمد بن سلمة الكعبي الهمذاني (٣٤٠-٤١٦) عن أبي بكر بن أبي علي (هو الإمام العالم المحدث الثقة، مسنِد خراسان، قاضي القضاة أحمد بن الحسن الحِيريّ النيسابوري ٣٢٥-٤٢١) قال: كان ابن المقرئ ـ هو الإمام الرَّحَّال الحافظ الثقة مسنِد أصبهان المعمَّر أبو بكر محمد بن إبراهيم بن علي بن عاصم بن زاذان (٢٨٥-٣٨١) ـ يقول: كُنْتُ أَنَا وَالطَّبَرَانِيُّ (٢٦٠-٣٦٠) وَأَبُو الشَّيْخِ (٢٧٤-٣٦٩) بِالمَدِيْنَةِ فضَاقَ بِنَا الوَقْتُ فَوَاصَلْنَا ذَلِكَ اليَوْمَ فلَمَّا كَانَ وَقتُ العِشَاءِ

حَضَرتُ القَبْرَ وَقُلْتُ يَا رَسُولَ الله الجُوْعَ! فَقَالَ لِي الطَّبَرَانِيُّ: اِجْلِسْ فَإِمَّا أَنْ يَكُونَ الرِّزْقُ أَوِ المَوْتُ فَقُمْتُ أَنَا وَأَبُو الشَّيْخِ فَحَضَرَ البَابَ عَلَوِيٌّ فَفَتَحْنَا لَهُ فَإِذَا مَعَهُ غُلَامَانِ بِقُفَّتَيْنِ فِيهِمَا شَيْءٌ كَثِيرٌ وَقَالَ: شَكَوْتُمُونِي إِلَى النَّبِيِّ ﷺ؟ رَأَيْتُهُ فِي النَّوْمِ فَأَمَرَنِي بِحَمْلِ شَيْءٍ إِلَيْكُمْ.

Aḥmad b. Ḥanbal's senior companion Abū Bakr al-Marwazī narrated in his *Mansak* that Imam Aḥmad himself recommended for one to make *tawassul* through the Prophet –upon him the blessings and peace of Allah– in every supplication in the same wording that the Prophet had taught the blind man in the well-known authentic hadith: **"O Allah! I am turning to you with your Prophet, the Prophet of mercy. O Muḥammad! I am turning with you to my Lord for the fulfillment of my need."**[39] The recommendation is adduced time and again in the books of the Ḥanbalī madhhab as it bears on the *adab* of *duʿāʾ* as a *fiqh* issue.[40]

This recommendation pre-empts the restrictions made up by a handful of non-*Salaf* writers that such *tawassul* must be (i) <u>only</u> through the *duʿāʾ* of the Prophet and not his person; and (ii) <u>only</u> in the lifetime of the Prophet and not after it. Such claims are innovations of misguidance that are disproved by the Umma's practice. More gravely yet, they constitute *taʿṭīl* (willful neglect) of the Prophet's abovementioned hadith.

---

[39] Narrated from ʿUthmān b. Ḥunayf by Aḥmad (28:478-480 §17240-17241); ʿAbd b. Ḥumayd, *Muntakhab*; Ibn Mājah (*Iqāmat al-ṣalāt, ṣalāt al-ḥāja*); Yaʿqūb b. Sufyān, *Mashyakha*; Nasāʾī, *Kubrā* (*ʿAmal al-yawm wal-layla, dhikr ḥadīth ʿUthmān b. Ḥunayf*); Ibn Khuzayma, *Ṣaḥīḥ*,; al-Ṭabarānī, *Duʿāʾ*, *Kabīr* and *Ṣaghīr*; Ibn al-Sunnī; Ḥākim; Bayhaqī; etc.

[40] Cf. Ibn ʿAqīl, *Tadhkira*; al-Sāmirī, *Mustawʿib*; Muḥ. b. Mufliḥ, *Furūʿ*; Ibrāhīm b. Mufliḥ, *Mubdiʿ*; Mardāwī, *Inṣāf* and *Taṣḥīḥ al-Furūʿ*; Buhūtī, *Kashshāf al-qināʿ*; al-Ḥajjāwī, *Iqnāʿ*. Aḥmad al-Ḥarrānī cites it in two places of his *Qāʿida fīl-tawassul wal-wasīla*—where he attributes it to "Imam Aḥmad and a group of the *Salaf*" from *Mansak al-Marwazī* as his source—and in his *Radd ʿalā al-Akhnāʾī* where he cites the text of the *duʿāʾ* in full, similar to the *duʿāʾ* of the blind man in al-Tirmidhī and with the wording *Yā Muḥammad*.

Ibn Abī al-Dunyā narrates in his book *Mujābū al-daʿwa* (Those whose prayers are answered) that a man diagnosed the trustworthy *muḥaddith* and physician ʿAbd al-Malik b. Ḥayyān b. Saʿīd b. al-Ḥasan b. Abjur (d. 150?/767?) as dying from a terminal *dubayla* (stomach ulcer). The latter turned to the wall and cried out, "Allah, Allah is my nurturing Lord, I do not associate anyone with Him. O Allah! Verily I am turning to you with your Prophet Muḥammad upon him blessings and peace, the Prophet of mercy. O Muḥammad! Verily I am turning with you to your nurturing Lord and my nurturing Lord asking that He grant me mercy against what is in me with a mercy with which He shall give me sufficiency and independence from all other than Him." He said it three times. Then he called the man. The latter palpated his belly and said, "You are cured! There is no sickness in you."

جَاءَ رَجُلٌ إِلَى عَبْدِ المَلِكِ بْنِ حَيَّانَ بْنِ سَعِيدِ بْنِ الحَسَنِ بْنِ أَبْجَرَ، فَجَسَّ بَطْنَهُ أي مَسَّهُ فقَالَ: بِكَ دَاءٌ لا يَبْرَأُ، قَالَ: مَا هُوَ؟ قَالَ هُوَ الدُّبَيْلَةُ، فَتحَوَّلَ الرَّجُلُ، فَقَالَ اللهُ، اللهُ رَبِّي لَا أُشْرِكُ بِهِ أَحَدًا. اللَّهُمَّ إِنِّي أَتوَجَّهُ إِلَيْكَ بِنَبِيِّكَ مُحَمَّدٍ ﷺ نَبِيِّ الرَّحْمَةِ. يَا مُحَمَّدُ، إِنِّي أَتوَجَّهُ بِكَ إِلَى رَبِّكَ وَرَبِّي أَنْ يَرْحَمَنِي مِمَّا بِي رَحْمَةً يُغْنِينِي بِهَا عَنْ رَحْمَةِ مَنْ سِوَاهُ - ثَلَاثَ مَرَّاتٍ - ثُمَّ دَعَا إِلَى ابْنِ أَبْجَرَ، فَجَسَّ بَطْنَهُ، فَقَالَ: بَرِئْتَ، مَا بِكَ عِلَّةٌ رواه ابن أبي الدنيا في مُجابُو الدّعوة

Al-Sakhāwī narrated in *al-Ḍawʾ al-Lāmiʿ* from the emir of Medina and others that Sardāḥ b. Muqbil b. Nakhbāz al-Ḥasanī al-Yanbuʿī (d. 833/1430) was blind for a long time after his eyes were burnt out with a hot iron by the sultan of Egypt and his brain became inflamed with pus. Then he headed for Medina, stood in front of the Prophet's Grave–upon him the blessings and peace of Allah–and complained to him of his suffering. Then he slept and saw the Prophet wiping over his eyes with his noble hand. In the morning he woke up and his eyes were better than before. Al-Sakhāwī commented, "And the matter is greater than that yet [i.e. there are far greater miracles than that yet]. For whoever uses his Prophetic majesty as his *wasīla* will never be disappointed!"

قال السخاوي في ترجمة سَرْدَاح بن مُقبِل بن نَخباز الحسني في الضوء اللامع بعد ذكر توسُّله عند قبر النبي ﷺ وتبرئته من داء كان فيه: **وَالْأَمْرُ أَعْظَمُ مِنْ هٰذَا؛ فَمَنْ تَوَسَّلَ بِجَنَابِهِ لَا يَخِيبُ**

Something similar is narrated about the *Salaf*'s visitation of the graves of the Awliya and their use of the latter's intermediacy.

XIX. The *Salaf* and *Khalaf* visited Awliya's graves to fulfill needs, especially the Ḥanbalīs with Imam Aḥmad's grave

It is narrated from many of the major pious predecessors that they would use the Awliya who had left this world as means for the fulfillment of needs. Al-Khaṭīb al-Baghdādī narrates from al-Ḥasan b. Ibrāhīm al-Khallāl in *Tārīkh Baghdād*, "Never did anything worry me whereupon I would visit the grave of Mūsā b. Ja'far (al-Kāẓim) to use his intermediacy except Allah facilitated for me what I liked;" and from Imam al-Shāfi'ī, "**Mūsā al-Kāẓim's grave is a *tiryāq mujarrab* (proven cure-all).**"

Ibrāhīm al-Ḥarbī, a Hadith master who authored one of the early encyclopedias of the difficult words of Hadith and another major companion of Imam Aḥmad b. Ḥanbal, would often say, "**The grave of Ma'rūf al-Karkhī is *al-tiryāq al-mujarrab* (the proven cure-all).**" Al-Sulamī narrated it from him in *Ṭabaqāt al-Ṣūfiyya* as did Ibn Abī Ya'lā in *Ṭabaqāt al-Ḥanābila*, Ibn al-Jawzī in *Ṣifat al-ṣafwa* and Dhahabī in the *Tārīkh* and the *Siyar*. Imam Qushayrī in his *Risāla* said all Baghdadis held this view. Khaṭīb and Abū Ṭāhir al-Silafī in *al-Mashyakha al-Baghdādiyya* narrated the same from 'Abd al-Raḥmān b. Muḥ. al-Zuhrī with the addition that "anyone that reads *Qul Huwa-l-Lāhu Aḥad* a hundred times there will have his request fulfilled." Both al-Khaṭīb and al-Silafī in the *Ṭuyūriyyāt* also narrated that the Qadi Ibn al-Maḥāmilī (d. 330/942) said, "**I have known Ma'rūf's grave for seventy years. No one suffering an affliction ever visited him except Allah lifted it from them.**" The Hadith scholars would sit around his grave to hold readings of Hadith as narrated by Ibn Ḥibbān in his *Ṣaḥīḥ* and Ibn al-Muqrī' in his *Mu'jam*.

Ibn Ḥajar in *Tahdhīb al-tahdhīb* cites al-Ḥākim al-Naysābūrī as narrating in *Tārīkh Naysābūr* that a large group of shaykhs went out to Tus (present-day northeast Iran) to visit the grave of 'Alī al-Riḍā b. Mūsā al-Kāẓim b. Ja'far al-Ṣādiq b. Muḥammad al-Bāqir, among them Ḥākim's grandshaykh the Imam of Hadith Ibn Khuzayma and his brother-in-law Abū 'Alī al-Thaqafī.

When they reached the grave Ibn Khuzayma "showed such a state of magnification for that spot, humbleness and plaintive supplication," the narrator said, "that we were bewildered."

نقل ابن حجر في تهذيب التهذيب والسخاوي في التحفة اللطيفة عن الحاكم في تاريخ نيسابور: سمعت أبا بكر محمد بن المؤمل بن الحسن يقول: **خَرَجْنَا مَعَ إِمَامِ أَهْلِ الحَدِيثِ أَبِي بَكْرِ بْنِ خُزَيْمَةَ وَعَدِيلِهِ أَبِي عَلِيٍّ الثَّقَفِيِّ مَعَ جَمَاعَةٍ مِنْ مَشَائِخِنَا - وَهُمْ إِذْ ذَاكَ مُتَوَافِرُونَ - إِلَى زِيَارَةِ قَبْرِ عَلِيِّ بْنِ مُوسَى الرِّضَا بِطُوس. قَالَ: فَرَأَيْتُ مِنْ تَعْظِيمِهِ - يَعْنِي ابْنَ خُزَيْمَةَ - لِتِلْكَ الْبُقْعَةِ وَتَوَاضُعِهِ لَهَا وَتَضَرُّعِهِ عِنْدَهَا مَا تَحَيَّرْنَا.**

Ibn Khuzayma's direct student and al-Ḥākim's teacher, the great Hadith master of Bost (present-day Lashkargah in south-western Afghanistan) Abū Ḥātim Muḥammad b. Ḥibbān al-Bustī, showed devotion similar to his teacher's in his reference to the same grave in his entry on ʿAlī al-Riḍā in *Kitāb al-thiqāt* (Biographical dictionary of the trustworthy masters):

> His grave is in Sanābādh outside Nawqān. It is famous and oft-visited. It is adjacent to [Hārūn] al-Rashīd's grave. I have certainly visited it many times. **Never did any hardship befall me at the time I resided in Tus, whereupon I would visit the grave of ʿAlī b. Mūsā al-Riḍā—Allah's blessings be on his grandfather and on him—and I supplicated Allah to remove it from me, except my prayer was answered and that hardship ended and left me.** This is something I have experienced repeatedly with the same result. May Allah cause us to die with love for the Elect one and his Family—upon him and them the blessings and peace of Allah.

قال شيخ خراسان ابن حبان البُستي في كتاب الثقات في ترجمة علي الرضا: **قَبْرُهُ بِسَنَابَاذ خَارِجَ النَّوْقَانِ مَشْهُورٌ يُزَارُ بِجَنْبِ قَبْرِ الرَّشِيدِ. قَدْ زُرْتُهُ مِرَارًا**

كَثِيرَةً وَمَا حَلَّتْ بِي شِدَّةٌ فِي وَقْتِ مُقَامِي بِطُوسٍ فَزُرْتُ قَبْرَ عَلِيِّ بْنِ مُوسَى الرِّضَا - صَلَوَاتُ الله عَلَى جَدِّهِ وَعَلَيْهِ - وَدَعَوْتُ اللهَ إِزَالَتَهَا عَنِّي إِلَّا اسْتُجِيبَ لِي وَزَالَتْ عَنِّي تِلْكَ الشِّدَّةُ. وَهٰذَا شَيْءٌ جَرَّبْتُهُ مِرَارًا فَوَجَدْتُهُ كَذٰلِكَ. أَمَاتَنَا اللهُ عَلَى مَحَبَّةِ الْمُصْطَفَىٰ وَأَهْلِ بَيْتِهِ ﷺ وَعَلَيْهِمْ أَجْمَعِينَ

There is even more explicit *tawassul*, love and reverence for the station of the Prophet and his Family by a greater authority yet than both of the above masters, namely Imam al-Shāfiʿī, who said in his *Dīwān*, as narrated by Bayhaqī in his *Manāqib*:

The Prophet's family are my resource,
and they're—alone—my means to him.
I hope through them to be given, tomorrow,
in the right hand the record of my deeds.

روى البيهقي مي مناقب الشافعي بسنده إلى محمد بن شعيب الترقفي الفقيه ينشد للشافعي رضي الله عنه:

آلُ النَّبِيِّ ذَرِيعَتِي وَهُمُ إِلَيْهِ وَسِيلَتِي
أَرْجُو بِأَنْ أُعْطَى غَداً بِيَدِي الْيَمِينِ صَحِيفَتِي

The above poetry shows that the foremost of the Imams of the *Salaf* viewed the Awliya themselves as consisting in a *wasīla* to the Prophet–upon him blessings and peace–and they viewed the Prophet as the arch-*wasīla* to Allah, as further illustrated by Shāfiʿī's *ṣalawāt tawassuliyya* (intercession-seeking invocations of blessings) at the opening of his *Risāla* (Epistle on legal theory):

May Allah bless our Prophet whenever he is mentioned by the rememberers and whenever the heedless omit to mention him! For truly Allah has rescued us from destruction through him. **No blessing has ever descended upon us**–hidden or visible, through which we have obtained spiritual and temporal gain or by which spiritual and temporal harm was dispelled or both–**but Muḥammad is the cause of its dispatch, the leader to its benefit and the guide to its uprightness**.

قال الإمام الشافعي رضي الله عنه في افتتاح رسالته: **صَلَّى اللهُ عَلَى نَبِيِّنَا كُلَّمَا ذَكَرَهُ الذَّاكِرُونَ وَغَفَلَ عَنْ ذِكْرِهِ الْغَافِلُون... فَإِنَّهُ أَنْقَذَنَا بِهِ مِنَ الهَلَكَةِ... فَلَمْ تُمْسِ بِنَا نِعْمَةٌ ظَهَرَتْ وَلَا بَطَنَتْ، نِلْنَا بِهَا حَظًّا فِي دِينٍ وَدُنْيَا أَوْ دُفِعَ بِهَا عَنَّا مَكْرُوهٌ فِيهِمَا، وَفِي وَاحِدٍ مِنْهُمَا: إِلَّا وَمُحَمَّدٌ صَلَّى اللهُ عَلَيْهِ سَبَبُهَا، الْقَائِدُ إِلَى خَيْرِهَا، وَالْهَادِي إِلَى رُشْدِهَا.**

The above vibrant passage was echoed by Shaykh al-Islam al-Taqī al-Subkī al-Kabīr in his *Fatāwā* (Vol. 1 p. 274) in the similar *ṣalawāt tawassuliyya* at the opening of the fatwa entitled *Tanazzul al-sakīna 'alā qanādīl al-Madīna* (The abundant descent of tranquility on the lanterns of Medina) in which he said,

To Allah belongs all praise, Who has blessed us with His Prophet–blessings and peace be upon him–with an endless felicity.

I bear witness that there is no deity but Allah alone without partner, the Protecting Friend, the Glorious.

I bear witness that Muḥammad is His servant and Messenger, the guide to every upright matter.

May Allah send blessings and peace upon him in a manner befitting His majesty, with a blessing rising ever higher and increasing,

and a superabundant greeting of peace until the Day of the Increase.

To proceed: Verily Allah knows that every goodness I bask in, and which He has bestowed upon me, is because of the Prophet, and that my recourse is to him,

and my reliance is upon him in seeking a means to Allah in every matter of mine.

Verily he is my means to Allah in this world and the next—

and how many of the blessings of Allah I am indebted to him for, both the hidden and the visible!

قال الإمام المجتهد شيخ الإسلام تقي الدين علي بن عبد الكافي السبكي الكبير في فتاويه الفتوى المسماة تنزُّل السكينة على قناديل المدينة: **بِسْمِ اللهِ الرَّحْمٰنِ الرَّحِيمِ وَبِهِ ثِقَتِي. الحَمْدُ للهِ الَّذِي أَسْعَدَنَا بِنَبِيِّهِ مُحَمَّدٍ ﷺ سَعَادَةً لَا تَبِيدُ، وَأَشْهَدُ أَنْ لَا إِلَهَ إِلَّا اللهُ وَحْدَهُ لَا شَرِيكَ لَهُ الْوَلِيُّ الحَمِيدُ، وَأَشْهَدُ أَنَّ مُحَمَّداً عَبْدُهُ وَرَسُولُهُ الهَادِي إِلَى كُلِّ أَمْرٍ رَشِيدٍ، صَلَّى اللهُ عَلَيْهِ وَعَلَى آلِهِ صَلَاةً تَلِيقُ بِجَلَالِهِ لَا تَزَالُ تَعْلُو وَتَزِيدُ، وَسَلَّمَ تَسْلِيماً كَثِيراً إِلَى يَوْمِ المَزِيدِ. وَبَعْدُ فَإِنَّ اللهَ يَعْلَمُ أَنَّ كُلَّ خَيْرٍ أَنَا فِيهِ وَمَنَّ عَلَيَّ بِهِ فَهُوَ بِسَبَبِ النَّبِيِّ ﷺ. وَالْتِجَائِي إِلَيْهِ، وَاعْتِمَادِي فِي تَوَسُّلِي إِلَى اللهِ فِي كُلِّ أُمُورِي عَلَيْهِ، فَهُوَ وَسِيلَتِي إِلَى اللهِ فِي الدُّنْيَا وَالْآخِرَةِ. وَكَمْ لَهُ عَلَيَّ مِنْ نِعَمٍ بَاطِنَةٍ وَظَاهِرَةٍ!**

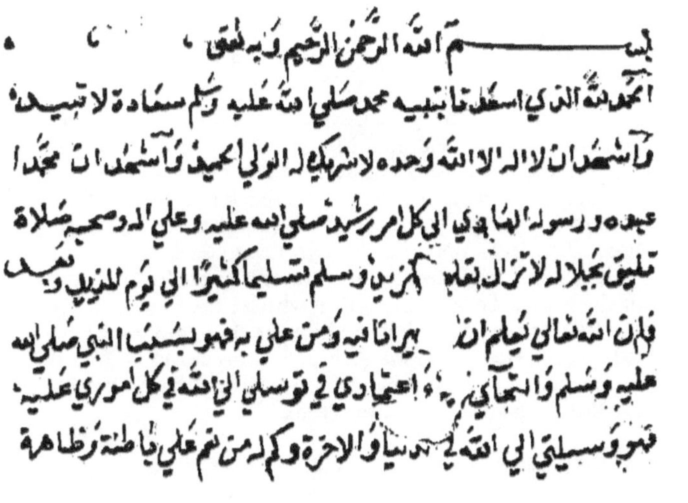
بسم الله الرحمن الرحيم وبه ثقتي
الحمد لله الذي اسعدنا بنبيه محمد صلى الله عليه وسلم سعادة لا تبيد
واشهد ان لا اله الا الله وحده لا شريك له الولي الحميد واشهد ان محمدا
عبده ورسوله الهادي الى كل امر رشيد صلى الله عليه وعلى اله وصحبه صلاة
تليق بجلاله لا تزال تعلو وتزيد وسلم تسليما كثيرا الى يوم المزيد وبعد
فان الله تعالى يعلم ان كل خير انا فيه ومن علي به فهو بسبب النبي صلى الله
عليه وسلم والتجائي اليه واعتمادي في توسلي الى الله في كل اموري عليه
فهو وسيلتي الى الله في الدنيا والاخرة وكم له من نعم علي باطنة وظاهرة

Abū Nuʿaym in the *Ḥilya*, Ibn al-Jawzī in the *Mujtabā* and the *Ṣafwa* and al-Dhahabī in the *Siyar* all narrate from Mujāhid that people would use the grave of Abū Ayyūb al-Anṣārī to perform the *istisqā'* (rain) prayer.

Ibn Bashkuwāl in *al-Ṣila fī tārīkh a'immat al-Andalus* (also Dhahabī in the *Tārīkh* and the *Siyar*) narrated that in the year 464/1072 the people of Samarqand suffered a drought and performed the prayer for rain repeatedly without receiving rain. One of the righteous told the Qadi of Samarqand to go to Khartank at al-Bukhārī's grave and pray for rain there. They did, whereupon it rained for seven straight days during which all of them were stranded in Khartank until the rain let off.

As for the grave of Imam Aḥmad b. Ḥanbal, none of the four Sunni schools ever emphasized the blessing of the grave of its Imam more than the followers of Imam Aḥmad have magnified the blessing of his grave. Qadi Ibn Abī Yaʿlā wrote the following in his entry on the Mufti of the Hanbalis in Baghdad—and one of the narrators of the *ʿaqīda* (credal doctrine) of Imam Ahmad —the Sharif Abū ʿAlī al-Ḥāshimī, in *Ṭabaqāt al-Ḥanābila*:

> Muhammad b. b. Aḥmad b. Mūsā Abū ʿAlī al-Hāshimī the qadi was of high standing, renowned fame, with a pre-eminent foothold and great influence with the two caliphs al-Qādir bi-l-Lāh and al-Qā'im bi-Amri-l-Lāh.[41] He heard Hadith from a group and authored *al-Irshād* in the [Ḥanbalī] madhhab. I saw fascicles of his commentary on al-Khiraqī's manual in his handwriting. His class was held in al-Manṣūr's Jāmiʿ Mosque. He would give fatwa and receive witnesses. He kept company with Abū al-Ḥasan al-Tamīmī and others of the shaykhs of the madhhab.... I heard Rizq Allāh [=Ibn Abī Yaʿlā's teacher Abū Muḥammad Rizq Allāh al-Tamīmī, he also narrates a creed from Aḥmad b. Ḥanbal] say, **"I visited Imam Aḥmad's grave in the company of the qadi al-Sharīf Abū ʿAlī, at which time I saw him kissing the foot of the grave. I asked him, 'Is there any report about this [act]?' He said to me, 'Aḥmad in my mind is something immense, and I do not believe that Allah will take me to task for this,' or something to that effect."**

[41] Respectively Abū al-ʿAbbās Aḥmad b. Isḥāq b. al-Muqtadir bi-l-Lāh and his son Abū Jaʿfar ʿAbd Allāh b. Aḥmad al-Qādir bi-l-Lāh.

Ibn al-Jawzī narrated in his *Manāqib al-Imām Aḥmad* from Abū Bakr b. Mukārim al-Ḥarbī:

> On a certain year torrential rains had fallen [in Baghdad] days before the beginning of Ramadan. One night during Ramadan **I slept and saw in my dream as if I had gone to visit—as was my habit—the grave of Imam Aḥmad.** I saw that his grave had become almost level with the ground to the point there remained only one or two brick rows between it and the ground. I said, "This must have happened because of the heavy rains." But I heard him say from the grave, "No, rather this is from awe before the All-True-Almighty and Exalted-because the All-True has visited me, so I asked Him about the secret of His visiting me every year and He said–Almighty and Exalted is He–'O Aḥmad! Because You have defended My Speech so that it will be disseminated and recited in the prayer-niches.'" Hearing this **I fell to my knees kissing his grave-side.** Then I said, "My master, why is it that **I kiss no other grave than your grave?**" He said, "My son, this is not a miraculous gift for me but rather it is a miraculous gift for the Messenger of Allah–upon him the blessings and peace of Allah–for I have with me a lock of his hair. Behold, let whoever loves me visit me in the month of Ramadan!"

The Damascene Hadith master 'Abd al-Ghanī al-Maqdisī —known as **Ibn Surūr—passed his hands, face and body over the grave of Imam Aḥmad** to seek a cure from boils which had left physicians helpless. His Damascene student the Hadith master al-Ḍiyā' al-Maqdisī heard it from him and narrated it in *al-Ḥikāyāt al-manthūra*, an autograph manuscript of which is kept in the Ẓāhiriyya library in Damascus.

Dhahabī also narrates from six scholars in *Tārīkh al-Islām* (Year 624/1227) in the entry of 'Abd al-Raḥmān b. Ibrāhīm b. Aḥmad, "the Imam, Bahā' al-Dīn Abū Muḥammad al-Maqdisī al-Ḥanbalī" that the latter had a son who sat in their gathering like an older shaykh and who became blind for seventy days, after which he was healed and his sight returned The six scholars said:

> We asked the Shaykh of the cause and he mentioned to us that he took his son to the grave of Imam Aḥmad and he prayed and supplicated. "I said, 'O Imam Aḥmad! I am

begging you! Do not refuse to intercede for him unto your nurturing Lord! O nurturing Lord, let him intercede for my son!' All the while my son was saying *āmīn*. Then we left. That night he woke up well-sighted."

روى الذهبي في تاريخ الإسلام لسنة ٦٢٤ ترجمة عبد الرحمن بن إبراهيم بن أحمد الإمام بهاء الدين أبي محمد المقدسي الحنبلي قال **سمعنا على ابن صِيلا وأبي شاكر السَّقْلَاطونيّ وتَجَنِّي وابنِ يَلْدَرْك ومَنُوجَهر وابنِ شاتيل: كان لَهُ [أي لبهاء الدين المقدسي] ابنٌ شيخٌ، إذا جَلَسنا تبيَّنَ كأَنَّه الأبُ، وعَمِيَ على كِبَرٍ، وبقي سبعين يوماً أعمى، ثمّ برئ وعادَ بصرُهُ ـ يعني الابن ـ فسألنا الشيخَ عن السبب فذكر لنا أَنَّه ذهب به إلى قبر الإِمام أحمد وأنّه دَعا وابتهلَ، [قال:] وَقُلْتُ: يَا إِمَامُ أَحْمَدُ أَسْأَلُكَ إِلَّا شَفَعْتَ فِيهِ إِلَى رَبِّكَ! يَا رَبِّ شَفِّعْهُ فِي وَلَدي! وَوَلَدِي يُؤَمِّنُ، ثُمَّ مَضَيْنَا. فَلَمّا كَانَ اللَّيلُ اسْتَيْقَظَ وَقَدْ أَبْصَرَ.**

The three common motives of all the above evidence, together with that of the preceding chapter, are that (i) pure monotheism is incomplete without the **witnessing that Muḥammad is the Messenger of Allah**; (ii) the latter witnessing culminates in the continuous **magnification of the Prophet**–upon him the blessings and peace of Allah–as the greatest mercy for the worlds and the arch-intercessor of all legally-qualified beings; and (iii) the completion of that magnification is the **acknowledgment of the blessing of the enduring presence of the Awliya who are his representatives** in blessing and intercession until the Day of Resurrection **and his only true inheritors in knowledge**.

XX. Great advice when visiting graves of Prophets and Awliya

The Afghan-Meccan Hadith scholar and faqih Mullā ʿAlī b. Sulṭān al-Qārī in his commentary on *al-Ḥiṣn al-ḥaṣīn* (The impregnable fortress)—a volume of supplications and *dhikr* written by the Imam and arch-expert of the Qurʾān Muḥammad Ibn al-Jazarī al-Dimashqī–Allah Most High have mercy on them–at the time Damascus was surrounded by the Mongols and the Crusaders—gave the following advice which we first cited in our *Visitations of Iraq* but which we repeat here for its benefit.

> When you visit the grave of a Prophet or wali or learned scholar or anyone besides them and you are in some terrible affliction, and you want for the soul of the dweller of that grave to be present for you to voice your complaint to him–i.e. with the tongue of your state or of your speech–so that he will intercede for you in the presence of the All-Sovereign of all, in order that He will suffice you against what has troubled you and cure you of your ailment, recite *Qul huwa-l-Lāhu aḥad* ten times (and if you precede it with the Heart of the Qurʾān—I mean the Sura of Yā Sīn —it will be better and faster [in response]), the two refuge-grantors [=Suras 113 and 114] three times each, the Opening of the Book, and the Beautiful Names after the beginning and the end of the Sura of al-Baqara. Close your eyes and collect all of your heart then say, *lā ilāha illā-l-Lāh* three times, *ALLĀH* three times with elongation of the *Ā*. Then pause and say, *assalāmu ʿalaykum wa-raḥmatu-l-Lāhi wa-barakātuh yā Sayyidī* [name], or *yā Shaykh*, or *yā Ustādhī*, or *yā Rasūla-l-Lāh*. And you expose what has befallen you of troubles to the one you are visiting: the All-Coverer of faults shall dispel them by the intercession of the dweller of the visitation. And this is among its greatest benefits.

The above text is from Mullā ʿAlī al-Qārī's commentary on *al-Ḥiṣn al-ḥaṣīn* cited by Shaykh Yūsuf al-Nabhānī in *Shawāhid al-ḥaqq*, quoting Imam Muṣṭafā al-Bakrī al-Khalwatī (1099-1162/1688-1749)—the student of ʿAbd al-Ghanī al-Nābulusī—who was citing al-Qārī.

The shahid and Mufti of Lebanon Shaykh Hasan Khalid (1921-1989) related from his teacher the Mufti of Syria Shaykh

Abū al-Yusr ʿĀbidīn that he would tell them to supplicate at the grave of Shaykh al-Islam the Quṭb Imam al-Nawawī–Allah have mercy on all of them–because supplication is answered there.

May Allah grant mercy to the seekers of intermediaries and to the intermediaries and may He benefit us and all Muslims with them except whoever refuses. Muwaffaq al-Dīn b. ʿAbd al-Raḥmān b. Makkī b. ʿUthmān al-Shāriʿī al-Shāfiʿī al-Anṣārī (d. 615/1218) described in *Murshid al-zuwwār ilā qubūr al-abrār* (The trusted guide of the visitors to the graves of the virtuous) twenty tasks in fulfillment of the etiquette of the visitation to the graves of the righteous including sincerity of intention, designating the day of Jumuʿa or the fourth day of the week [=Wednesday], preferably seeking the graves of Prophets, the Prophetic family, the Companions and one's relatives—spiritual and biological—together with the recitation of the Qur'ān, the invocation of blessings on the Prophet–upon him the blessings and peace of Allah, supplication for oneself, the mention of the virtues of the one being visited at his grave, and other than that. Success is all from Allah.

XXI. Miracles of Awliya are truth and part of the Sunni creed

The objector said—may Allah guide him—"likewise I have come across strange matters, among them his claim that Imam 'Alī would restore to people the limbs that had been cut off from them!"

Yes. This is from a report mentioned by Imam Fakhr al-Dīn al-Rāzī in the excursus on the *karāmāt* (miraculous gifts) of the Awliya in his *Tafsīr* (Kahf 18:9-12) followed by Niẓām al-Dīn al-Naysābūrī in *Gharā'ib al-Qur'ān wa-ra ghā'ib al-Furqān* and al-Shirbīnī in *al-Sirāj al-munīr* which Qadi Nabhānī cited in *Jāmi' karāmāt al-awliyā'* in the chapter on our liege lord 'Alī b. Abī Ṭālib–Allah be well-pleased with him, whereby al-Rāzī said,

> It is related that one of those who loved him [='Alī] committed a theft. He was a black slave. He was brought to 'Alī who asked him, "Did you steal?" He said yes, whereupon he had his hand cut off. He left Ali's presence and came upon Salmān al-Fārisī and Ibn al-Ḥawwā'. The latter asked, "Who cut off your hand?" He replied, "The Commander of the believers, the mighty one of the Muslims, the Messenger's son-in-law, the husband of the Virgin." He said, "He cut off your hand yet you eulogize him?" He replied, "Why should I not eulogize him when he cut off my hand rightly and delivered me from hellfire?" Salmān heard that and reported it to 'Alī. The latter summoned the black slave, placed his maimed hand on his forearm and covered it with a cloth then he made some supplications, whereupon a voice was heard from the sky saying, "Remove the cloth from the hand." They lifted it and the hand had been healed by the permission of Allah and His beautiful handiwork.

In other sources there is the addition that 'Alī said, "Did I not tell you, O Ibn al-Kawa, that we have lovers who, even if we cut them down limb by limb, they would only increase in their love for us? And we have haters who, even if we spoon-fed them honey, they would only increase in their hatred for us."

There is another report about the miraculous healing of a man who had been affected with hemiplegia on his right side, whereupon our liege lord 'Alī supplicated for him after praying some cycles of prayer, then he said to him, "O blessed one, rise!" He rose and walked and was hale like before. Our liege lord 'Alī then said to him, "Were it not that you swore your father was well-pleased with you I would not have supplicated for you." Ibn al-Subkī mentioned it in *Ṭabaqāt al-Shāfi'iyyat al-kubrā.*

We ask, what is the obstacle for such miracles—whether rationally or legally—when it is well-established that the Messenger of Allah–upon him the blessings and peace of Allah–would restore to people the organs that had been severed from them? Among them was Qatāda b. al-Nu'mān when his eye was thrown out of its socket at the battle of Badr, whereupon the Messenger of Allah–upon him the blessings and peace of Allah–put it back and he was healed, and it became the better-sighted one of his eyes as narrated by Abū Ya'lā, Ibn Ḥibbān, Ṭabarānī, al-Ḥākim and others. Identical and similar miracles are related about Abū Dharr with his eye at Uḥud (Abū Ya'lā); Rifā'a b. Rāfi' b. Mālik with his eye also at Badr (Ibn Abī Shayba, al-Bazzār, al-Ṭabarānī, Ḥākim and Bayhaqī); 'Alī b. Abī Ṭālib's ophthalmia at the battle of Khaybar (Bukhārī and Muslim); and 'Abd Allāh b. 'Atīk who had broken his leg in a fall (Bukhārī).

All the above five reports are cited in full in the chapter on the bodily miracles of the Prophet–upon him the blessings and peace of Allah–in al-Nabhānī's *Ḥujjat Allāh 'alā al-'ālamīn bi-mu'jizāt Sayyid al-Mursalīn* (The overwhelming proof of Allah over the worlds with the staggering miracles of the Master of the Messengers). The probative connection of these hadiths with the Awliya was demonstrated in the chapter entitled *Fī ithbāt al-karāmāt wa-tamyīzihā min al-mu'jizāt* (On the affirmation of the truth of miraculous gifts and their being distinct from staggering miracles) in Imam al-Ḥaramayn's *al-Irshād* in which he said that "**it is possible for every staggering miracle of a Prophet to be a miraculous gift for his followers.**" He also said, "**The acceptable position for us is that the breaches of natural custom are possible in the course of *karāmāt*** (miraculous gifts)."

This is the undisputed position of *Ahl al-Sunna wal-jamā'a*. Tāj al-Dīn Ibn al-Subkī said in *Ṭabaqāt al-Shāfi'iyyat al-kubrā*:

> Know that **every *karāma* that has emerged at the hand of any Companion or any wali, or shall ever emerge until the Day people rise for the nurturing Lord of the worlds, is verily a *mu'jiza* for the Prophet**–upon him the blessings and peace of Allah–because its worker only obtained it through being a follower of his–upon him the blessings and peace of Allah–and confessing that **he is the first and foremost in all the creation of Allah, their purest quintessence and the master of humankind from whose ocean are extracted the pearls and from whose life-giving help the rainfall is sought**. This meaning is fit to be a reason for general consensus in its emergence especially in the time of the Companions–may Allah be well-pleased with them–because when the believers saw what would take place at their hands of breaches of custom, they would believe in their Prophet–upon him the blessings and peace of Allah–and they would realize that he was speaking the truth. It is probable that this was a reason for their display.

The above explanations by Imam al-Ḥaramayn and Ibn al-Subkī are explained in greater detail in al-Nabhānī's introduction to *Ḥujjat Allāh*. We translated this introduction in full at the beginning of *The Prophet Muhammad's Knowledge of the Unseen*.

It is enough to clarify that **the *karāmāt* of Awliya or saints' miracles in Islam are a truth that is categorically obligatory to believe** in the Muslim creed just as the pious predecessors of the Umma and their epigones have stated, including al-Ṭaḥāwī in his *'Aqīda* and al-Laqānī who said in *Jawharat al-tawḥīd*,

وَأَثْبِتَنْ لِلأَوْلِيَا الكَرَامَةْ وَمَنْ نَفَاها فَانْبِذَنْ كَلامَهْ

and fully affirm the Awliya's miraculous gifts,
and whoever denies it, toss away what he says.

Aḥmad al-Ḥarrānī declared the same in his *'Aqīda Wāsiṭiyya*, as did Ibn 'Ābidīn in the chapter on *thubūt al-nasab* in the book of *Ṭalāq* (divorce) in his *Ḥāshiyat Radd al-muḥtār*, citing al-Nasafī's *'Aqā'id*.

XXII. Awliya conversing with Allah and even seeing Him

The objector also said, "and [he claims] that one of the Awliya might address Allah Most High and that Allah replies to him!"

This specific *karāma* (miraculous gift) is related by many authorities of the *Salaf* and *Khalaf* as having taken place for them in dream. Among the Awliya and Hadith masters who were famously reported to have conversed with or seen Allah that way are Raqaba b. Maṣqalat al-ʿAbdī; Imam al-Awzāʿī; Yaḥyā b. Saʿīd al-Qaṭṭān—a principal teacher of Imam Aḥmad; Imām Aḥmad himself; Surayj b. Yūnus; Ibrāhīm b. Muḥammad al-Qaṣrī (he also saw the Prophet–upon him blessings and peace–60 times); the shahid Rabīʿ b. Sulaymān b. ʿAṭā'āh al-Qurashī; Yazīd b. Hārūn; Fatḥ b. Shakhraf (he spent seven years in the wilderness after that); Ḥasan b. al-ʿAbbās al-Aṣbahānī; ʿAlī b. al-Muwaffaq al-ʿĀbid; Imam Abū al-Qāsim al-Qushayrī; and others. Nabhānī related hearing Allah in dream at the end of *al-Asālīb al-badīʿa.*

We have established in the previous chapter the Sunni position on the relation of the staggering miracles of Prophets and the miraculous gifts of non-Prophets. Allah Most High said, *and Messengers We have recounted to you before, and Messengers We have not recounted to you; and the One God spoke to Mūsā with express speech* (al-Nisā' 4:164); and He said, *and when My slaves ask you about Me, then verily, I am near! I answer the call of the supplicant when he supplicates* (al-Baqara 2:186); and He said, *verily there is in that indeed a reminder for anyone that has a heart or gives ear while he is presently witnessing* (Qāf 50:37).

The Imam and *Quṭb* of renewal, al-Ḥabīb ʿAbd Allāh al-Ḥaddād al-Ḥaḍramī replied the following when he was asked about the meaning of Ḥujjat al-Islām al-Ghazālī's statement,

لَيْسَ كُلُّ أَحَدٍ لَهُ قَلْبٌ

"Not everyone has a heart."

يُرِيدُ - رحمه الله تعالى ونفع به - الْقَلْبَ الحَقِيقِيَّ الَّذِي يَفْقَهُ وَيَعْقِلُ عَنِ الله تَعَالَى، وَهُوَ مَعْنًى شَرِيفٌ قَائِمٌ بِهَذا الْقَلْبِ الصَّنَوْبَرِيِّ اللَّحْمِيِّ المَوْجُودِ لِكُلِّ أَحَدٍ، وَعَلَى مَا ذُكِرَ يَتَنَزَّلُ قَوْلُهُ تَعَالَى ﴿ إِنَّ فِي ذَٰلِكَ لَذِكْرَىٰ لِمَن كَانَ لَهُۥ قَلْبٌ أَوْ أَلْقَى ٱلسَّمْعَ وَهُوَ شَهِيدٌ ﴿٣٧﴾ ﴾ ق أي قَلْبٌ يَفْقَهُ عَنِ الله تَعَالَى. وَفِي آيَةٍ أُخْرَى أَثْبَتَ لَهُمُ الْقُلُوبَ الصُّورِيَّةَ وَنَفَى عَنْهُمُ الْفِقْهَ الَّذِي هُوَ المُرَادُ وَالمَقْصُودُ، فَقَالَ تَعَالَى: ﴿ لَهُمْ قُلُوبٌ لَّا يَفْقَهُونَ بِهَا وَلَهُمْ أَعْيُنٌ لَّا يُبْصِرُونَ بِهَا وَلَهُمْ ءَاذَانٌ لَّا يَسْمَعُونَ بِهَآ ﴾ من الآية ١٧٩ الأعراف.

He means–may Allah grant him mercy and benefit us with him–*al-qalb al-ḥaqīqī* (the real heart) that truly comprehends and understands what Allah sends. It is a noble meaning that subsists in this pinecone-like heart of flesh that everyone has. It is in the sense of what he said that one must give consideration to the statement of Allah, *verily there is in that indeed a reminder for anyone that has a heart* (Qāf 50:37). I.e. a heart that deeply understands what Allah says. In another verse He has affirmed for them the formal hearts but has negated from them the comprehension that is intended and which is the whole objective, by saying, *they have hearts with which they do not understand; they have eyes with which they do not see; they have ears with which they do not hear* (al-Aʿrāf 7:179).[42]

The Messenger of Allah–upon him the blessings and peace of Allah–said, "**How many an unkempt, begrimed servant is pushed out of doors—but if he swore by Allah, He would indeed fulfill his oath!**"[43] And he said–upon him the blessings and

[42] ʿAbd Allāh b. ʿAlawī al-Ḥaddād, *al-Nafā'is al-ʿulwiyya fil-masā'il al-ṣūfiyya* (The supernal gems concerning the Sufi questions), p. 105 §78.
[43] Narrated from Anas, Abū Hurayra and Muʿādh b. Jabal by Aḥmad, Muslim, al-Tirmidhī and Ibn Mājah.

peace of Allah–"**Each one of you is conversing intimately (*yunājī*) with his nurturing Lord.**"[44] And the Ṣiddīq said–may Allah be well-pleased with him–"I converse intimately with my nurturing Lord and He certainly knows my need."[45] And he said, "Verily I have let Him with whom I converse intimately hear."[46] More than all of the above, Allah Most High said in the report known as "the ḥadith of the Awliya"—as narrated by al-Bukhārī in his *Ṣaḥīḥ* from Abū Hurayra, from the Prophet–upon him the blessings and peace of Allah–from Allah Most High—"**When I love him** [=My servant] **I become his hearing with which he hears and his sight with which he sees.**" The opening of this hadith contains a dire warning to those who oppose the Awliya: "**Whoever comes against one of My Awliya I have certainly declared war against him!**"

The above hadith is cited by the author of *Madārij al-sālikīn* who interprets it to refer to the hearing of the heart: "the best audition is the audition of he who hears by Allah what is heard from Allah, namely His speech. It is the audition of the beloved lovers, as in the hadith found in *Ṣaḥīḥ al-Bukhārī* [etc.]. And the heart is affected by the audition in proportion with the love it contains. So when it fills up with the love of Allah and **it hears the Speech of its Beloved**..."

Ibn al-Jawzī narrated in *Manāqib al-Imām Aḥmad* that 'Abd Allāh the son of Aḥmad heard his father say, "I saw the Lord of Might and Glory in my dream. I said, 'O nurturing Lord! What is the best thing by which those that are near to You have drawn near to You?' He said, 'My Speech, Aḥmad.' I said, 'O nurturing Lord! With understanding or without understanding?' He said, *bi-fahmin wa-bi-ghayri fahm* (with understanding and without)."

[44] Narrated from (i) Abū Sa'īd al-Khudrī by 'Abd al-Razzāq, *Muṣannaf*; al-Ḥākim; al-Bayhaqī, *Shu'ab* and *Sunan*; (ii) 'Adī b. Ḥātim by Abū Bakr b. Khallād al-Naṣībī; Abū Nu'aym, *Ḥilya* and *Ma'rifat al-Ṣaḥāba*.

[45] Narrated from Ibn Sīrīn by Sa'īd b. Manṣūr, Ṭabarī, Ibn al-Mundhir, al-Ḥakīm al-Tirmidhī, al-Tha'labī and al-Bayhaqī in the *Shu'ab*.

[46] Narrated from Abū Qatāda by Abū Dāwūd and al-Tirmidhī.

There are many more such examples of divine conversations and sightings. The ulema of credal doctrine have concurred that it is possible for the believer to see Allah in this world in a state of wakefulness on the basis of the request made by the Prophet Mūsā–upon him peace–to Allah Most High, *let me see, that I may look at You* (Aʿrāf 7:143), for Prophets never ask something impossible or absurd. It is in this vein that the Prophetic definition of *iḥsān* (excellence) as "**for you to worship Allah as if you see Him, and if you do not see Him then He sees you**" was described by Imam al-Nawawī in *Sharḥ al-Arbaʿīn* as *maqām al-mushāhada*, "**the station of mutual witnessing**." May Allah grant us His witnessing and not deprive us of seeing Him.

XXIII. Awliya do not legislate but they infer sound rulings

The objector said, "And he claimed that one of the gnostics knows the unseen and makes up laws!"

As for his claim that Habib 'Alī al-Jafrī claimed that "one of the gnostics makes up laws," it is a lie and a fabrication. Allah Most High said, *and if only, when you heard it, you had said, "It would never be for us to speak such a thing. Glorified are You! This is an enormous calumny"* (Nūr 24:16). Habib 'Alī explicitly said in his public lecture in Jāmi' al-Īmān in the Mazra'a neighborhood of Damascus in Rabi' al-Awwal 1425/May 2004 that "whoever says that the wali gives laws has certainly committed disbelief." This lecture was attended by thousands and it is the only time that Shaykh Sa'īd al-Būṭī allowed anyone to speak in his place in the history of his teaching in that mosque. Būṭī died as a shahid in 1434/2013 sitting in the very same lectern.

It is possible that the basis of the objector's accusation is another accuser's charge that "Habib 'Alī al-Jafrī said, 'It was transmitted from the gnostic ulema that whoever stands in 'Arafāt thinking that Allah will never forgive him, has committed an enormity,' and this is never the case, for I found none of the four Imams or their recognized followers stipulating such a ruling. So it is established that al-Jafrī means the non-jurist ulema, and they are the ones he named the *'ārifīn* (gnostics)!"

Note that the latter remark typifies the abhorrent *kibr* (arrogance) of the immature scholars of external knowledge towards the Sufis which Imam Aḥmad b. Ḥanbal denounced when he told certain students of his, "May Allah forgive you! Is anything meant by knowledge other than what Ma'rūf [al-Karkhī] has attained?"[47] Abū Bakr al-Marwazī similarly narrated in his book *al-Wara'* (scrupulous Godfearingness) that when Aḥmad was

[47] Narrated by al-Khaṭīb, *Tārīkh*; Ibn Abī Ya'lā, *Ṭabaqāt al-Ḥanābila*; al-Dhahabī, *Siyar*; Ibn Mufliḥ, *al-Maqṣad al-arshad*.

asked on his deathbed who would succeed him as the Imam of the school he said, "Put all your questions to 'Abd al-Wahhāb [al-Warrāq]." One of those present, Fatḥ b. Abī al-Fatḥ, said: "But he does not have much learning!" Aḥmad replied, "He is a *rajul ṣāliḥ* (saintly man): one such as him is granted success in speaking the truth."[48] Al-Qushayrī put to rest the delusion that the ulema are above the Awliya at the very beginning of his famous *Qushayriyya* epistle to the Sufis when he said:

قال الإمام القشيري في طليعة رسالته: هٰذِهِ رِسَالَةٌ كَتَبَهَا الْفَقِيرُ إِلَى اللهِ تَعَالَىٰ عَبْدُ الْكَرِيمِ بْنُ هَوَازِنَ الْقُشَيْرِيُّ إِلَى جَمَاعَةِ الصُّوفِيَّةِ بِبُلْدَانِ الْإِسْلَامِ فِي سَنَةِ سَبْعٍ وَثَلَاثِينَ وَأَرْبَعِمِائَةٍ. أَمَّا بَعْدُ: رَضِيَ اللهُ عَنْكُمْ! فَقَدْ جَعَلَ اللهُ هٰذِهِ الطَّائِفَةَ صَفْوَةَ أَوْلِيَائِهِ وَفَضَّلَهُمْ عَلَىٰ الكَافَّةِ مِنْ عِبَادِهِ بَعْدَ رُسُلِهِ وَأَنْبِيَائِهِ

"This is a treatise that the pauper in need of Allah Most High, 'Abd al-Karīm b. Hawāzin al-Qushayrī, has written for the assembly of the Sufis in all Muslim countries in the year 437/1046. May Allah be well-pleased with you! For Allah has indeed made this group the chosen quintessence of His friends and He has preferred them to the totality of His servants after His Messengers and His Prophets."

Likewise Imam al-Ghazālī lambasted the same delusion in the chapter on *ādāb al-muta'allim wal-mu'allim* (manners of the learner and the teacher) in the book of *'ilm* (knowledge), the very first book of the *Iḥyā'*, after which he said:

قال حجة الإسلام في الإحياء كتاب العلم: الرُّتْبَةُ الْعُلْيَا لِلْأَنْبِيَاءِ ثُمَّ الْأَوْلِيَاءِ ثُمَّ الْعُلَمَاءِ الرَّاسِخِينَ فِي الْعِلْمِ ثُمَّ لِلصَّالِحِينَ عَلَى تَفَاوُتِ دَرَجَاتِهِمْ

"The highest rank belongs to the Prophets, then the *awliyā'* (friends of Allah), then the well-grounded ulema, and then

[48] Abū Bakr al-Marwazī, *al-Wara'*; al-Khaṭīb, *Tārīkh*; Ibn Abī Ya'lā, chapter on al-Warrāq in *Ṭabaqāt al-Ḥanābila*.

the righteous, according to their widely-differing levels!"

Sulṭān al-'ulamā' al-'Izz Ibn 'Abd al-Salām al-Sulamī endorsed both these statements in his *Fatāwā* and went further:

قال سلطان العلماء العز ابن عبد السلام السُلَمي في الفتاوى المصرية له: **أَمَّا تَفْضِيلُ الْعَارِفِينَ بِاللهِ عَلَى الْعَارِفِينَ بِأَحْكَامِ الشَّرْعِ فَقَوْلُ الْأُسْتَاذِ وَأَبِي حَامِدٍ فِيهِ مُتَّفَقٌ عَلَيْهِ، وَلَا يَشُكُّ عَاقِلٌ أَنَّ الْعَارِفِينَ بِمَا يَجِبُ لله مِنْ أَوْصَافِ الْجَلَالِ وَنُعُوتِ الْكَمَالِ وَبِمَا يَسْتَحِيلُ عَلَيْهِ مِنَ الْعَيْبِ وَالنُّقْصَانِ أَفْضَلُ مِنَ الْعَارِفِينَ بِالْأَحْكَامِ، بَلِ الْعَارِفُونَ بِاللهِ أَفْضَلُ مِنْ أَهْلِ الْفُرُوعِ وَالْأُصُولِ.**

Nor was the statement that "whoever stands in 'Arafāt thinking that Allah will never forgive him, has committed an enormity" forwarded by "non-jurist ulema" since it is found in *Qūt al-qulūb*, *Iḥyā' 'ulūm al-dīn* and *al-Ghunya*, so the reference is to the authors of those works—Abū Ṭālib al-Makkī, al-Ghazālī and 'Abd al-Qādir al-Jaylānī.

In reality the abovementioned authorities based themselves on the manifest locution of three reports: (i) the hadith narrated from Ibn 'Umar whereby the Prophet–upon him blessings and peace–said, "**Verily the one with the worst offense among people is he that leaves 'Arafāt thinking that Allah Almighty and Exalted has not forgiven him**;"[49] (ii) the report that Ibn al-Mubārak found his teacher Sufyān al-Thawrī on the evening of 'Arafa and asked him, weeping, "Who in this crowd is in the worst state?" He replied, "The one who thinks Allah will not forgive him;"[50] (iii) the report that a man asked Ibn al-Mubārak the same question on the way from 'Arafa to Muzdalifa and he gave him the same reply.[51]

[49] Narrated by al-Khaṭīb in *al-Muttafiq wal-muftariq* with a weak chain.
[50] Narrated from Muḥammad b. Bashīr by Ibn Abī al-Dunyā in *Ḥusn al-ẓann bi-l-Lāh*.
[51] Cited by Abū Ṭālib al-Makkī in *Qūt al-qulūb*.

All of the above scholars without exception were jurists of the first rank in addition to being major Sufis, including Sufyān who was reputed as the Faqih of Kufa, the *zāhid* (ascetic) of his time and the Commander of the Believers in Hadith. He said, **"The best of creation are five types: an ascetic scholar, a Sufi jurisprudent, a humble person of wealth, a grateful pauper and a Sunni sharif."** It is narrated with their chains by Qushayrī in the *Risāla*, ʿAbd Allāh al-Harawī al-Anṣārī in his *Ṭabaqāt al-Ṣūfiyya*, Ibn al-Jawzī in *Ṣifat al-ṣafwa* and others.

قال إمام أهل الكوفة الفقيه الزاهد المجتهد المطلق أمير المؤمنين في الحديث سفيان الثوري:
أَعَزُّ الخَلْقِ خَمْسَةُ أَنْفُسٍ: عَالِمٌ زَاهِدٌ، وَفَقِيهٌ صُوفِيٌّ، وَغَنِيٌّ مُتَوَاضِعٌ، وَفَقِيرٌ شَاكِرٌ، وَشَرِيفٌ سُنِّيٌّ. رواه القشيري عن ابن الأعرابي في الرسالة والهروي الأنصاري في طبقات الصوفية وابن الجوزي في صفة الصفوة وصاحب مدارج السالكين

The ruling that whoever stands in ʿArafāt thinking that Allah will never forgive him has committed an enormity, furthermore, is supported by the strong Prophetic and Divine hadiths describing the Day of ʿArafa as (i) the very best of all days (Jābir by al-Bazzār, Abū Yaʿlā, Ibn Ḥibbān, al-Ṭabarānī), (ii) in which Allah frees more servants from hell than any other day (ditto); (iii) the day of the very best of all supplications (ʿAbd Allāh b. ʿAmr by al-Tirmidhī); and (iv) the day in which Allah takes His angels to witness that He is proud of the people of ʿArafa and has forgiven them all (Jābir by Ibn Khuzayma, al-Laʾlakāʾī and al-Bayhaqī; Abū Hurayra by Abū Nuʿaym and Ibn Bishrān). Thus **whoever leaves ʿArafa on that day thinking he is unforgiven has disbelieved in all of the above or disregarded it, which is an enormity.**

XXIV. Prophets and their inheritors do receive God-given knowledge of the unseen; meaning of *Nabī* and *Nubuwwa*

As for knowledge of the unseen, it is firmly established by definition as the province of the Prophets. The literal meanings of *al-nabīy* are (i) "the announcer of news on the part of Allah" (*Kitāb al-ʿayn*) "from a *nubūw* (height)" (*Jamharat al-lugha*) and (ii) *al-ṭarīq al-wāḍiḥ* (the crystal-clear way) (*Muʿjam maqāyīs al-lugha*; *Kitāb al-afʿāl*) while *nubuwwa* (Prophethood) is "*safāra* (mediatorship) between Allah and *dhawī al-ʿuqūl* (the possessors of minds) among His servants for the removal of their *ʿilla* (impairment) in the matter of their great return and their livelihood" (*Mufradāt alfāẓ al-Qurʾān*). The deniers of that mediatorship in the name of *tawḥīd* are deniers of the second half of the *shahāda*.

By virtue of the inheritance of the Prophets consisting not in gold and silver but in knowledge—per the Prophetic hadith narrated from Abū al-Dardāʾ in Aḥmad and the *Sunan*—it follows that **knowledge of the unseen is also part of the legacy of the Prophet's inheritors among the Awliya**. In both cases–for Prophets and Awliya–such knowledge is per the rule established in chapter XXI **in the sense of God-given partial knowledge, neither all-encompassing, nor absolute, nor inherent, nor independent**. The deniers of the Prophet's knowledge of the unseen are worse than the deniers of mediatorship because the latter are simple ignorants while the former are complex ignorants.

Furthermore, there are levels to that relative knowledge and it is far from monolithic and undifferentiated, contrary to the oversimplifications of the abovementioned two types. Thus the knowledge of ordinary people is like a drop in the ocean of the knowledge of a wali, the knowledge of Awliya is like a drop in the ocean of the knowledge of a Prophet, the knowledge of the first and the last, Prophets and Awliya is like a drop in the ocean of the knowledge of the Seal of Prophets, and the knowledge of the Seal of Prophets is like a drop in the superinfinite ocean of the knowledge of Allah Most High.

Qadi Yūsuf al-Nabhānī gathered the Prophetic hadiths to that effect in the chapter on the knowledge of the unseen in his encyclopedia of the staggering miracles of the Prophet–upon him the blessings and peace of Allah–entitled *Ḥujjat Allāh 'alā al-'ālamīn bi-mu'jizāt Sayyid al-Mursalīn*, which is the largest chapter of that 900-page book.[52] Among them:

> The Prophet–upon him the blessings and peace of Allah–stood among us [speaking] for a long time and did not leave out one thing from that time until the rising of the Final Hour except he told us about it. Whoever remembers it remembers it and whoever forgot it forgot it. All those who are present know this. Some of it I might have forgotten, then I see it [happen] and remember it just as someone would remember a man who had been away and then appears before him and he instantly recognizes him.[53]

عن حذيفة رضي الله عنه قال: **قَامَ فِينَا رَسُولُ الله ﷺ مَقَامًا مَا تَرَكَ شَيْئًا يَكُونُ فِي مَقَامِهِ ذَلِكَ إِلَى قِيَامِ السَّاعَةِ إِلاَّ حَدَّثَ بِهِ حَفِظَهُ مَنْ حَفِظَهُ وَنَسِيَهُ مَنْ نَسِيَهُ قَدْ عَلِمَهُ أَصْحَابِي هَؤُلاَءِ وَإِنَّهُ لَيَكُونُ مِنْهُ الشَّيْءُ قَدْ نَسِيتُــهُ فَأَرَاهُ فَأَذْكُرُهُ كَما يَذْكُرُ الرَّجُلُ وَجْهَ الرَّجُلِ إِذَا غَابَ عَنْهُ ثُمَّ إِذَا رَآهُ عَرَفَهُ** رواه أحمد والبخاري ومسلم وهذا لفظه وأبو داود ومثله عن أبي سعيد وعمر رضي الله عنهما

Bukhārī and Muslim also narrated from Anas that the Messenger of Allah–upon him blessings and peace of Allah–came out when the sun passed the zenith and he prayed the noon prayer. Then he stook on the pulpit and he mentioned

[52] See its translation in Haddad, *The Prophet Muhammad's Knowledge of the Unseen*.

[53] Narrated from Ḥudhayfa by Aḥmad, Bukhārī, Muslim (this is his wording) and Abū Dāwūd. It is also narrated from Abū Sa'īd al-Khudrī and 'Umar by Aḥmad, al-Tirmidhī (*ḥasan ṣaḥīḥ*) and al-Bukhārī.

the Hour. He mentioned that it contained tremendous matters then he said, "Whoever likes to ask something, let him ask. You will not ask me about anything except I will tell you for as long as I stand here." People were weeping a lot and he kept saying, "Ask me!"

وعن أنس أَنَّ رَسُولَ اللهِ ﷺ خَرَجَ حِينَ زَاغَتِ الشَّمْسُ، فَصَلَّى الظُّهْرَ فَقَامَ عَلَى الْمِنْبَرِ، فَذَكَرَ السَّاعَةَ، فَذَكَرَ أَنَّ فِيهَا أُمُورًا عِظَامًا، ثُمَّ قَالَ: مَنْ أَحَبَّ أَنْ يَسْأَلَ عَنْ شَيْءٍ فَلْيَسْأَلْ، فَلاَ تَسْأَلُونِي عَنْ شَيْءٍ إِلَّا أَخْبَرْتُكُمْ مَا دُمْتُ فِي مَقَامِي هَذَا. فَأَكْثَرَ النَّاسُ فِي الْبُكَاءِ، وَأَكْثَرَ أَنْ يَقُولَ: سَلُونِي. متفق عليه.

Muslim also narrated that Abū Zayd ʿAmr b. Akhṭab al-Anṣārī said, "The Prophet–upon him the blessings and peace of Allah–prayed the dawn prayer with us then he climbed the pulpit and addressed us until the time came for *ẓuhr*, then he descended and prayed. Then he climbed the pulpit and addressed us until the time came for *ʿaṣr*, whereupon he descended and prayed. Then he climbed the pulpit and addressed us until the sun set. He informed us about all that was to happen until the Day of Resurrection. The most knowledgeable of us is he who has memorized the most."

عن أبي زيد يعني عمرو بن أخطب رضي الله عنه قال: صَلَّى بِنَا رَسُولُ اللهِ ﷺ الْفَجْرَ وَصَعِدَ الْمِنْبَرَ فَخَطَبَنَا حَتَّى حَضَرَتِ الظُّهْرُ فَنَزَلَ فَصَلَّى ثُمَّ صَعِدَ الْمِنْبَرَ فَخَطَبَنَا حَتَّى حَضَرَتِ الْعَصْرُ ثُمَّ نَزَلَ فَصَلَّى ثُمَّ صَعِدَ الْمِنْبَرَ فَخَطَبَنَا حَتَّى غَرَبَتِ الشَّمْسُ فَأَخْبَرَنَا بِمَا كَانَ وَبِمَا هُوَ كَائِنٌ فَأَعْلَمُنَا أَحْفَظُنَا أحمد ومسلم

Tirmidhī narrated from Mu'ādh b. Jabal, "The Messenger of Allah–upon him the blessings and peace of Allah–was delayed from coming out to us one morning to pray the dawn prayer until we were about to see the sun rise, whereupon he came out in a hurry, the final call to prayer was raised and the Messenger of Allah prayed and made his prayer brief. When he gave salam he called out with a loud voice and said to us, 'Verily I shall tell you what kept me from coming out to you this morning. Verily I rose and prayed in part of the night. I made ablution and prayed whatever was apportioned to me, then I became drowsy in my prayer and my eyes felt heavy. Lo and behold, I beheld my nurturing Lord in the most beautiful form! He said to me, "O Muḥammad!" I said, "Twice at your service, my nurturing Lord!" He said, "What do the highest angels argue about?" I said, "I do not know, my nurturing Lord." He said it three times. Then I saw Him place His palm between my shoulder-blades until I felt the coolness of His fingers between my breasts. Then **everything uncovered itself to me and I knew**'" (*ḥasan ṣaḥīḥ*). It was also narrated from Ibn 'Abbās by Aḥmad and al-Tirmidhī in the wording, "**and I knew what was in the skies and what was on earth.**" The latter also narrated it in the wording, "**and I knew whatever was between the east and the west.**"

عن معاذ بن جبل قال: **احْتُبِسَ عَنَّا رَسُولُ اللهِ ﷺ ذَاتَ غَدَاةٍ مِنْ صَلَاةِ الصُّبْحِ حَتَّى كِدْنَا نَتَرَاءَى عَيْنَ الشَّمْسِ، فَخَرَجَ سَرِيعًا فَثُوِّبَ بِالصَّلَاةِ، فَصَلَّى رَسُولُ اللهِ ﷺ وَتَجَوَّزَ فِي صَلَاتِهِ، فَلَمَّا سَلَّمَ دَعَا بِصَوْتِهِ فَقَالَ لَنَا: عَلَى مَصَافِّكُمْ كَمَا أَنْتُمْ. ثُمَّ انْفَتَلَ إِلَيْنَا فَقَالَ: أَمَا إِنِّي سَأُحَدِّثُكُمْ مَا حَبَسَنِي عَنْكُمُ الغَدَاةَ. إِنِّي قُمْتُ مِنَ اللَّيْلِ فَتَوَضَّأْتُ فَصَلَّيْتُ مَا قُدِّرَ لِي فَنَعَسْتُ فِي صَلَاتِي فَاسْتَثْقَلْتُ، فَإِذَا أَنَا بِرَبِّي تَبَارَكَ**

وَتَعَالَى فِي أَحْسَنِ صُورَةٍ، فَقَالَ: يَا مُحَمَّدُ قُلْتُ: لَبَّيْكَ رَبِّ، قَالَ: فِيمَ يَخْتَصِمُ الْمَلَأُ الأَعْلَى؟ قُلْتُ: لَا أَدْرِي رَبِّ، قَالَهَا ثَلَاثًا. قَالَ: فَرَأَيْتُهُ وَضَعَ كَفَّهُ بَيْنَ كَتِفَيَّ حَتَّى وَجَدْتُ بَرْدَ أَنَامِلِهِ بَيْنَ ثَدْيَيَّ، فَتَجَلَّى لِي كُلُّ شَيْءٍ وَعَرَفْتُ. الحديث. قال الترمذي: هذا حديث حسن صحيح ورواه أحمد والترمذي عن ابن عباس بلفظ فَعَلِمْتُ مَا فِي السَّمَاوَاتِ وَمَا فِي الْأَرْضِ ورواه الأخير أيضاً بلفظ فَعَلِمْتُ مَا بَيْنَ الْمَشْرِقِ وَالْمَغْرِبِ

Aḥmad in his *Musnad* (1:218 §45) and Imam Mālik in the *Muwaṭṭā'* respectively narrated from 'Ā'isha the report of Abū Bakr al-Ṣiddīq's *tafarrus* (foresight) of his death on *yawm al-ithnayn* (the second day of the week i.e. Monday) and of the birth of a girl to him—"I am shown that it will be a daughter." Umm Kulthūm bint Abū Bakr was born after his death. These are two miraculous gifts of his.

Another famous *karāma* of the unseen is the story of 'Umar's perceiving from his pulpit in Medina in the year 23/644 that the troops of the Companion Sāriya b. Zunaym al-Du'alī were in difficulty in Persia at a month's distance, and his shouting to him to take their stand against the enemy army on the mountain instead of the valley. When the troops' emissary reached Medina he said to 'Umar, "We were going to be routed then we heard a voice shouting, 'Sāriya, the mountain!' three times, so we took our positions with the mountain at our backs, after which Allah routed the enemy.'"[54] "The miracle was vision and voice for 'Umar but voice only for Sāriya" (Shaykh Hisham).

[54] Narrated from Ibn 'Umar by al-Wāqidī, Sayf b. 'Umar, Ibn Sa'd, al-Ṭabarī in his *Tārīkh*, Abū Bakr al-Naṣībī in his *Fawā'id*, al-Sulamī in *al-Arba'ūn fil-taṣawwuf*, Abū Nu'aym in the *Dalā'il*, Bayhaqī in *al-I'tiqād*, al-Lā'lakā'ī in *Sharḥ al-Sunna*, 'Āqūlī in his *Fawā'id*, Ibn al-A'rābī in *Karāmāt al-awliyā'* and Ibn Hajar in *al-Iṣāba*.

The Qadi Abū Bakr b. al-'Arabī al-Ma'āfirī al-Mālikī said of the abovementioned miracle, "It constitutes a tremendous rank and an evident gift from Allah, and **it is present in all of the righteous incessantly until the Day of Resurrection**."[55] Al-Kharā'iṭī (240-327/854-939) said of 'Umar's *firāsa*[56] in *I'tilāl al-qulūb* (The ailment of hearts):

قال الإمام الحافظ أبو بكر محمد بن جعفر بن محمد الخرائطي عن فراسة عمر بن الخطاب رضي الله عنه في كتاب إعتلال القلوب **مَا كَانَ أَنْظَرَهُ بِنُورِ اللهِ فِي ذَاتِ اللهِ وَأَفْرَسَهُ! كَانَ ـ وَاللهِ! ـ كَمَا قَالَ الشَاعِرُ:**

بَصِيرٌ بِأَعْقَـابِ الأُمُورِ بِرَأْيِهِ　　كَأَنَّ لَهُ فِي الْيَوْمِ عَيْناً عَلَى غَدِ

> He was so perceptive with the light of Allah for the sake of Allah Himself, and insightful! He was—by Allah!—as the poet said,
>
> *discerning of the upshots of things in his view,*
> *as if his eyes, today, did behold the morrow.*

It is also narrated that our liege lord 'Uthmān b. 'Affān said to Anas who had happened to look at a woman in the souk before visiting him, "One of you comes in with the trace of fornication in his eyes!" Anas said, "What! Is there revelation after the Messenger of Allah?" He replied, "No, but there is *burhān* (proof) and *firāsa* (insight) and *ṣidq* (truthfulness)."[57] Qurṭubī cited it in his *Tafsīr* (al-Ḥijr 15:75) and commented, "Many such examples are related from the Companions and the Successors." For more on the Companions' *karāmāt* see al-Nabhānī's *Ḥujjat Allāh 'alā al-'ālamīn* towards the very end.

[55] Ibn al-'Arabī al-Mālikī, *'Āriḍat al-aḥwadhī* (13:150).

[56] See next chapter, second footnote.

[57] Narrated by al-Qushayrī in his *Risāla* (*Futuwwa*) and cited by Muḥibb al-Dīn al-Ṭabarī in *al-Riyāḍ al-naḍira* and Ibn al-Subkī in *Ṭabaqāt al-Shāfi'iyyat al-kubrā*.

XXV. Affirmation of the Awliya's knowledge of the unseen by the putative founders of "Salafism"

Shams al-Dīn al-Zurʿī said in his book *Madārij al-sālikīn*:

> What causes *firāsa* (spiritual insight) is a light that Allah casts into His servant's heart by which the latter can differentiate between truth and falsehood.... Its reality is that of a fleeting thought that pounces on the heart, defeating what opposes it. Its morphology is like that of *wilāya* (rule), *imāra* (commandership) and *siyāsa* (governance). This *firāsa* is in proportion to belief: the stronger one's belief is, the sharper his *firāsa* will be. Abū Saʿīd al-Kharrāz (d. 226/841)[58] said, "Whoever looks with the light of *firāsa* has looked with the light of the All-True, and the materials of his knowledge will be with the All-True without inadvertence or heedlessness, but rather a true ruling that courses on His servant's tongue." [Abū Bakr] al-Wāsiṭī (d. 320/932) said, "***Firāsa*** **consists in rays of light that sparkle in the hearts and enable knowledge of some secrets of the unseen en bloc from one unseen to the next until one witnesses things from wherever the All-True shows them to him, so he can tell what people think.**" [Abū Sulaymān] al-Dārānī (140-215/757-830) said, "*Firāsa* is the unveiling of the soul and the eyeing of the unseen, and it is one of the stations of belief." One of them said it is the utterance of the secrets of creatures based on witnessing, not based on conjecture and reckoning. ʿAmr b. Nujayd (d. 365/976) said that Shāh al-Kirmānī (d. after 270/883) was sharp in

[58] The Imam of the Sufis in Baghdad in his time and the best-spoken of them after al-Junayd according to al-Sulamī. He was a companion of Sarīy al-Saqaṭī, Bishr al-Ḥāfī and Dḥu al-Nūn al-Miṣrī and teacher to Muḥammad b. ʿAlī al-Kattānī. Among his sayings: "Every inward state the outward state belies is falsehood" and "Whoever thinks he will reach without effort it is wishful thinking, and whoever thinks he will reach through effort is only toiling." An edition and translation of his *Kitāb al-ṣidq* (Book of Truthfulness) was published by A.J. Arberry in 1937.

firāsa and never wrong, and that he would say, "Whoever keeps his gaze away from forbidden matters and abstains from pleasures builds up his inward state through permanent watchfulness and his outward state by following the Sunna, and accustoms himself to halal sustenance, his *firāsa* will not err." Aḥmad b. 'Āṣim al-Anṭākī (140-215/757-830) said "when you sit with the people of truthfulness keep truthfulness for they are the spies of the hearts. They enter your hearts and exit them unawares to you." Al-Junayd (d. 297/910) was speaking to a group of people one day when a young man asked him, "O Shaykh, what is the meaning of the Prophet's statement, 'Beware of the *firāsa* of the believer, for verily he sees with the light of Allah'?"[59] Thereupon al-Junayd bowed his head and kept silent. After a while he raised his head and said to the young man, "Submit! For the time has come for you to submit." The young man submitted and became Muslim.

Al-Zur'ī's teacher, Aḥmad b. 'Abd al-Ḥalīm al-Ḥarrānī, said in his *Fatāwā*:

> The dream of Prophets is revelation and the dream of the believers is one fortysixth part of Prophethood as is established from the Prophet–upon him the blessings and peace of Allah–in the sound compilations. 'Ubāda b. al-Ṣāmit said —and it is also narrated as a Prophetic hadith—that "**The dream of the believer is speech spoken by the nurturing Lord to His servant *fil-manām* (in sleep), and likewise *fil-***

[59] Narrated from (i) Abū Sa'īd al-Khudrī by Abū Ḥanīfa in his *Musnad Abī Ḥanīfata riwāyat al-Ḥaṣkafī*; Bukhārī, *al-Tārīkh al-kabīr*; Tirmidhī; Ṭabarī (Ḥijr 15:75); Ṭabarānī, *Awsaṭ*; and others; (ii) Ibn 'Umar by al-Ṭabarī (ditto); Abū Nu'aym, *Ḥilya*; (iii) Abū Umāma by al-Ḥakīm al-Tirmidhī, *Nawādir*; Ṭabarānī, *Awsaṭ*; *Kabīr*; *Musnad al-Shāmiyyīn* with a fair chain per Haythamī, *Majma' al-zawā'id* (10:268), a fair hadith per Suyūṭī, *La'āli'*; Ibn Naṣr al-Sāmarrī, *Fawā'id*; Abū Nu'aym, *al-Arba'ūn 'alā madhhab al-mutaḥaqqiqīn min al-Ṣufiyya*; *al-Ṭibb al-Nabawī*; *Ḥilya* and others; (iv) Abū Hurayra by Abū al-Shaykh, *Amthāl al-Ḥadīth*; Ibn Bishrān, *Amālī*; (v-vi) Jābir and Abū al-Dardā' by al-Fuwaṭī, *Majmā' al-ādāb*; and (vii) Thawbān by al-Ṭabarī (ditto). Al-Khaṭīb said al-Junayd is not known to have related any other hadith.

yaqaẓa* (wakefulness).**" For it is firmly established in the *Ṣaḥīḥ* from the Prophet–upon him the blessings and peace of Allah–that he said, "**In the nations before you there were *muḥaddathūn* (people who are communicated to by the angels), although they were not Prophets.** If there is any of them in my Community, truly it is 'Umar b. al-Khaṭṭāb."[60] There is another version in the *Ṣaḥīḥ* that has *mukallamūn* (people who are spoken to). And He–Most High–has said, *and when I inspired to the close companions that, "Believe in Me and in My Messenger!"* (Mā'ida 5:111), and He said, *and We inspired to Mūsā's mother that, "Breastfeed him"* (Qaṣaṣ 28:7). So **this *waḥy (inspiration) **can take place for non-Prophets; it can be in wakefulness or in sleep; and it can be in the form of a voice calling, and the voice will be in oneself and not outside of oneself, in wakefulness or in sleep, just as the light that one might see will be in oneself.**[61]

Most of the above is part of what attackers of Sufis strive to deny as being part of Islam. When they are informed that even their own putative authorities say it, they will also try to deny that. But "truth is truth, and falsehood is falsehood" (Ibn Ḥazm). In reality the above excerpts carry no authority except insofar as they more or less accurately reflect the divine and Prophetic sources of which they are but a drop in the ocean.

Let the deniers read for themselves the countless amount of proofs for the God-given knowledge of the unseen of Prophets and Awliya that are documented in the commentaries on the Book of Allah, in the compilations of the Prophetic reports and the sayings of the Companions and the Imams, and in the chapters that are specific to the unveiling of the knowledge of the unseen in such as the following works:

[60] Narrated from Abū Hurayra and 'Ā'isha by al-Bukhārī and Muslim, the latter without the words "although they were not Prophets."

[61] Aḥmad al-Ḥarrānī, *Majmū' al-fatāwā*, 37 vols. (Medina: Mujamma' al-Malik Fahd, 1425/2004) 12:398.

- the books of Prophetic *khaṣā'iṣ* by Qadi 'Iyāḍ, Ibn al-Mulaqqin, Ibn Diḥya, al-Khayḍarī, al-Is'ardī, al-Suyūṭī, Ibn Ṭūlūn, al-Kattānī and others;

- the books of *Dalā'il al-Nubuwwa* by al-Firyābī, Abū Nu'aym al-Aṣbahānī, al-Bayhaqī, Qawwām al-Sunna al-Taymī, Sa'īd Bāshanqar and others;

- al-Nabhānī's encyclopedia of the Prophetic miracles already cited;

- and the compilations on the histories of the Companions and of the later Sufis such as *Ḥilyat al-Awliyā* by Abū Nu'aym, the *Ṭabaqāt al-Awliyā* compilations by Ibn al-Mulaqqin, al-Sakhāwī and Munāwī, Ibn al-Jawzī's *Ṣifat al-ṣafwa*, Sulamī's and al-Harawī al-Anṣārī's *Ṭabaqāt al-Ṣūfiyya*, Ibn Abī al-Dunyā's *al-Awliyā*, al-Khallāl's *al-Awliyā*, al-La'lakā'ī's *Karāmāt al-awliyā*, and Nabhānī's *Jāmi' karāmāt al-awliyā* to name a few.

XXVI. Affirmation that ʿAlī b. Abī Ṭālib possessed *ʿilm ladunnī* (knowledge from the divine side)

Al-Ḥakīm al-Tirmidhī, one of the foremost Sufi masters of the early generations, said in commentary on the Prophetic hadiths cited in the previous chapters:

> The *muḥaddathūn* (recipients of inspiration) have levels. **Some are given a third of prophethood, some half, and some more than that, all the way to the level of the one who receives the most—he who possesses the seal of *wilāya* (sainthood).** Someone says: "It shocks me to say that some-one other than Prophets may possess any part of Prophet-hood!" Have you not heard the hadith of the Messenger of Allah–upon him the blessings and peace of Allah–"**Following a middle course** *(al-iqtiṣād)*, **right guidance** *(al-hady)* **and good demeanor** *(al-samt al-ṣāliḥ)* **are one in twenty-four parts of Prophethood**"?[62] If *those who follow a middle course* possess the aforementioned portions of Prophethood, then what about *he that is foremost in good deeds*?"[63] [A reference to the Quranic verse, *of them is he that is following a middle course, and of them is he that is foremost in obtaining the good things* (Fāṭir 35:32).]

To the *muʿaṭṭil* (anarchic) claim that "since the hadith says, 'If there is anyone in my Umma then it is 'Umar,' it follows that the number of such inspired people is at most one, namely

[62] Narrated from I. 'Abd Allāh b. Sarjis al-Muzanī with *al-ta'uda* (gentleness) instead of *al-hady* by Tirmidhī (*ḥasan*), Maqdisī, *Mukhtāra*, 'Abd b. Ḥumayd, *Musnad* and Khaṭīb, *Tārīkh* and *Jāmiʿ*; II. Ibn 'Abbās with the wording "one in twenty-five parts" by Aḥmad, Bukhārī in *al-Adab al-mufrad*, Abū Dāwūd, Ṭabarānī, *Awsaṭ*, and al-Khaṭīb, *Jāmiʿ*; III. with the wording "one in twenty-seven parts" from Ibn 'Abbās by al-Ṭabarānī; and IV. with the wording "one in seventy parts" from Ibn 'Abbās by al-Bukhārī in *al-Adab al-mufrad*.

[63] al-Ḥakīm al-Tirmidhī, *Khatm al-Awliyā'* (pp. 346-347), chapter ten (*'alāmāt al-awliyā'*).

'Umar," Ibn Ḥajar replied with the reminders that it is wrong to think that other Communities had many but this Community only one; that in the Prophet's time predominance was given to Prophetic revelation, but after the latter finished, inspiration began for those whom Allah specified because there would be safety from confusion in that; and anyone that denies it despite its abundance and fame, is just showing arrogance. Thus what is meant by the hadith is the perfection of the quality of *ilhām* (inspiration) in 'Umar, not its lack in other Muslims.[64] Another proof is that Abū Bakr was even more inspired than 'Umar by the Consensus of *Ahl al-Sunna*. This is shown by Abū Bakr's unique leadership at the time of the Prophet's death–upon him the blessings and peace of Allah–and, again, when he took up arms to exact the *zakat* from the rebellious Arab tribes. "And **examples of that have occurred for other than 'Umar which are beyond count**."[65]

We cite once again from the author of *Madārij al-sālikīn* because, although he is a late scholar, nevertheless he is held by the 'Salafi' sectarians as an object of blind imitation and they place him and his teacher above the actual *Salaf*—including the Four Imams and the Companions! He said in the section he entitled *darajāt al-'ilm* (levels of knowledge):

> The third level is a *'ilm ladunnī* (knowledge from the side of Allah).... There is no veil between it and the unseen. By the *'ilm ladunnī*, the Folk [=Sufis] refer to what takes place for the servant without intermediary but rather through inspiration from Allah and an imparting of knowledge on His part to His servant, as took place with al-Khiḍr without the intermediary of Mūsā. Allah Most High said, *whereupon they found one of our slaves whom We had given mercy from Our presence, and whom We had taught, from Our side, a certain knowledge* (Kahf 18:65). He differentiated between mercy

[64] Ibn Ḥajar, *Fatḥ al-Bārī* (7:50-51, 12:376).
[65] Ibn Ḥajar, *Fatḥ al-Bārī* (6:516).

and knowledge and He made them respectively from His presence and from His side—for he had not obtained them at the hand of a human being—but "from His side" is more special yet than "from His presence." This is why He said, *and appoint for me, from Your side, an all-sustaining authority* (Banū Isrā'il/Isrā' 17:80), as it is the most special and the closest of what is in His presence… whereby He opens up for him of the understanding of the Book and the Sunna in a way that He makes specific to him, as 'Alī b. Abī Ṭālib said when he was asked, **"Has the Messenger of Allah–upon him the blessings and peace of Allah–given you [plural=the people of the Prophetic House] something special exclusively of people?"** He replied, **"No—by Him Who has cleaved the grain and created the soul!—except a certain understanding Allah might give to a servant in regard to His Book"** [Bukhārī and Ibn Mājah]. So this is the real *'ilm ladunnī.*

XXVII. ʿAlawī b. ʿAbbās al-Mālikī's fatwa on *kashf* (spiritual unveiling)

Sayyid ʿAlawī b. ʿAbbās b. ʿAbd al-ʿAzīz al-Mālikī al-Makkī (1327-1391/1910-1971) said in his *Majmūʿ fatāwā wa-rasāʾil* (Compendium of fatwas and articles)—which I received from the hand of its publisher, namely his son in his house—in an article entitled *Bayān madhhab al-Ṣūfiyyati wal-uṣūliyyīn fil-ilhām* (Exposition of the positions of the Sufis and the legal theorists concerning inspiration) which he abridged from Sayyid ʿAlawī's Maghrebine teacher Muḥammad ʿAlī b. Ḥusayn al-Mālikī al-Makkī's (1287-1368/1870-1948) treatise entitled *Manāhil al-riyāsa wal-kiyāsa fī mawārid ʿadhb al-firāsa* (The springs of leadership and wisdom concerning the drinking-points of the fresh water of spiritual insight):

> The *ʿārifūn* (possessors of spiritual knowledge) have said that *ilhām* (inspiration) and *firāsa* (spiritual insight) are a *ḥujja* (conclusive proof) from him whom Allah has protected in all his outward and inward acts while the *uṣūliyyūn* (legal theorists) have said that *ilhām* and *firāsa* are not a *ḥujja*. The latter [distinction] is understood as [addressing] *ilhām* that issues from other than the abovementioned type and is outside the rule and basis of the sound *firāsa*—an unsound insight. So the disagreement of the legal theorists and the jurists with the Sufi masters is not a denial of *ilhām* at its root.
>
> The upshot is that the *ʿārifīn* Imams, in their statement that it constitutes a conclusive proof, have looked at the hearts of the minority which are demonstrably protected from the enticements of satanic whisperings. Such hearts are invariably mistrusting of any likely locus of wrong to the point that they never judge other than on the basis of truth, so they declared it permissible to follow their fatwa. And how rare they are! Nay, this is only for Wābiṣa (see three paragraphs down) and whoever is on the same foothold.

ʿIṣām [=ʿIṣām al-Dīn Ibrāhīm b. Muḥammad b. ʿArab Shāh al-Samarqandī al-Isfarāyīnī (873-945/1468-1538)] in his gloss on [the commentary by al-Taftāzānī on] the *ʿAqā'id al-Nasafiyya*, inferred the probative force of *ilhām* through explicit analogy. He concluded that if *ilhām* were not a conclusive proof in other than Prophets on the pretext that one's fleeting thoughts cannot be trusted in other than the infallible one–upon him blessings and peace of Allah–it would have to follow that the same must be said of dreams, but the latter concomitance is invalid in light of the Prophetic hadith that **the believer's dream is truth and it is one fortysixth part of Prophethood,**[66] on top of what was transmitted concerning inspiration, "**Consult your heart no matter what fatwa they give you.**"

The latter quotation, like the preceding restriction to Wābiṣa and his kind, is a reference to the famous hadith of the Companion Wābiṣa b. Maʿbad al-Asadī:

> I came to the Messenger of Allah–upon him the blessings and peace of Allah–not wanting to leave out anything about virtue and vice except I would ask him about it. There was a crowd around him so I began to step over [the shoulders of] the people. They said: "Away! Away with you, Wābiṣa, from the Messenger of Allah!" But I said: "So I am Wābiṣa! Leave me so I can get near him! I love no one more that I want to get near to!" He–upon him blessings and peace–said to me: "Come near, Wābiṣa, come near, Wābiṣa!" I approached until my knees touched his. He said, "Wābiṣa! Shall I tell you what you came to ask me about, or do you want to ask me first?" I said, "Messenger of Allah, tell me!" He said, "You came to ask me about virtue and vice." I said, "Yes, by the One Who sent you with the truth!" He–upon him the blessings and peace of Allah–joined three fingers together and poked my chest and said, '**Wābiṣa, *istafti qalbak*** (consult your heart)! *Taqwā* (Godfearingness) is right here! *Birr* (piety) is what-

[66] Narrated from the Companions in the *Musnad*, *Ṣaḥīḥ*s and *Sunan*.

ever your chest becomes relaxed in doing while *ithm* (iniquity) is whatever your chest becomes constricted in doing, regardless of what they recommend.[67] So **consult your heart no matter what fatwa they give you**, and leave what seems dubious to you for what does not seem dubious to you.'"[68]

Al-Tūrabishtī (d. 661/1263) makes the following observations on this hadith in his commentary on al-Baghawī's *Maṣābīḥ al-Sunna* entitled *al-Muyassar fī sharḥi Maṣābīḥ al-Sunna*:

> This hadith is subsumed under the evidences of Prophethood because Wābiṣa had come with an intent he had kept to himself to ask him about that, and he hardly gave him any time before he himself said, "You came to ask such and such." One of the perspicuous scholars viewed that the sign recommended by the Messenger of Allah–upon him the blessings and peace of Allah–to distinguish between the two matters [of right and wrong][69] was not part of what is for the general public, but rather something specific to the people of perspicuous knowledge and possessors of spiritual insights with pure hearts and weathered souls. This position, even if it is not far-fetched, nevertheless the view that it is indeed for the general public—among those who have in common the word of Godfearingness and whom the province of the faith encompasses—musters more truth and more guidance. It is not necessary for us to divert his statement to the particular when we can very well construe it as meant for the universal.

[67] Also translatable as, "Virtue is whatever sets the heart and soul at rest, while vice is what pricks the conscience [lit. 'becomes fixed in the heart'] and nags the breast no matter what people keep recommending to you."

[68] Narrated in various wordings from (i-v) Abū Hurayra, Anas, Abū Tha'laba al-Khushanī, al-Nawwās b. Sim'ān and Wābiṣa himself by 'Abd al-Razzāq, Aḥmad, Dārimī, Muslim, Tirmidhī (*ḥasan*), Nasā'ī, al-Ṭabarānī, Abū Ya'lā, Ibn Ḥibbān, Abū Nu'aym, Bayhaqī and others. Wābiṣa is also famous for the Prophetic hadith ordering him to repeat his prayer after he had joined the congregation behind the last row in a row formed exclusively of himself.

[69] I.e. the heart's signal.

XXVIII. The human being is Allah's *khalīfa* (vicegerent)[70]

Imam al-Shāfiʿī said in his poetry,

شَهِدْتُ بِأَنَّ اللهَ لَا شَيْءَ غَيْرُهُ   وَأَشْهَـدُ أَنَّ البَعْثَ حَقٌّ وَأُخْلِصُ

وَأَنَّ عُرَىٰ الْإِيمَانِ قَوْلٌ مُحَسَّنٌ   وَفِعْـلٌ زَكِيٌّ قَـدْ يَزِيـدُ وَيَنْقُـصُ

وَأَنَّ أَبَـا بَكْرٍ خَلِيفَةُ رَبِّهِ   وَكَانَ أَبُو حَفْصٍ عَلَى الخَيْرِ يَحْرِصُ

رواه البيهقي في المناقب وابن عساكر في التاريخ وغيرهما عن الرَّبيع بن سليمان المُرادي
وأبي إبراهيم المُزَني ـ الأخير بلفظ مُبَيَّنٌ ـ كلاهما عن الإمام الشافعي

"I bear witness that Allah—there is nothing other than He; and I bear witness that Resurrection is truth—and I have pure conviction—and that the ropes of belief are a beautified, definite statement and a pure, fruit-bearing act—it can increase and decrease—and that **Abū Bakr was the Caliph of his nurturing Lord** and Abū Ḥafṣ [ʿUmar] was keen on goodness."[71]

Shaykh al-Islām al-Tāj Ibn al-Subkī said the same of the second Caliph as well:

> Imam al-Ḥaramayn–Allah have mercy on him–said in *al-Shāmil* that there was an earthquake in the time of ʿUmar–Allah be well-pleased with him–[in the year 20/641 per al-Suyuṭī in *Kashf al-ṣalṣala ʿan waṣf al-zalzala* (The alarm disclosing the character of earthquakes)] so he praised Allah

[70] This chapter was written in refutation of Shaykh ʿAbd al-Raḥmān b. Ḥasan Ḥabannaka's (1927-2004) book *Lā yaṣiḥḥu an yuqāla al-insānu khalīfatun ʿani-l-Lāhi fī arḍih* (It is invalid to say the human being is a caliph from Allah on His earth).

[71] Narrated from (i) al-Rabīʿ b. Sulaymān al-Murādī and (ii) Abū Ibrāhīm Ismāʿīl b. Yaḥyā al-Muzanī by al-Bayhaqī, *Manāqib al-Shāfiʿī* (1:440, 2:68); Qawwām al-Sunna Ismāʿīl al-Aṣbahānī, *Siyar al-Salaf al-ṣāliḥin*; al-Salmāsī, *Manāzil al-aʾimmat al-arbaʿa*; Ibn ʿAsākir, *Tārīkh* (5:410, 51:312); Ibn Kathīr, *Ṭabaqāt al-Shāfiʿiyyīn*; Ibn Taghrī Bardī al-Atābakī, *al-Nujūm al-zāhira fī mulūk Miṣar wal-Qāhira*; and others.

and glorified Him while the earth continued to tremble and quake, after which he struck it with the whip and said, "Be quiet! Did I not practice justice on you?" Thereupon it became still. 'Umar was the Commander of the Believers in the literal sense, outwardly and inwardly, and **the Caliph of Allah on His earth and over the dwellers of His earth**.

قال شيخ الإسلام التاج ابن السبكي في طبقات الشافعية الكبرى قَالَ إِمَامُ الْحَرَمَيْنِ رَحِمَهُ اللهُ فِي كِتَابِ الشَّامِلِ إِنَّ الْأَرْضَ زُلْزِلَتْ فِي زَمَنِ عُمَرَ رَضِيَ اللهُ عَنْهُ [قال السيوطي في كشف الصلصلة ص ٦٦ ط المدينة: قال هشام ـ أي الكلبي ـ وذلك في سنة عشرين من الهجرة] فَحَمِدَ اللهَ وَأَثْنَى عَلَيْهِ وَالْأَرْضُ تَرْجُفُ وَتَرْتَجُّ ثُمَّ ضَرَبَهَا بِالدِّرَّةِ وَقَالَ أَقِرِّي! أَلَمْ أَعْدِلْ عَلَيْكِ؟ فَاسْتَقَرَّتْ مِنْ وَقْتِهَا. قُلْتُ ـ أي ابن السبكي ـ كَانَ عُمَرُ رَضِيَ اللهُ عَنْهُ أَمِيرَ الْمُؤْمِنِينَ عَلَى الْحَقِيقَةِ فِي الظَّاهِرِ وَالْبَاطِنِ وَخَلِيفَةَ اللهِ فِي أَرْضِهِ وَفِي سَاكِنِي أَرْضِهِ.

The evidence for their statement that the human being is the caliph of Allah on earth is well-established in the sound hadiths.

The Messenger of Allah–upon him blessings and peace–said to Ḥudhayfa b. al-Yamān, "Then the callers unto misguidance shall rise. **If you see in those days the Caliph of Allah on earth then stick to him even if he flails your body and takes your property**. If you do not see him then flee anywhere on earth even if it means you die while biting on some tree-stump!" Ḥudhayfa said, "What happens after that?" He said, "After that the Dajjāl shall come out." Ṭayālisī, Aḥmad, Abū Dāwūd and al-Ḥākim narrated it. Abū Dāwūd has, "**In those days if there is a caliph of Allah on earth that lashes you on the back and takes your property then stick to him all the same!** Otherwise die biting on some tree-stump!"[72]

---

[72] "I.e. isolate yourself and endure the bitterness and harshness of the times" per al-Bayḍāwī, *Tuḥfat al-abrār sharḥ Maṣābīḥ al-Sunna*.

قال رسول الله ﷺ لحذيفة اليماني رضي الله عنه **ثُمَّ تَنْشَأُ دُعَاةُ الضَّلَالَةِ فَإِنْ رَأَيْتَ يَوْمَئِذٍ خَلِيفَةَ اللهِ فِي الْأَرْضِ فَالْزَمْهُ وَإِنْ نَهَكَ جِسْمَكَ وَأَخَذَ مَالَكَ فَإِنْ لَمْ تَرَهُ فَاهْرَبْ فِي الْأَرْضِ وَلَوْ أَنْ تَمُوتَ وَأَنْتَ عَاضٌّ بِجِذْلِ شَجَرَةٍ. قَالَ ثُمَّ مَاذَا؟ قَالَ ثُمَّ يَخْرُجُ الدَّجَّالُ.** رواه أحمد وأبو داود

قال البيضاوي: أي: إن لم يكن لله في الأرض خليفة فعليك بالعزلة والصبر على مضض الزمان والتحمّل لمشاقه وشدائده.

The Messenger of Allah–upon him the blessings and peace of Allah–also said, "When you see the black banners having come from Khorasan then join them, for **among them is the Caliph of Allah, the Mahdi**."[73]

روى أحمد وابن ماجه والبزار والحاكم جميعهم عن ثوبان قال رسول الله ﷺ: **إِذَا رَأَيْتُمُ الرَّايَاتِ السُّودَ قَدْ جَاءَتْ مِنْ خُرَاسَانَ فَأْتُوهَا فَإِنَّ فِيهَا خَلِيفَةَ اللهِ الْمَهْدِيَّ.** وصحح إسناده كل من البزار والحاكم والبوصيري في مصباح الزجاجة

In another report the Prophet–upon him blessings and peace–said, "**Whoever commands goodness or forbids wrongdoing then truly he is the caliph of Allah on His earth, and the caliph of His Book, and the caliph of the Messenger of Allah**."[74]

[73] Imam Aḥmad narrated it in his *Musnad*, as did Bazzar in his *Musnad*, Ibn Mājah in his *Sunan* and Ḥākim in the *Mustadrak*, all of them from Thawbān. Bazzar, al-Ḥākim and Shihāb al-Dīn al-Būṣīrī in *Miṣbāḥ al-zujāja fī zawā'id Ibni Mājah* all said it has a sound chain.

[74] Narrated from (i) 'Ubāda b. al-Ṣāmit by Ibn 'Adī in *al-Kāmil fīl-ḍu'afā'* and Ibn Surūr al-Maqdisī in *al-Amr bil-ma'rūf*; (ii) al-Ḥasan al-Baṣrī in *mursal* mode from Ibn Ma'bad al-Raqqī in *al-Ṭā'a wal-ma'ṣiya* and al-Tha'labī in his *Tafsīr* (Āl 'Imrān 3:104). Zayla'ī in *Takhrīj aḥādīth al-Kashshāf* and Ibn Ḥajar in *al-Kāfī al-shāf fī takhrīj aḥādīth al-Kashshāf* and *Lisān al-mīzān* cited the above chains. Nu'aym b. Ḥammād narrated it in the *Fitan* earlier than all of the above but in anonymized *maqṭū'* mode from (iii) 'Abd Allāh b. Nu'aym al-Ma'āfirī's authorities.

وعنه ﷺ **مَنْ أَمَرَ بِمَعْرُوفٍ وَنَهَى عَنْ مُنْكَرٍ فَهُوَ خَلِيفَةُ اللهِ فِي الْأَرْضِ وَخَلِيفَةُ كِتَابِهِ وَخَلِيفَةُ رَسُولِ اللهِ صَلَّى اللهُ عَلَيْهِ وَسَلَّمَ** رواه نعيم بن حماد مقطوعاً على مشيخة عبد الله بن نعيم المعافري ورواه ابن عدي وابن سرور المقدسي في الأمر بالمعروف عن عبادة بن الصامت مرفوعاً ورواه ابن مَعْبَد الرَّقِّي في الطاعة والمعصية والثعلبي في التفسير عن الحسن مرسلاً.

Al-Shāfiʿī narrated in *al-Sunan al-maʾthūra* (*Ḥajj, mā jāʾa fī fidyat al-adhā*, 16th or 23rd report depending on the edition) and *al-Umm* (*Ṣalāt al-jamāʿa, ṣifat al-aʾimma* at the very end) that ʿAbd Allāh b. Jaʿfar b. Abī Ṭālib said, "Abū Bakr governed us—**the best Caliph of Allah, His most merciful one and His most favorably disposed over us.**"[75]

روى المُزَني عن الشافعي في السنن المأثورة وفي كتاب الأم بإسناد الشافعي إلى عبد الله بن جعفر بن أبي طالب قال: **وَلِيَنَا أَبُو بَكْرٍ رَضِيَ اللهُ عَنْهُ خَيْرُ خَلِيفَةِ اللهِ عَزَّ وَجَلَّ أَرْحَمُهُ بِنَا وَأَحْنَاهُ عَلَيْنَا** وكذا رواه أحمد والدارقطني كلاهما في فضائل الصحابة والحاكم وصحح إسناده والبيهقي في معرفة السنن وابن عساكر في التاريخ

The Ṣiddīq himself relatedly said in his sermon when the Arabs fell into *ridda* (apostasy):

> By Allah! I shall certainly keep upholding the command of Allah and struggle in the way of Allah until Allah accomplishes for us His promise and gives us His covenant in full, whereby whoever of us gets killed, gets killed as a shahid in Paradise, and **whoever of us remains, remains as a Caliph of Allah on His earth** and an inheritor of the worship of the All-True. For verily Allah Most High has told us—and there is no breach to His statement—*The One God has promised those of you who believe and do righteous deeds that He shall*

[75] Narrated by Aḥmad, *Faḍāʾil*; Dāraquṭnī, *Faḍāʾil al-Ṣaḥāba*; Ḥākim (*ṣaḥīḥ al-isnād*); Bayhaqī, *Maʿrifat al-Sunan wal-āthār*; Ibn ʿAsākir.

indeed grant them succession in the land just as He granted those who were before them succession; and that He shall indeed empower for them their faith-system with which He is well-pleased for them; and that He shall indeed give them in exchange, after their fear, safety, as they worship Me without associating anything with Me. But whoever disbelieves after that, then those ones—they are the depraved (al-Nūr 24:55).[76]

عن ابن عمر قال أبو بكر الصديق رضي الله عنهم في خطبته لمّا ارتدّت العرب: **وَاللهِ لا أَبْرَحُ أَقُومُ بِأَمْرِ اللهِ وَأُجَاهِدُ فِي سَبِيلِ اللهِ حَتَّى يُنجِزَ اللهُ لَنَا وَعْدَهُ وَيَفِيَ لَنَا بِعَهْدِهِ، فَيُقْتَلُ مَنْ قُتِلَ مِنَّا شَهِيدًا فِي الجَنَّةِ وَيَبْقَى مَنْ بَقِيَ مِنَّا خَلِيفَةَ اللهِ فِي أَرْضِهِ، وَوَارِثَ عِبَادَةِ الحَقِّ. فَإِنَّ اللهَ تَعَالَى قَالَ لَنَا وَلَيْسَ لِقَوْلِهِ خُلْفٌ ﴿ وَعَدَ ٱللَّهُ ٱلَّذِينَ ءَامَنُوا۟ مِنكُمْ وَعَمِلُوا۟ ٱلصَّٰلِحَٰتِ لَيَسْتَخْلِفَنَّهُمْ فِى ٱلْأَرْضِ كَمَا ٱسْتَخْلَفَ ٱلَّذِينَ مِن قَبْلِهِمْ وَلَيُمَكِّنَنَّ لَهُمْ دِينَهُمُ ٱلَّذِى ٱرْتَضَىٰ لَهُمْ وَلَيُبَدِّلَنَّهُم مِّنۢ بَعْدِ خَوْفِهِمْ أَمْنًا ۚ يَعْبُدُونَنِى لَا يُشْرِكُونَ بِى شَيْـًٔا ۚ وَمَن كَفَرَ بَعْدَ ذَٰلِكَ فَأُو۟لَٰٓئِكَ هُمُ ٱلْفَٰسِقُونَ ﴿٥٥﴾ ﴾** النور. رواه الخطيب في الرواة عن مالك.

Likewise Saʿīd b. al-Jubayr's reply in answer to the tyrant al-Ḥajjāj al-Thaqafī's question, "What do you say about Abū Bakr?" Ibn Jubayr replied, "**The Ṣiddīq, the Caliph of Allah**, he went with a glorious memory and he lived blessed!" Abū Nuʿaym narrated it from al-Ḥasan al-Baṣrī in the *Ḥilya*.

سَأَلَ الحَجَّاجُ سَعِيدَ بْنَ جُبَيْرٍ مَا تَقُولُ فِي أَبِي بَكْرٍ؟ قَالَ: الصِّدِّيقُ خَلِيفَةُ اللهِ مَضَى حَمِيدًا وَعَاشَ سَعِيدًا رواه أبو نعيم في الحلية عن الحسن البصري

[76] Narrated from Ibn ʿUmar by al-Khaṭīb in *al-Ruwāt ʿan Mālik*.

Abū Nu'aym likewise narrated from Mubārak Abū Ḥammād the admonition Sufyān al-Thawrī gave to 'Alī b. al-Ḥasan al-Salīmī, "Know, my brother, that Allah Most High does not make anyone enter Paradise through rebellious sins and that **Dāwūd–upon him peace–the Caliph of Allah on earth**, faced what he faced because of a single sin which, if we ourselves had done its like, we would have said it is not a sin. So guard yourself from Allah, my brother!"

روى أبو نعيم في حلية الأولياء بسنده عن مبارك أبي حماد مولى إبراهيم بن سام قال سمعت سفيان الثوري يقرأ على علي بن الحسن السَّلِيمي ومن جملته قال **وَاعْلَمْ يَا أَخِي أَنَّ اللهَ تَعَالَى لَا يُدْخِلُ أَحَدًا الجَنَّةَ بِالمَعَاصِي وَأَنَّ دَاوُدَ عَلَيْهِ السَّلَامُ خَلِيفَةَ اللهِ فِي الْأَرْضِ نَزَلَ مَا نَزَلَ بِهِ بِخَطِيئَةٍ وَاحِدَةٍ وَلَوْ أَنَّا عَمِلْنَا مِثْلَهَا لَقُلْنَا لَيْسَتْ بِخَطِيئَةٍ فَاتَّقِ اللهَ يَا أَخِي**

The Mālikī-Shāfi'ī Imam of Egypt Ibn 'Abd al-Ḥakam narrated in his *Sīrat 'Umar b. 'Abd al-'Azīz* that when **a man called 'Umar b. 'Abd al-'Azīz, "O Caliph of Allah on earth**!" he said to him, "When I was born my parents called me 'Umar. When I matured I chose the teknonym Abū Ḥafṣ. When you put me in charge of your affairs you called me Commander of the believers. So if you called me any of these I would answer you [variant: I would love you]. But as for 'Caliph of Allah on earth,' I am certainly not so! Rather, they are Dāwūd the Prophet and his like. Allah Most High said, *O Dāwūd! Verily We have appointed you as a caliph on earth* (Ṣād 38:26).'

قال ابن عبد الحكم في كتاب سيرة عمر بن العزيز على ما رواه الإمام مالك بن أنس وأصحابه **نَادَى رَجُلٌ عُمَرَ بْنَ عَبْدِ الْعَزِيزِ فَقَالَ يَا خَلِيفَةَ اللهِ فِي الْأَرْضِ فَقَالَ لَهُ عُمَرُ مَهْ إِنِّي لَمَّا وُلِدْتُ اخْتَارَ لِي أَهْلِي اسْماً فَسَمَّوْنِي عُمَرَ فَلَوْ نَادَيْتَنِي**

يَا عُمَرَ أَجَبْتُكَ فَلَمَّا كَبُرْتُ اخْتَرْتُ لِنَفْسِي الْكُنَى فَكُنِّيْتُ بِأَبِي حَفْصٍ فَلَوْ نَادَيْتَنِي يَا أَبَا حَفْصٍ أَجَبْتُكَ فَلَمَّا وَلَّيْتُمُونِي أُمُورَكُمْ سَمَّيْتُمُونِي أَمِيرَ الْمُؤْمِنِينَ فَلَوْ نَادَيْتَنِي يَا أَمِيرَ الْمُؤْمِنِينَ أَجَبْتُك - في نسخة: أَحْبَبْتُكَ في الثلاثة - وَأَمَّا خَلِيفَةَ اللهِ فِي الْأَرْضِ فَلَسْتُ كَذٰلِكَ وَلٰكِنْ خُلَفَاءُ اللهِ فِي الْأَرْضِ دَاوُدُ النَّبِيُّ عَلَيْهِ السَّلَامُ وَشَبَهُهُ قَالَ اللهُ تَبَارَكَ وَتَعَالَى يَٰدَاوُۥدُ إِنَّا جَعَلْنَٰكَ خَلِيفَةً فِي ٱلْأَرْضِ من سورة صٓ ٢٦

It is clear from the usage of the Prophet, the Companions and the Imams that 'Umar b. 'Abd al-'Azīz said his disclaimer out of humbleness, not because it was incorrect to call him so. When our liege lord 'Uthmān b. 'Affān was murdered, the very same Ḥudhayfa b. al-Yamān who reported the Prophetic hadith already cited above (calling the political caliph "the caliph of Allah on earth"), said, "Have you seen the Day of the house arrest? It was a universal fitna for the Muslims. Glory to Allah, glory to Allah! **The Caliph of Allah, and they killed him unjustly!** Verily it was the first of the fitnas, and the last one will be the false Messiah."[77] One of the Awliya of the *Tābi'īn*, Abū Muslim al-Khawlānī, said to that effect, "They killed the she-camel of Allah (al-A'rāf 7:73-78, Hūd 11:64-67, Shams 91:11-15), and **you have killed the Caliph of Allah**! I bear witness before my nurturing Lord that His Caliph is dearer to Him than His she-camel."[78]

[77] Narrated from Zayd b. Wahb by al-Khallāl, *al-Sunna*.

[78] Narrated by al-Khaṭīb, *Tālī talkhīṣ al-mutashābih*; Ibn 'Asākir, *Tārīkh*.

XXIX. Epilogue and Supplications

This is what was facilitated of the necessary clarification of certain recurring questions on *taṣawwuf* (sufism) in rebuttal of the "Salafi" movement, also known as Wahhabis—the innovated, sourceless, self-generated, revisionist sect that have been opposing the fiqh of the Four Sunni Schools, minimizing the status of the Prophet and his inheritors and promoting the attribution of limbs to Allah for the past 250 years–and, in particular, their calumnies against the Sufis who are the elite of the Umma.

It is a continuation of what has been clarified over the past forty years in the books of seven of our teachers: Muḥammad b. ʿAlawī al-Mālikī (*Mafāhīm yajib an tuṣaḥḥaḥ* and *Manhaj al-Salaf fī fahm al-nuṣūṣ*), Yūsuf al-Rifāʿī (*al-Radd al-muḥkam al-manīʿ ʿalā munkarāt wa-shubuhāt Ibn Manīʿ* and *Naṣīḥa li-ikhwāninā ʿulamāʾ Najd*), Zayn b. Sumayṭ (*al-Ajwibat al-ghāliya fī ʿaqīdat al-firqat al-nājiya*), Mawlana Shaykh Hisham Kabbani (*The "Salafi" Movement Unveiled*, *The Doctrine of Ahl al-Sunna Versus the "Salafi" Movement* and *The Encyclopedia of Islamic Doctrine*), Muḥammad Saʿīd Būṭī (*al-Lāmadhhabiyyatu akhṭaru bidʿatin tuhaddidu al-sharīʿata al-islāmiyya* and *al-Salafiyya marḥalatun tārīkhiyya mubārakatun lā madhhabun islāmī*), Muḥammad Sāmir al-Naṣṣ (*al-Wasīla ilā fahmi ḥaqīqat al-tawassul*) and ʿAbd al-Hādī Kharsa (*al-Radd ʿalā kitāb "Ilā ayn ayyuhā al-Ḥabīb?"* and *The Scholars of the Sufis: They Are the Genuine Followers of the Salaf*) among others.

We had already touched on such topics and we have been exposing for 25 years the Wahhabis' heresies in their open war on the soul of Sunnism—Ashʿaris, Maturidis and Sufis—in ten previous works such as *ʿAlawī b. Aḥmad b. Ḥasan b. al-Quṭb ʿAbd Allāh al-Ḥaddād's "Miṣbāḥ al-anām wa-jilāʾ al-ẓalām fī radd shubah al-bidʿī al-Najdī al-latī aḍalla bihā al-ʿawāmm"* (The lamp of mankind and the illumination of darkness: refutation of the Najdi innovator's fallacies by which he has led astray the common people) (1999); *Albānī and His Friends: A Concise Guide to the "Salafi" Movement* (2004, 2009); *Sunna Notes: Studies in Hadith & Doctrine I-III* (2005-2010); *From the Two Holy Sanctuaries: A Hajj Journal* (2006); *The Four Imams and Their Schools: Abu Hanifa, Malik, al-Shafi'i, Ahmad* (2007); *Ibn Jahbal al-Kilabi's Refutation of Him (al-Ḥarrānī) Who Attributes Direction to Allah* (2008); *The Muhammadan Light in the Qur'an, Sunna, and Companion-Reports* (2012); *Mulla 'Ali al-Qari's Encyclopedia of Hadith Forgeries* (2013); *The Rightly-Guided Caliphs: Abū Bakr, 'Umar, 'Uthmān, 'Alī* (2023); and *The Visitations of Iraq to the Stations of Interlife* (2024).

This is from the bounty of my nurturing Lord (al-Naml 27:40) and from the injunction of my two arch-masters, Mawlana al-Shaykh Muhammad Nazim al-Haqqani who had given me his copy of Ḥabīb 'Alawī b. Aḥmad's *Miṣbāḥ al-anām* in Damascus to work on, and Mawlana Shaykh Hisham Kabbani who instructed me time and again that such work must continue tirelessly "because they are like Ya'jūj and Ma'jūj and they will never stop creeping up."

We live in the end times of strifes and tribulations predicted in the Hadith. The Prophet–upon him the blessings and peace of Allah–advised that nothing shall remain at that time but to break one's sword, withdraw from public involvement and become one of the scatter rugs of one's house. Mawlana's last word remains the last word of Allah and His Prophet. Whatever is for Allah remains, and you are with the one you love.

Mawlana Shaykh Hisham rejoined eternal life during the finishing touches to this book. It reflects nothing but his pure voice that always stood for the All-True in defense of the Holy Prophet and the honor of his inheritors and his whole Umma, while the elite and the rank and file of the Umma continue to sleep at the wheel from east to west. It had been the case long before and continues thereafter. Such is the stuff that we are made of, Mawlana, but for a rarer than rare few such as yourselves among the Muhammadan Inheritors, the forerunners of the Mahdi! May Allah receive you in His mercy and shed of it on us, because of you, that for which we may thank Him with every fiber of our being and hope to carry on until we meet again.

Allah we ask that He reunite the voice of Muslims. May He grant us the best perspective on things, the best management of affairs, the best wisdom in all the matters of the world and the faith. O Allah! Reform the Umma of our liege lord Muḥammad–upon him the blessings and peace of Allah–and grant us victory over our lower selves and the other corrupters of this world.

O Allah! Enlighten the eyesights of our ulema and students of knowledge with the secrets of *be lordly ones by virtue of your past teaching of Scripture and what you have studied* (Āl 'Imrān 3:79) and *so We made it understood to Sulaymān* (Anbiyā' 21:79), and illumine their heart-sights with the secret of *say, "I do not ask you over it any wage but only affectionate love towards near kindred"* ('Ayn Sīn Qāf/al-Shūrā 42:23). Do not leave them to ignorance and their enemies—else how can they serve and protect humankind and the leaders of humankind?

O Allah! Link us with whoever links us to You, and reunite us with whoever reunites us on You, and grant us righteousness in any case, and shower Your purest blessings and holiest salutations on our liege lord Muḥammad, his Family, his Companions, his Awliya and all his Umma. Praise belongs to Allah the nurturing Lord of the worlds.

Mid-Rajab 1446
January 2025

Bibliography

Aḥmad b. Muḥammad b. Ḥanbal b. Hilāl b. Asad al-Shaybānī, Abū ʿAbd Allāh. *Faḍāʾil al-Ṣaḥāba*. Ed. Waṣiyyullāh Muḥ. ʿAbbās. 2 vols. Beirut, Muʾassasat al-Risāla, 1403/ 1983.

______. *al-ʿIlal wa-maʿrifat al-rijāl riwāyat ʿAbd Allāh b. Aḥmad*. Ed. Waṣiyyullāh Muḥ. ʿAbbās. 2nd ed. 3 vols. Riyadh: Dār al-Khānī, 1422/2001.

______. *Masāʾil al-Imām Aḥmad b. Ḥanbal riwayat Isḥāq b. Hānīʾ al-Naysābūrī*. Ed. Zuhayr al-Shāwīsh. 2 vols. Beirut: al-Maktab al-Islāmī, 1394-1400/1974-1980.

______. *al-Musnad*. Ed. Shuʿayb al-Arnāʾūṭ et al. 50 vols. Beirut: Muʾassasat al-Risāla, 1999-2001.

______. *al-Zuhd*. Ed. Muḥ. ʿAbd al-Salām Shāhīn. Beirut: Dār al-Kutub al-ʿIlmiyya, 1420/1999.

al-Bayḍāwī, Nāṣir al-Dīn Abū Saʿīd Abū al-Khayr ʿAbd Allah b. ʿUmar b. Muḥammad b. ʿAlī. *Tuḥfat al-abrār sharḥ Maṣābīḥ al-Sunna*. ed. Nūr al-Dīn Ṭālib et al., 3 vols. Ṣāliḥiyya, Kuwait: Idārat al-Thaqāfa al-Islāmiyya; Beirut and Damascus: Dār al-Nawādir, 1433/2012.

al-Bayhaqī, Abū Bakr Aḥmad b. al-Ḥusayn. *Dalāʾil al-Nubuwwa wa-maʿrifat aḥwāl Ṣāḥib al-sharīʿa*. Ed. ʿAbd al-Muʿṭī Qalʿahjī. 7 vols. Beirut: Dār al-Kutub al-ʿIlmiyya and Dār al-Rayyān lil-Turāth, 1408/ 1988.

______. *al-Iʿtiqād wal-hidāya ilā sabīl al-rashād ʿalā madhhab al-salaf wa-aṣḥāb al-Ḥadīth*. Ed. Aḥmad Abū al-ʿAynayn. Riyadh: Dār al-Faḍīla, 1420/1999.

______. *al-Madkhal ilā al-Sunan al-kubrā*. Ed. Muḥ. Ḍiyāʾ al-Raḥmān Aʿẓamī. 2nd ed. 2 vols. Riyadh: Maktabat Aḍwāʾ al-Salaf, 1420/ 1990.

______. *Manāqib al-Shāfiʿī*. Ed. al-Sayyid Aḥmad Ṣaqr. 2 vols. Cairo: Maktabat Dār al-Turāth, 1390/1970.

______. [*Shuʿab al-īmān*]. *al-Jāmiʿ li-shuʿab al-īmān*. Ed. ʿAbd al-ʿAlī ʿAbd al-Ḥamīd Ḥāmid. 14 vols. Riyadh: Maktabat al-Rushd, 1423/ 2003.

al-Dārimī, Abū Muḥammad ʿAbd Allāh b. ʿAbd al-Raḥmān b. al-Faḍl. *Sunan al-Dārimī*. See al-Ghamrī, *Fatḥ al-Mannān*.

al-Dhahabī, Muḥammad b. Aḥmad b. ʿUthmān al-Turkmānī. *Muʿjam al-shuyūkh al-kabīr*. Ed. Muḥ. Ḥabīb al-Hayla. 2 vols. Ṭāʾif: Maktabat al-Ṣiddīq, 1408/1988.

_______. *Siyar aʿlām al-nubalāʾ*. Ed. Muḥibb al-Dīn al-ʿAmrāwī. 19 vols. Beirut: Dār al-Fikr, 1996.

_______. *Siyar aʿlām al-nubalāʾ*. Ed. Shuʿayb al-Arnāʾūṭ et al. 3rd ed. 25 vols. Beirut: Muʾassasat al-Risāla, 1405/1985.

_______. *Tadhkirat al-ḥuffāẓ*. Ed. ʿAbd al-Raḥmān Yaḥyā al-Muʿallamī. Ed. Muḥammad Zāhid b. Ḥasan b. ʿAlī al-Kawtharī. 3rd ed. 5 vols. in 3. Hyderabad Deccan: Dāʾirat al-Maʿārif al-ʿUthmāniyya, 1376-1377/ 1956-1958. Rept. Beirut: Dār Iḥyāʾ al-Turāth al-ʿArabī, n.d.

_______. *Tārīkh al-Islām wa-wafayāt al-mashāhīr wal-aʿlām*. Ed. ʿUmar ʿAbd al-Salām Tadmurī. 2nd ed. 52 vols. Beirut: Dār al-Kitāb al-ʿArabī, 1409/ 1989.

al-Ghamrī, Abū ʿĀṣim Nabīl. *Fatḥ al-Mannān sharḥ wa-taḥqīq kitāb al-Dārimī Abī Muḥammad ʿAbd Allāh b. ʿAbd al-Raḥmān*. 10 vols. Beirut: Dār al-Bashāʾir al-Islāmiyya, 1419/1999.

al-Ḥaddād, ʿAbd Allāh b. ʿAlawī b. Muḥammad. *al-Nafāʾis al-ʿulwiyya fil-masāʾil al-ṣūfiyya*. [Bshāmūn, Lebanon:] Dār al-Ḥāwī, 1414/1993.

al-Ḥaddād, ʿAlawī b. Aḥmad b. Ḥasan b. ʿAbd Allāh. *Miṣbāḥ al-anām wa-jilāʾ al-ẓalām fī radd shubah al-bidʿī al-Najdī al-latī aḍalla bihā al-ʿawāmm*. Cairo: al-Maṭbaʿat al-ʿĀmira al-Sharafiyya, 1325/1907.

al-Ḥākim al-Naysābūrī, Abū ʿAbd Allāh Muḥ. b. ʿAbd Allāh b. al-Bayyiʿ. *al-Mustadrak ʿalā al-Ṣaḥīḥayn*. With Dhahabī's *Talkhīṣ al-Mustadrak*. 4 vols. Hyderabad Deccan: Dāʾirat al-Maʿārif al-Niẓāmiyya, 1334-1342/1916-1923. Rept. in 5 vols. Beirut: Dār al-Maʿrifa, 1986 with indices by Yūsuf al-Marʿashlī.

al-Ḥakīm al-Tirmidhī, Abū ʿAbd Allāh Muḥ. b. ʿAlī b. al-Ḥasan. *Nawādir al-Uṣūl fī Maʿrifat Akhbār al-Rasūl*. Ed. Nūr al-Dīn Shukrī al-Būrdurī. 5 vols. Jeddah: Dār al-Minhāj, 1436/2015.

Ḥaqqī al-Burūsawī, Ismāʿīl b. Muṣṭafā b. Čawush. *Tafsīr rūḥ al-bayān*. Ed. Ḥāfiẓ Muḥ. Khayrī and Aḥmad Rifʿat. 10 vols. Istanbul: al-Maṭbaʿat al-ʿUthmāniyya, 1330-1346/1912-1928.

[al-Ḥarrānī, Aḥmad b. ʿAbd al-Ḥalīm.] *al-ʿAqīdat al-Wāsiṭiyya*. Ed. Ashraf ʿAbd al-Maqṣūd. 2nd ed. Riyadh: Aḍwāʾ al-Salaf, 1430/1999.

al-Haytamī al-Makkī, Abū al-Faḍl Aḥmad b. Muḥammad b. Ḥajar. *al-Jawhar al-munaẓẓam fī ziyārat al-qabri al-mukarram*. Ed. ʿAbd al-Ghanī Ṣāliḥ al-Jaʿfarī. Cairo: Dār Jawāmiʿ al-Kalim, 1992.

_______. *al-Zawājir ʿan iqtirāf al-kabāʾir*. 2 vols. in 1. Būlāq: al-Maṭbaʿat al-Khadīwiyya, 1284/1868.

Ibn Abī al-Dunyā al-Baghdādī al-Qurashī, Abū Bakr ʿAbd Allāh b. Muḥ. b. ʿUbayd. *Kitāb mujābī al-daʿwa*. Ed. Ziyād Ḥamdān. Beirut: Muʾassasat al-Kutub al-Thaqāfiyya, 1413/1993.

Ibn Abī Khaythama Zuhayr b. Ḥarb, Abū Bakr Aḥmad. *al-Tārīkh al-kabīr al-ma'rūf bi-tārīkh Ibn Abī Khaythama*. Ed. Ṣalāḥ b. Fatḥī Halal. 4 vols. Cairo: al-Fārūq al-Ḥadītha, 1424-1427/2004-2006.

Ibn 'Asākir, Thiqat al-Dīn Abū al-Qāsim 'Alī b. al-Ḥasan b. Hibat Allāh al-Dimashqī. *Mu'jam al-shuyūkh*. Ed. Wafā' Taqī al-Dīn. 3 vols. Beirut: Dār al-Bashā'ir al-Islāmiyya, 1421/2000.

______. *Tārīkh madīnat Dimashq*. Ed. Muḥibb al-Dīn al-'Amrawī. 80 vols. Beirut: Dār al-Fikr, 1421/2001.

Ibn Ḥajar al-'Asqalānī, Shihāb al-Dīn Abū al-Faḍl Aḥmad b. 'Alī. *Fatḥ al-Bārī bi-sharḥ Ṣaḥīḥ al-Bukhārī*. Ed. Muḥ. Fu'ād 'Abd al-Bāqī and Muḥibb al-Dīn al-Khaṭīb. 13 vols. Beirut, Dār al-Ma'rifa, 1379/1959.

______. *al-Iṣāba fī tamyīz al-Ṣaḥāba*.Ed. 8 vols. in 4. Cairo: al-Maṭba'at al-Sharafiyya, 1327/1909. Rept. in 5 vols. with indices Beirut: Dār al-Kutub al-'Ilmiyya, n.d.

______. *al-Kāfī al-shāf fī takhrīj aḥādīth al-Kashshāf*. Beirut: Dār Iḥyā' al-Turāth al-'Arabī, 1418/1997.

______. *Lisān al-Mīzān*. Ed. 'Abd al-Fattāḥ Abū Ghudda. 10 vols. Beirut: Dār al-Bashā'ir al-Islāmiyya, 2002.

______. *Mukhtaṣar zawā'id Musnad al-Bazzār 'alā al-kutub al-sitta wa-Musnad Aḥmad*. Ed. Ṣabrī Abū Dharr. 2 vols. Beirut: Mu'assasat al-Kutub al-Thaqāfiyya, 1412/1992.

______. *Taghlīq al-ta'līq 'alā Ṣaḥīḥ al-Bukhārī*. Ed. Sa'īd 'Abd al-Raḥmān al-Qizqī. 2nd ed. 5 vols. Beirut: al-Maktab al-Islāmī; Amman: Dār 'Ammār, 1409/1989.

______. *Tahdhīb al-Tahdhīb*. 12 vols. Hyderabad Deccan: Dā'irat al-Ma'ārif al-Niẓamiyya, 1326/1908.

______. *Talkhīṣ al-ḥabīr fī takhrīj aḥādīth al-Rāfi'ī al-Kabīr*. Ed. Abū 'Āṣim Ḥasan b. 'Abbās. 4 vols. Cairo: Mu'assasat Qurṭuba, 1416/1995.

Ibn Jamā'a al-Kinānī al-Shāfi'ī, 'Izz al-Dīn 'Abd al-'Azīz b. Muḥammad b. Ibrāhīm. *Hidāyat al-sālik ilā al-madhāhib al-arba'ati fil-manāsik*. Ed. Ṣāliḥ al-Khuzayyim. 4 vols. Dammam: Dār Ibn al-Jawzī, 1422/2002.

Ibn al-Jawzī al-Qurashī al-Baghdādī, Abū al-Faraj 'Abd al-Raḥmān b. 'Alī b. Muḥ. *al-Madhhab al-aḥmad fī madhhab al-Imām Aḥmad*. Ed. Sālim al-Sayyid al-Jallād, 'Abd Allāh Ismā'īl Mutawallī and Muḥ. Shawqī Amīn. 2nd ed. Riyadh: al-Mu'assasat al-Sa'īdiyya, 1401/1981.

______. *Manāqib al-Imām Aḥmad*. Ed. 'Abd Allāh al-Turkī. Giza: Hajar, 1988.

______. *al-Mawḍū'āt min al-aḥādīth al-marfū'āt*. Ed. Nūr al-Dīn b. Shukrī Būyājīlār. 4 vols. Riyadh: Aḍwā' al-Salaf, 1418/1997.

______. *Al-Mujtabā min al-mujtanā*. Ed. Ayman 'Abd al-Jabbār al-Buḥayrī and 'Alī Jumu'a. Cairo: Dār al-Āfāq al-'Arabiyya, 1419/1999.

______. *Muthīr al-gharām al-sākin ilā ashraf al-amākin*. Ed. Muṣṭafā Muḥ. Ḥusayn al-Dhahabī. Cairo: Dār al-Ḥadīth, 1415/1995.

______. *Ṣifat al-ṣafwa*. Ed. Maḥmūd Fākhūrī and Muḥ. Rawwās Qal'ahjī. 2nd ed. 4 vols. Beirut: Dār al-Ma'rifa, 1979.

______. *al-Taḥqīq fī masā'il al-khilāf*. With al-Dhahabī's *Tanqīḥ al-Taḥqīq*. Ed. 'Abd al-Mu'ṭī Qal'ajī 12 vols. Aleppo: Dār al-Wa'y al-'Arabī, 1419/1998.

______. *al-Thabāt 'inda al-mamāt*. Ed. 'Abd Allāh al-Laythī al-Anṣārī. Beirut: Mu'assasat al-Kutub al-Thaqāfiyya, 1406/1986.

______. *al-Wafā bi-aḥwāl al-Muṣṭafā*. Ed. Muṣṭafā 'Abd al-Qādir 'Aṭā. Beirut: Dār al-Kutub al-'Ilmiyya, 1408/1988.

Kabbani, Shaykh Muhammad Hisham. *Encyclopedia of Islamic Doctrine*. 2nd ed. 7 vols. Mountain View, CA: As-Sunna Foundation of America, 1998.

al-Kalābādhī, Abū Bakr Muḥ. b. Abī Isḥāq b. Ibrāhīm. *Baḥr al-fawā'id al-mashhūr bi-Ma'ānī al-akhbār*. Ed. Wajīh Kamāl al-Dīn Zakī. 2 vols. Cairo: Dār al-Salām, 1429/ 2008.

al-Khaṭīb al-Baghdādī, Abū Bakr Aḥmad b. 'Alī b. Thābit. [*Tārīkh Baghdād*.] *Tārīkh Madīnat al-Salām wa-Akhbār Muḥaddithīhā wa-Dhikr Quṭṭānihā al-'Ulamā'*. Ed. Bashshār 'Awwād Ma'rūf. 17 vols. Beirut: Dār al-Gharb al-Islāmī, 1422/2001.

al-Maqrīzī, Taqī al-Dīn Aḥmad b. 'Alī b. 'Abd al-Qādir b. Muḥammad. *Imtā' al-asmā' bi-mā lil-Nabiyyi min al-aḥwāl wal-matā'*. Ed. Muḥ. al-Numaysī, 15 vols. Beirut: Dār al-Kutub al-'Ilmiyya, 1999.

al-Nabhānī, Yūsuf b. Ismā'īl. *al-Asālīb al-badī'a*, see *Shawāhid al-ḥaqq*.

______. *Ḥujjat Allāh 'alā al-'ālamīn bi-mu'jizāt Sayyid al-Mursalīn*. Beirut: al-Maṭba'at al-Adabiyya, 1317/1900.

______. *Jāmi' karāmāt al-awliyā'*. Ed. Ibrāhīm 'Aṭwah 'Awaḍ. 2 vols. Beirut: al-Maktabat al-Thaqāfiyya, 1411/1991.

______. *Shawāhid al-ḥaqq fīl-istighātha bi-Sayyid al-khalq*. With his *al-Asālīb al-badī'a fī faḍli al-Ṣaḥābati wa-iqnā' al-Shī'a*. Cairo: al-Maṭba'at al-Maymaniyya (=Muṣṭafā Bābī al-Ḥalabī), 1323/1905. Rept. Beirut: Dār al-Fikr, 1978.

al-Nābulusī, 'Abd al-Ghanī b. Ismā'īl. *al-Ḥaḍrat al-unsiyya fīl-riḥlat al-qudsiyya*. Ed. Akram Ḥasan al-'Ulbī. Beirut: al-Maṣādir, 1411/1990.

______. *Kashf al-nūr 'an aṣḥāb al-qubūr*. Ed. Aḥmad Farīd Mazyadī. Beruwala, Sri Lanka: Dār al-Āthār al-Islāmiyya, 1428/2007.

al-Naṣṣ, Sāmir b. Mamdūḥ. *al-Wasīlatu ilā fahmi ḥaqīqati al-tawassul.* Beirut: Dar al-Tawfīq, 2003.

al-Nawawī, Muḥyī al-Dīn Abū Zakariyyā Yaḥyā b. Sharaf b. Marīy al-Dimashqī. *Sharḥ matn al-arbaʿīn al-Nawawiyya fīl-aḥādīth al-ṣaḥīḥat al-Nabawiyya*. 2nd ed. Cairo: Muṣṭafā al-Bābī al-Ḥalabī, 1385/1966.

_______. *Sharḥ Ṣaḥīḥ Muslim*. Ed. Muḥ. Afandī b. ʿAbd al-Laṭīf. 18 vols. Cairo: al-Maṭbaʿat al-Miṣriyya bil-Azhar, 1347-1349/1929-1930.

Qawwām/Qiwām al-Sunna. See al-Taymī al-Aṣfahānī.

al-Sakhāwī, Abū al-Khayr Shams al-Dīn Muḥammad b. ʿAbd al-Raḥmān b. Muḥammad. *al-Ḍaw' al-Lāmiʿ li-Ahl al-Qarn al-Tāsiʿ*. 12 vols. in 6. Cairo: Maktabat al-Qudsī, 1354/1935. Rept. Beirut: Dār al-Jīl, 1412/1992.

_______. *al-Maqāṣid al-Ḥasana fī Bayān Kathīr min al-Aḥādīth al-Mushtahara ʿalā al-Alsina*. Ed. ʿAbd Allāh Muḥ. al-Ṣiddīq. Cairo: Maktabat al-Khānjī, 1955.

_______. *al-Qawl al-badīʿ fīl-ṣalāt ʿalā al-Ḥabīb al-shafīʿ*. Ed. Muḥ. ʿAwwāma. Medina: Mu'assasat al-Rayyān, 1422/2002.

al-Shinqīṭī, Muḥ. al-Amīn b. Muḥ. al-Mukhtār b. ʿAbd al-Qādir Jakanī. *Aḍwā' al-bayān fī īḍāḥ al-Qur'ān bil-Qur'ān*. 3rd ed. 7 vols. Mecca: Dār ʿIlm al-Fawā'id, 1426/2005. With *Tatimmat Aḍwā' al-bayān* by ʿAṭiyya Muḥammad Sālim. 2nd ed. 2 vols. N.p.: S.n. 1400/1980.

al-Shinqīṭī, Muḥ. al-Khaḍir b. ʿAbd Allāh b. Aḥmad b. Māya'bā al-Jakanī. *Kawthar al-maʿānī al-darārī fī kashfi khabāya Ṣaḥīḥ al-Bukhārī*. 14 vols. Beirut: Mu'assasat al-Risāla, 1415/1995.

al-Ṭabarānī, Abū al-Qāsim Sulaymān b. Aḥmad b. Ayyūb al-Lakhmī al-Shāmī. *al-Aḥādīth al-Ṭiwāl*. Ed. ʿAbd al-Majīd al-Salafī. 2nd ed. Beirut: al-Maktab al-Islāmī, 1419/1998.

_______. *al-Muʿjam al-Awsaṭ*. Ed. Ṭāriq ʿAwaḍ Allāh and ʿAbd al-Muḥsin al-Ḥusaynī. 10 vols. Cairo: Dār al-Ḥaramayn, 1415/1995.

_______. *al-Muʿjam al-Kabīr*. Ed. Ḥamdī ʿAbd al-Majīd al-Salafī. 2nd ed. 25 vols. Baghdad: Wizārat al-Awqāf, 1984-1990. Rept. Cairo: Maktabat Ibn Taymiyya, n.d.

_______. *al-Muʿjam al-Ṣaghīr*. Ed. ʿAbd al-Raḥmān Muḥ. ʿUthmān. 2 vols. Medina: al-Maktaba al-Salafiyya, 1388/1968. Rept. 2 vols. Beirut: Dār al-Kutub al-ʿIlmiyya, 1403/1983.

_______. *Musnad al-Shāmiyyīn*. Ed. Ḥamdī ʿAbd al-Majīd al-Salafī. 4 vols. Beirut: Mu'assasat al-Risāla, 1405/1984.

al-Taymī al-Aṣbahānī, Qiwām/Qawwām al-Sunna Abū al-Qāsim Ismāʿīl b. Muḥ. b. al-Faḍl b. ʿAlī al-Qurashī al-Ṭulayḥī. *Dalā'il al-Nubuwwa*. Ed. Musāʿid al-Ḥamīd. 4 vols. Riyadh: Dār al-ʿĀṣima, 1412/1992.

_______. *Siyar al-salaf al-ṣāliḥīn*. Ed. Karam Ḥilmī Farḥāt Aḥmad. 4 vols. Riyadh: Dār al-Rāya, 1420/1999.

Zayn al-ʿĀbidīn [b. Ibrāhīm b. Sumayṭ] b. al-ʿAlawī. *Al-Ajwibat al-ghāliya fī ʿaqīdat al-firqat al-nājiya*. [Damascus?:] n.p., 1421/2000.

[al-Zurʿī al-Dimasqhī], Shams al-Dīn Muḥammad b. Abī Bakr b. Ayyūb. *Madārij al-sālikīn fī manāzil al-sā'irīn*. Ed. Muḥ. Ajmal al-Iṣlāḥī and Sirāj Munīr. 2nd ed. 4 vols. Beirut: Dār Ibn Ḥazm, 1441/2019.

_______. *Iʿlām al-muwaqqiʿīn ʿan Rabb al-ʿālamīn*. Ed. Mashhūr Ḥasan Salmān. 7 vols. Dammam: Dār Ibn al-Jawzī, 1423/2002.

_______. *Jilā' al-afhām fī faḍl al-ṣalāt wal-salām ʿalā khayri al-anām*. Ed. Zā'id Aḥmad al-Nushayrī. Mecca: Dār 'Ilm al-Fawā'id, 1433/2012.

_______. *al-Rūḥ*. Ed. Yūsuf Budaywī. Damascus: Dār Ibn Kathīr, 1998.

Index of Reports

Abū Ayyūb al-Anṣārī rested his face on the Grave.....88-89, 119
Abū Bakr al-Ṣiddīq foresaw the day of his death....................153
Abū Bakr was the best Caliph of Allah ('Abd Allāh b. Ja'far) 170
Abū Bakr was the Caliph of his nurturing Lord (Shāfi'ī).......167
Abū Bakr, the Ṣiddīq, the Caliph of Allah (Ibn Jubayr) 171
Abū Hurayra traveled to Sinai to pray at the Mount..........23, 67
Abū Hurayra habitually placed his hand on the pommel........22
Abū Ṭālib's *islām* is dearer to me than my father's (Abū Bakr)55
after that, the Dajjāl shall come out...168
Ā'isha told them to open a skylight above his noble grave....112
Allah has angels roaming the earth and conveying to me........95
Allah forbade the earth to consume the bodies of Prophets....93
Allah is the Giver and I am the distributor 111, 117
and we have none but you to flee to (Labīd) 115
be quiet! Did I not practice justice on you? ('Umar) 168
beautify the invocation of blessing on me...............................108
belief is Yemeni and wisdom is Yemeni 16
belief is Yemeni, and I am Yemeni..14
the believer's dream is truth and 1/46th of Prophethood......164
the best of creation are a scholar, a Sufi faqih (Sufyān)..........148
the best of men are the people of Yemen..................................14
beware Allah in my Companions, do not take them as targets60
beware the believer's *firāsa* for he sees with Allah's light.......156
Bilal came to the Prophet's grave and said 'Ask for rain'.......113
Bilāl traveled to Medina to visit the noble Prophetic Grave....67
the Book of Allah and my *'itra* (intimate family).....................58
the Caliph of Allah whom they killed unjustly (Ḥudhayfa)...173
certain understanding Allah might give to a servant ('Alī)....161
come near, Wābiṣa, come near, Wābiṣa! 164
the Companions would touch the pommel of the pulpit.22, 118
consult your heart no matter what fatwa they give you..164-165
convey from me if only a verse and narrate from Israelites.....41

cupping and its timings....36
the Day of 'Arafa Allah frees the most servants from hell....148
the Day of 'Arafa Allah takes His angels to witness....148
the Day of 'Arafa is that of the very best of supplications....148
the Day of 'Arafa is the very best of all days....148
do not make my grave a *'īd*....79
do not make your houses graves....79
do not pray towards the graves....83
do not saddle up except to go to the Three Mosques....72, 73
do not weep over the faith when its people are in charge of it 89
the dream of a believer is speech by Allah to His servant....156
the dust of Medina is a cure from leprosy....51
each of you converses intimately with his nurturing Lord....143
everything uncovered itself to me and I knew....152
firāsa is unveiling and eyeing of the unseen (Dārānī)....155
the first to corrupt my Sunna is a man of the Banū Umayya..48
five verses in al-Nisā' I would not give away (Ibn Mas'ūd)...116
following a middle course, right guidance....159
go to 'Umar and tell him, 'You are going to have rain'....113
hadith of the demolishing of magnified graves....66
hadith of performing ablution with fermented fruit mash....34
has anything crowned our heads except *Ahl al-Bayt*?....56
he [Hasan] resembles the Prophet not you O 'Alī (Abū Bakr) 55
he has perished and failed, the worshipper of money....102
He placed His palm between my shoulder-blades until I felt the coolness of His fingers....152
healing of 'Abd Allāh b. 'Atīk's broken leg....138
healing of Abū Dharr's eye at Uḥud....138
healing of 'Alī b. Abī Ṭālib's ophthalmia at Khaybar....138
healing of Qatāda's eye at Badr....138
healing of Rifā'a's eye at Badr....138
his sanctity after death is as his sanctity alive (Imam Malik) 103
how many an unkempt begrimed servant pushed out....142
I am the city of knowledge and 'Alī is its door....27

I am the one who can intercede 112, 117
I am shown that it will be a daughter (Abū Bakr) 153
I beheld my nurturing Lord in the most beautiful form 152
I came to the Messenger, not to a stone! (Abū Mūsā)........ 88-89
I go seek help with the Prophet's grave (Ibn al-Munkadir).....89
I have left you that which, if you hold fast to it, you will never go astray after me...58
I let Him with whom I converse intimately hear (Abū Bakr) 143
I have memorized two containers of Hadith (Abū Hurayra)..47
I remind you of Allah about the people of my House 58
Ibn 'Umar and Ḥafṣa used Prophet's *jubba* for medication...119
Ibn 'Umar put his hand on the seat of the Prophet's pulpit ..118
If I were to take a friend in my Umma it would be Abū Bakr..53
If you see in those days the Caliph of Allah, stick to him.......168
In the Masjid of Khayf is the grave of seventy Prophets 86
In the nations before you were *muḥaddathūn*........................157
Invoke blessings upon me abundantly on Jumu'a 108
It is not I that have furnished you with mounts but Allah.....120
Jews, Christians took their Prophets' graves as temples.....81, 87
keep careful watch of Muhammad in the people of his House55
knowledge comes by learning, fiqh by learning fiqh 112
leave what seems dubious for what does not seem dubious..165
may intercession fail me if I do not love Abū Bakr and 'Umar57
the Messenger of Allah died on the second day of the week ...22
the Messenger of Allah was delayed one morning..................152
Messenger of Allah! Hunger! 122
the most knowledgeable memorized most ('Amr b. Akhṭab).151
my Companions are like the stars 27
my father be his [al-Ḥasan's] ransom (Abū Bakr) 55
my life is a great good for you and my death a greater good.105
my Umma never ceases to stand on truth, prevailing 111-112
no Prophet dies and resides in his grave forty mornings.........95
the noble Prophetic Grave is the purest of all the spots on earth and in the seven skies..64

none greets me but Allah has returned my life to me......... 94-95
none invokes blessings on me but it is shown to me 107
not everyone has a heart (Ghazali).. 141
O Allah! Bring over their hearts to obedience of You 14
O Allah! I turn to you with your Prophet. O Muḥammad! ... 123
O Allah! I seek refuge in You from unbeneficial knowledge... 38
O best of those whose bones are buried in the mound ('Utbī)... 74
O blessed one, rise ('Alī) 138
on my night Journey I passed by Mūsā at the red dune as he was standing in prayer in his grave.. 96
one does not travel but to the three Mosques.... 23-24, 67-71, 76
one of you comes in with fornication in his eyes ('Uthmān) 154
one who rendered me the greatest services is Abū Bakr 53
people of truthfulness are spies of hearts (Aḥmad b. 'Āṣim) .. 156
people of Yemen are part of me and I am part of them 15
a people will tell you what you and your fathers never heard . 18
people with our complexion saying the same as what we do .. 18
perish the worshipper of gold and silver and silk................... 102
the Prophet did not leave out anything but told us about it .. 150
the Prophet informed us about all that was to happen........... 151
the Prophet looked towards Iraq, Syro-Palestine and Yemen 14
the Prophet met with the Prophets on the night of *isrā'* 94
the Prophet named the Umayyads *sufahā*, *Luka' b. Luka'*, *ṣibyān*, *tāfih*, *safīh*, *ruwaybiḍa* and *fuwaysiq*......................... 47
the Prophet ordered us to give people their due stations......... 33
the Prophet prayed *fajr* with us then climbed the pulpit 151
the Prophet stood among us [speaking] for a long time 150
the Prophet supplicated, whereupon it rained........................ 115
the Prophet's family are my resource (al-Shāfi'ī) 129
the Prophets are alive in their graves with a real and full life .. 93
the Prophets are alive in their graves, praying.......................... 96
remove the cloth from the hand ('Alī) 137
the rescuing wind of the All-Beneficent hails from Yemen 16
the ruin of my Umma befalls at the hands of Quraysh boys ... 45

Sāriya, the mountain! ('Umar) 153
the saved Group 57
shall I say what you came to ask or do you wish to ask first .. 164
the sneezer is blessed thrice 35
that which, if you hold fast to it, you will never ever go astray after me 59
the thigh is nakedness 32
then the callers unto misguidance shall rise 49, 168
there is none dearer to me than who sits by me (Ibn 'Abbās) . 61
there will be towards the end of time anti-Christ arch-liars 18
they are your people, O Abū Mūsā 13
they for whom Allah wants immense goodness, He grants ... 111
they took their Prophets' graves as places of prostration ... 81, 87
they killed Allah's camel, you killed His Caliph (Abū Muslim) 173
this Umma always prevails over opponents 111-112
those that call at the gates of Hellfire, whoever answers 18
those that follow what I and my Companions follow 57
those that will ruin my Umma are this tribe of Quraysh ... 45-46
tomorrow there shall come over people with softer hearts 15
tomorrow we meet the beloved (Anas) 15
touching the pulpit of the Prophet 118
truth is truth and falsehood is falsehood (Ibn Ḥazm) 157
the two of them never separate until they come to the Basin .. 59
'Umar came out to pray for rain through al-'Abbās 114
the Umma will never concur on misguidance 64
visit the graves 68, 73
Wābiṣa, consult your heart! *Taqwā* is right here 164
Wābiṣa! Consult yourself, no matter what they recommend 165
Wall up every private access to this Mosque but Abū Bakr's .. 53
we have lovers who, even if we cut them limb by limb ('Alī) 137
we've come to you, best of all creatures (Labīd) 115
were it not you swore your father was pleased with you ('Alī) 138
what ails me I saw Banū al-Ḥakam sauntering on my pulpit? 46
what do the highest angels argue about? 152

when I love him I become his hearing with which he hears..143
when one of you has sex with his wife 35
when the maker of a judgment makes his judgment striving..44
when you see the black banners from Khorasan join them...169
whoever clings to the sultan is seduced 23
whoever comes against any wali of Mine I wage war on him 143
whoever lies against me or rejects something I have ordered.41
whoever deliberately lies against me, let him sit in Hell...........41
whoever invokes blessings upon me at my grave I hear him...96
whoever likes to ask something, let him ask 151
whoever remains remains as a Caliph of Allah (Abū Bakr)...170
whoever orders good or forbids wrong is a caliph of Allah...169
whoever visits me after my death is as if he visited me in life .80
whoever visits my grave, my intercession has become certain 80
whoever worshipped Muḥammad (Abū Bakr)........................102
will you leave alone my Companion for me?.............................52
worship Allah as if you see Him, and if you do not see Him.144
the worst of the ulema are those that go to the emirs...............23
the worst offender leaves 'Arafāt thinking he is unforgiven..147
you are displayed to me with your names and your traits.....108
you are the nearest means to Allah (Sawād b. Qārib).............117
you came to ask me about virtue and vice...............................164
you have certainly been forgiven...74
you will not ask me about anything except I will tell you......151
your deeds are shown to your deceased relatives and kin......108
your deeds will be displayed to me...106

www.ingramcontent.com/pod-product-compliance
Lightning Source LLC
Chambersburg PA
CBHW030521080526
44586CB00011B/284
* 9 7 8 1 9 3 8 0 5 8 8 6 8 *